Contents

INSIGHTS

General Editor: Clive Bloom

Editorial Board: Clive Bloom, Brian Docherty, Gary Day, Lesley Bloom

Insights brings to academics, students and general readers the very best contemporary criticism on neglected literary and cultural areas. It consists of anthologies, each containing original contributions by advanced scholars and experts. Each contribution concentrates on a study of a particular work, author or genre in its artistic, historical and cultural context.

Published titles

Clive Bloom (*editor*)
JACOBEAN POETRY AND PROSE: Rhetoric, Representation and the Popular Imagination
TWENTIETH-CENTURY SUSPENSE: The Thriller Comes of Age
SPY THRILLERS: From Buchan to le Carré
AMERICAN DRAMA

Clive Bloom, Brian Docherty, Jane Gibb and Keith Shand (*editors*)
NINETEENTH-CENTURY SUSPENSE: From Poe to Conan Doyle

Clive Bloom and Brian Docherty
AMERICAN POETRY: The Modernist Ideal

Dennis Butts
STORIES AND SOCIETY: Children's Literature in a Social Context

Gary Day (*editor*)
READINGS IN POPULAR CULTURE: Trivial Pursuits?
THE BRITISH CRITICAL TRADITION: A Re-evaluation

Gary Day and Clive Bloom (*editors*)
PERSPECTIVES ON PORNOGRAPHY: Sexuality in Film and Literature

Brian Docherty (*editor*)
AMERICAN CRIME FICTION: Studies in the Genre
AMERICAN HORROR FICTION: From Brockden Brown to Stephen King
TWENTIETH-CENTURY EUROPEAN DRAMA

Rhys Garnett and R. J. Ellis (*editors*)
SCIENCE FICTION ROOTS AND BRANCHES: Contemporary
  Critical Approaches

Robert Giddings (*editor*)
LITERATURE AND IMPERIALISM

Robert Giddings, Keith Selby and Chris Wensley
SCREENING THE NOVEL: The Theory and Practice of Literary
  Dramatisation

Dorothy Goldman (*editor*)
WOMEN AND WORLD WAR 1: The Written Response

Paul Hyland and Neil Sammells (*editors*)
IRISH WRITING: Exile and Subversion

Maxim Jakubowski and Edward James (*editors*)
THE PROFESSION OF SCIENCE FICTION: Writers on their Craft
  and Ideas

Mark Lilly (*editor*)
LESBIAN AND GAY WRITING: An Anthology of Critical Essays

Christopher Mulvey and John Simons (*editors*)
NEW YORK: City as Text

Adrian Page (*editor*)
THE DEATH OF THE PLAYWRIGHT? Modern British Drama and
  Literary Theory

Frank Pearce and Michael Woodiwiss (*editors*)
GLOBAL CRIME CONNECTIONS: Dynamics and Control

John Simons
FROM MEDIEVAL TO MEDIEVALISM

Jeffrey Walsh and James Aulich (*editors*)
VIETNAM IMAGES: War and Representation

Gina Wisker (*editor*)
BLACK WOMEN'S WRITING

American Poetry:
The Modernist Ideal

Edited by

CLIVE BLOOM
Middlesex University

and

BRIAN DOCHERTY
Goldsmiths' College, University of London

MACMILLAN

First published 1995 by
MACMILLAN PRESS LTD
Houndmills,. Basingstoke, Hampshire RG21 6XS
and London
Companies and representatives
throughout the world

ISBN 0–333–53288–0 hardcover
ISBN 0–333–53289–9 paperback

A catalogue record for this book is available
from the British Library.

10   9   8   7   6   5   4   3   2   1
04 03 02 01 00 99 98 97 96 95

Printed in Great Britain by
Mackays of Chatham PLC
Chatham, Kent

Preface

The modernist tradition in American poetry traces its origins back to Walt Whitman. Whitman's poetry, like the modernists' poetry of this century, is epic, inclusive and concerned with 'making it new': each time seeing the world in radical and revolutionary terms equal to the universalising vision of America and its concept of democracy. For the modernist poets of this century Whitman's legacy is an unfinished one and Whitman waits to greet their efforts at the dawn of the twenty-first.

Modernist poetry was not confined to a few great though eccentric writers at the beginning of this century, rather it has been an enduring tradition embracing writers from the east coast, mid west and Pacific coasts: imagist, objectivist, beat. International in flavour and structure but determined first and foremost by its affinity with the language and conditions of mass American democracy and the constant imperative to renew and reawaken, this poetry finds its voice in its complexity and epic quality.

With its detailed introduction and scholarly essays this volume helps define the American modernist canon, its obsessions and its structure. Students will find the essays detailed and comprehensive, together giving a real feeling for the major poets not only of the modernist canon but also of America. Academics and serious readers will find a range of approaches and variety of subject matter which provide an important contribution to current poetic debate. This book is one of the few available to address the full variety, history and movement of American modernist poetry across this century.

Notes on the Contributors

Ian F. A. Bell is Professor of English and American Literature at the University of Keele. His books include *Critic as Scientist: The Modernist Poetics of Ezra Pound*; *Henry James and the Past: Readings into Time*; *Washington Square: Styles of Money*; and he has edited *Ezra Pound: Tactics for Reading*; *Henry James: Fiction as History* and *American Literary Landscapes* (with D. K. Adams).

Clive Bloom is the author of several books on literature, cultural theory and popular fiction. He has recently edited *Literature and Culture in Modern Britain: 1900–1929* and *American Drama in the Twentieth Century*, and is the author of *Pulp: from Sweeney Todd to Stephen King* (forthcoming).

Richard Bradbury is a lecturer in English and American literature at the University of Exeter. He contributes regularly to the **Insights** series.

Lorrayne Carroll teaches at the University of South Maine.

Brian Docherty is a poet and tutor in English at Goldsmiths' College, London. He is the editor of several books, including *American Crime Fiction*, *Twentieth-Century European Drama* and *The Beats*.

Thomas Evans is an independent scholar and writer who lives in Hertford, England.

Nancy K. Gish is Professor of English at the University of South Maine and is the author of several works on literature and poetry, including *Hugh MacDiarmid: The Man and His Work*.

Eric Mottram is Emeritus Professor of English and American Literature at King's College, University of London. He has published over a dozen books on modern literature and culture including studies on William Faulkner, Allen Ginsberg and William S. Burroughs.

Pat Righelato is a Tutor in Literature for the Open University.

David Seed lectures at Liverpool University, is the author of numerous articles and of full-length studies of Thomas Pynchon and Joseph Heller.

Gavin Selerie is a Tutor in Literature for Birkbeck College Centre for Extra-Mural Studies. He is editor of the Riverside series of interviews with Gregory Corso, Lawrence Ferlinghetti, Allen Ginsberg and others.

Geoff Ward is a Lecturer in the English Department at the University of Liverpool. The author of many articles on poetry from the Romantics to the present day, he has recently completed *Statues of Liberty: The New York School of Poets* and *Language, Poetry and the American Avant-Garde*. He is currently editing *The Bloomsbury Guide to Romantic Literature*, and is the author of six collections of poetry.

Alistair Wisker teaches at the University of East Anglia. He is the author of many articles and essays as well as a full-length study, *The Writing of Nathaniel West*.

Gregory Woods is a Lecturer for Manchester Metropolitan University. He is author of *Articulate Flesh: Male Homo-Eroticism and American Poetry*.

1

Introduction

CLIVE BLOOM

An American
is a complex of occasions,
themselves a geometry
of spatial nature.

Charles Olson, *Maximus Poems*

The founding figures of American modernist poetry are Whitman and Poe, but they do not stand in equal relationship to one another. Through Poe, we enter the reticent, traditionalist, religionistic and conservative world of T. S. Eliot (via French poetry), John Crowe Ransom and the Southern Agrarians; through Whitman we enter the Western, democratic, irreverent and individualist world of, among others, Ezra Pound (despite many of his views), William Carlos Williams and Allen Ginsberg. A minor note is struck by the Wordsworthian chords of those whose work explores the dilemmas of the personality via a detailed description of the natural world, poets such as Marianne Moore.

Throughout these strains the search for authenticity in voice and form is the central quest. In the context of American poetry and despite differing poets' adherence to similar original models, the message from these models is one decidedly against the grain. Whitman's message was one that taught the democratic poet that authenticity could only come from differentiation – a fresh start with a fresh language: Ezra Pound's 'Make it New', or, as William Carlos Williams put it, 'a reexamination of the means – on a fresh-basis'. Yet this language had to be both individual and universal; poetic and vernacular; a withdrawal into the self as an expansion of the self into the conceptual space of 'America'.

1

This search for authenticity, a search conducted essentially around language, gained urgency in the twentieth century with the influx of millions of new immigrants and with the highlighting of indigenous forms of American spoken by ordinary working people from the mid-west or the cities. This could be differentiated from the English spoken across the Atlantic and the European cultural norms that such speech implied. There is no equivalent of Georgianism in American poetry and even those Americans who left the United States in horror at the changes at home *brought* those particularly American concerns about language structure which found little common ground amongst English poets. Pound, 'H. D.', and Amy Lowell came and left. Eliot, in becoming a perfect Englishman in his 'fourpiece suit' (to use Virginia Woolf's satiric comment), struggled with the problem of being an American-manqué, up to and beyond the Second World War, as *The Four Quartets* testify and as the original title to *Sweeney Agonistes*, provisionally titled *Wanna Go Home, Baby*, gives notice. By 1939, Britain's own leading poet, W. H. Auden, had left for citizenship in America.

Whitman's poetic and inferential message, about America and its language (the structure of American *sensibility*), was reformulated and expanded by the poetic theorising of Ezra Pound ('make it new'), the geographical artistic shift to Chicago and the monumental meditation on the American language by H. L. Mencken published in 1919. By 1941, Mencken's preface to the fourth edition could state:

[T]he pull of American has become so powerful that it has begun to drag English with it, and in consequence some of the differences once visible have tended to disappear. The two forms of the language, of course, are still distinct in more ways than one, and when an Englishman and an American meet they continue to be conscious that each speaks a tongue that is far from identical with the tongue spoken by the other. But the Englishman, of late, has yielded so much to American example, in vocabulary, in idiom, in spelling and even in pronunciation, that what he speaks promises to become, on some not too remote tomorrow, a kind of dialect of American, just as the language spoken by the American was once a dialect of English. The English writers who note this change lay it to the influence of the American movies and talkies, but it seems to me that there is also something more, and something deeper. The American people now constitute by far the largest fraction of the English-speaking race, and since the World War they have shown in increasing inclination to throw off their old subservience to English precept and example. If only by the force of numbers, they are bound to exert a dominant influence upon the course of the common language hereafter.

The linguistic shift here suggested, a shift of structure and therefore of sensibility, makes the task of the American poet one dedicated to exploring the peculiarities and strangenesses of the liberal American condition. Indeed, 'the [very] first American colonists had perforce to invent Americanisms, if only to describe the unfamiliar landscape'. Origins and strangeness, beginnings and newness, these qualities, and the structural imperative of these explorations keep the American poetic imagination in tune with the ideas of Whitman, Pound, Williams, and Olson. America is a country overburdened with history, which none the less lives as if it had none. But if the authentic America is an America both lost and yet always new, a contradiction between metaphysics and history, where does America lie? If in the now, America is always without a memory; if in the 'then', it is already lost in history (indeed it has become 'Europe').

How often the poet will return to the puritan, or slave, or native American, origin of the continent, in order to rethink *anew* the epic of American democratic consciousness. Such rethinking brings its own structural imperatives, its own idiosyncratic grammar, its own oddities of typography in order to force a *new* perspective, and a new universal vision. This is the *rediscovery* of an authentic, lost origin of Americaness, rethought in the tracery of a hard and complex language, both highly personal (lyric) and highly public (epic). From Whitman to Ginsberg this is the pattern, whether the writer is, for example, William Carlos Williams, Charles Olson or Gregory Corso. Paragraphic and urgent, these writers attempt to capture the essence of the 'now' and the 'new' by a return to beginnings and an unfinished history of the past: one which is both their own (their family's) and the nation's. Travelling backwards in imagination they travel *forward* to meet their poetic forebears – the authentic always being the new, the beginning and (as Eliot pointed out) the end. These poets move forward to reconcile themselves (to justify themselves?) with Whitman.

The universal epic of the mind must be played out it the national particularities of the culture, and the poet cannot escape those particularities. Such particularities offer a subject matter and a *mode* but they also restrict and control. Unlike many other artists, poets are poets only intermittently and on their days off. Unlike W. B. Yeats, who wrote on his passport 'poet', or Amy Lowell, who enjoyed a private income, other poets have to 'hide' their vocation beneath a daytime job. Some may be school teachers, office clerks, publishers (T. S. Eliot); some may be small-town doctors (William Carlos Williams); some may be insurance executives (Wallace Stevens); some may become itinerants (Vachel Lindsay) or simply dropouts (Hart Crane; Gary Snyder); but the vast majority will, since the 1940s, go into academia teaching literature courses. As Randall Jarrell commented, ' the gods who had taken away the poet's audience had given him students'. Even those obtaining high public office (Archibald MacLeish) and burdened (or recognised) with prizes may still find the role of poet only recognised in contrast to what they do in their 'real' lives. In this way, for many of the poets, their everyday existence is a type of disguise: the poet busy doing other things, things authentic in another way; secondary realities.

In this excursion into the working lives of poets may be found some central contrasting motifs with that other literary form of immediacy, voice and authenticity, the drama. Elsewhere, I have pointed out the special role drama found for itself in America. There, I suggested 'enough for the reader to gather that the staged-drama in America has created its own space between and often outside of the dynamic forms of both film and television. Such a space requires our acceptance of a type of primary authenticity which unravels or questions the inauthenticity of popular consumer culture and the values of the American System'.

Such a statement suggests that both drama and poetry share a common goal based on common aims. This is not, perhaps, the case. The serious drama of America uses popular culture and the imagery of the popular imagination in order to turn it against itself and thereby show it as phoney, because manipulative of the popular mind. This seems not the case with the modernist poet, who never relinquishes the *idiom* and *structure* of popular culture. Neither Pound nor Eliot rejected mass culture *in toto*, nor, as with Woody Allen and Neil Simon, have such poets sentimentalised the popular imagination and its pleasures. The *rhythms* of the popular (jazzy and metropolitan; beat and junk culture) inform the best poets and even influence their technique (cummings and Olson).

The poet is therefore different from the playwright, more isolated, more removed from the everyday bustle of the culture business, and not required to earn a living as a poet. Indeed, saved by the daytime job, the poet is neither a 'professional' artist nor a collaborative one. Compromise is not a prerequisite and no other medium beckons. This isolation curiously keeps the poet within the community and its linguistic strengths even if the poet has not been of the community since the beginning of the century. Poetry in modern America is a specialisation but it is not a profession, nor does it reject business *per se* because it is not dependent upon it, hence Wallace Stevens's 'Money is a kind of Poetry'.

The complexities of the modernists are well known and need not detain us here, although a few comments may help to define the phenomenon. The modernist movement in America corresponds with the technological and industrial advances in that country which led to its commercial and cultural domination of the twentieth century. Beginning both in Chicago (Harriet Monroe) and London (by Pound and other expatriots) before the First World War, the movement spread into Europe and by the 1930s was receiving European avant-gardists fleeing from Hitler. By the 1940s and 1950s the movement was firmly established in America on the West Coast, in New York and in the Mid-West, taking its strength from the vibrancy, technology and commercialism of America's mass culture and popular idioms.

At once compressed and epic, modernist poetry drew its strength from oriental and classical sources in order to synthesise symbolist and romantic models. Elite and exclusive, poets nevertheless strove to revitalise democratic expression (especially during the 1940s and late 1950s). Eclectic in approach, both through lifestyle and through artistic temperament, American poets also combined an awareness of European modes but adapted them to American demotics, creating for themselves a language both unique to itself and, because of the rapid extension abroad of American culture, truly international.

Looking away from Europe and especially English models, poets internalised the American mythic mode; looking backward to Whitman they sought to *reinvent* themselves through a poetry that *reinvented* 'America'. Revolutionary and obsessed with the new, modernism nevertheless sought a rapprochement with the determining ideals of the puritan founding fathers, ideals they still saw as unachieved and as universal determinants for the future of all mankind. Thus newness and a new beginning became synonymous with authority, with a contract to make their work public and rooted; at once the end and the beginning of tradition (see Eliot or Hart Crane) – radical yet eternal.

This high, all embracing, transcendent way of approaching poetry was predicated on the central problem of organisation: structure would be meaning, not just carry the meaning of the content. This structure would bear the burden of visibility – the more perfect the structure and the formal conditions of the work so the better the work would close around itself, perfectly solipsistic because perfectly all embracing; an epic of structure and therefore of abstracted mental space (the individual poet as heroic and Whitmanesque) as well as national and public (the individual poet as everybody). Regardless of any particular political message in any particular poet (say Ginsberg), this general approach to poetry has the hallmark of an American sensibility and therefore of an American *political* disposition. Indeed, the conditions governing the aesthetics of modernism can be directly related to the commercial and industrial culture which grew up in America between the 1900s and the 1950s.

Moreover, for writers such as cummings and Olson *the very technology* of the modern determined their approach to their work. For cummings, the transfer from pen to typewriter meant imaginative liberation in the anonymous space of typography. At once freed from personality (as in Eliot's prescription), cummings's use of lower typecase for his name also aligned him with 'ordinary' readers: the poet e. e. cummings as everyman and anonymous, 'citizen of immortality . . . [the] poet is a little more than everything, he is democracy; he is alive: he is ourselves'. Ideally suited to formally rearranging the blank page, the use of the typewriter for composition opened the way for modernist poets to explore structures determined by a machine (therefore impersonal, public, denying genius and the egotistical sublime), but guided by a uniquely 'tuned' individual (closer to the nature of the real). Taken up by Charles Olson in his idea of 'Projective Verse' (the poem as a battery full of 'energy'), the typewriter liberates the poet *beyond* language and into the abstract space of a music *controlled* by new *formal* conventions:

> The irony is, from the machine has come one gain not yet sufficiently observed or used, but which leads directly on toward projective verse and its consequences. It is the advantage of the typewriter that, due to its rigidity and its space precisions, it can, for a poet, indicate exactly the breath, the pauses, the suspensions

even of syllables, the juxtapositions even of parts of phrases, which he intends. For the first time the poet has the stave and the bar a musician has had. For the first time he can, without the convention of rime [sic] and meter, record the listening he has done to his own speech and by that one act indicate how he would want any reader, silently or otherwise, to voice his work.

These complexities were, in all cases, determined by the defining struggle with structure. For the modernist, structural organisation is both a way of 'knowing' and of acting *within* the world. Thus representation, as a second-order reality, is rejected in favour of a mimetic technique which attempts to *be the real* in deed: Pound's *image*, William Carlos Williams's 'poem as a field of action' and Olson's objectivism. In striving to secure the 'real' and the deep structure of the individual and national temper, the poem's own inner structure becomes a principle of perception which goes beyond that represented. Such tension between content and structure within a poem redefines the conditions governing representation as 'copy' and representation as 'art': doing as becoming. Here is the difficulty of such poetry – the reader *knows* by becoming altered by the structure, *not* by extracting its meaning as is traditional. In such poetry, the community is estranged from itself and this estrangement is its reality – both new and already known – an archeology of personality and nation. Here the personality becomes synonymous with the national temper and the lyric with the epic. The intensely personal then resonates with a *public* urgency.

Monumental and yet fragile, such poetry negotiates a space between the structures of state (as representative of eternality, law and government) and those of the community (fluid, organic and impermanent). Although politicised at this level, modernist poetry tends to display an indifference to the intervention of immediacy in favour of an intervention at the level of grammar. Thus the 'eternal' quality of modernist poetry is predicated on the urgent and immediate need to intervene at the level of deep structure.

Such an intervention falls within an aesthetic approach which attempts to avoid the politicisation of content as an avoidance of partisanship – this is, of course, simply partisan. The new content of poetry during and after the 1950s was and is no more than a symptomatic shift in the battle over *structure* – a battle both aesthetic and political as it is a tussle over the ownership of the 'real' itself as a determinant of the factual. As such it is an *a priori activity*.

For the American modernist poet, poetry is an act within and conditional upon mass popular culture. This poetry recognises its connection to the life of mass culture at the level of organisation and linguistic structure. Such poetry is always *engaged* at the structural level, a level which is both aesthetic and deeply politicised as critique. This can be seen in Pound, with his insistence on seeing the thing clearly and which leads to his pronouncements on the 'image'.

> An 'Image' is that which presents an intellectual and emotional complex in an instant of time. I use the term 'complex' rather in the technical sense employed by the newer psychologists[.]

He continues, 'it is the presentation of such a "complex" instantaneously which gives that sense of sudden liberation'. This 'liberation' is the creed of the American contract: a frontier concern, both revolutionary and emancipatory, the fulfilment of the enlightenment humanist project.

For T. S. Eliot, anglicised through and through, the adherence to tradition (one specifically 'invented' by Eliot himself) liberates the individual into the world both of the technician and of the old-fashioned puritan craftsman: a maker rather than a genius (thus he answered W. B. Yeats's 1900 essay 'Symbolism and Poetry' with 'Tradition and the Individual Talent': 'the poet has, not a personality to express, but a particular medium'. 'The analogy [being] that of the catalyst'.

For William Carlos Williams, the poem is a 'field of action', in which the editorial niceties of T. S. Eliot are already too English. For Williams, poetry must be part of the modern world:

> What, by this approach I am trying to sketch, what we are trying to do is not only to disengage the elements of a measure but to seek (what we believe is there) a new measure or a new way of measuring that will be commensurate with the social, economic world in which we are living as contrasted with the past. It is in many ways a different world from the past calling for a different measure.

And as American poetry it must be as fecund as American industry.

It is as though for the moment we should be profuse, we Americans; we need to build up a mass, a conglomerate maybe, containing few gems but bits of them ... . Stop a minute to emphasize our own position: It is not that of Mr Eliot. We are making a modern bolus.

In this making poetry new at the level of structure, the poet must (*faux naif*) return to a mid-western language just discovering itself and awaiting its Whitman. Williams continues,

In any case we as loose, disassociated (linguistically), yawping speakers of a new language are privileged (I guess) to sense and so to seek to discover that possible thing which is disturbing the metrical table of values ... .
The yeast animating Whitman and all the 'moderns'. ...
This isn't optimism, it is chemistry: Or better physics.

Here the origin finds the present, and the urgency of Whitman and the atomic bomb become one. And why, asks Williams, did W. H. Auden 'flee' to America, if it wasn't to know himself in 'that instability in the language where innovations would be at home'. The objective, then, is not 'experimentation but *man*'. The Universal man, new and eternal, is an American. The poetry of this new creation must be as Olson suggests, galvanic: a battery full of energy determined, to use the jargon of the 1950s, by 'the *kinetics* of the thing', the poet both technician and frontiersman. And so, for all these poets, 'all poetry is experimental poetry' and 'one reads poetry with one's nerves'.

The writers in this volume represent an enduring and indicative strain in American poetry. Despite revisions and revocations they still demand our full attention and a seriousness, perhaps, temporarily forgotten.

2

H.D. (Hilda Doolittle)

DAVID SEED

In 1913 the first three poems were published by 'H.D., Imagiste'. Pound had attached his famous label, he explained in a letter of 1927, as a promotional tactic: 'the name was invented to launch H.D. and Aldington'.[1] This statement reads disingenuously because, at the time, Pound's activities on behalf of Imagism formed part of a sustained programme for encouraging experimentation in poetry, and his 'cautions' (as he called them), 'A Few Don'ts', articulated a direction which that experimentation might take. Pound's undoubted energy as a publiciser of new work paid off with a vengeance in the case of H.D. because the label 'imagiste' stuck long after it had ceased to be applicable to her poetry. More seriously, Pound's injunctions about poetic expression ('the natural object is always the *adequate* symbol', 'go in fear of abstractions', etc.) privileged a critical vocabulary which centred on the concrete, the actual, and the 'hard'.[2] H.D.'s biographer Barbara Guest, for instance, persists in reading the former's early poems through Pound's spectacles. Calling her the 'finest Imagist', Guest declares that 'her poetry of this period is always concrete, never abstract'.[3]

As a comment on the poems collected in *Sea Garden* (1916) this is woefully superficial because it ignores their main characteristics of mobility and allusion. If we consider 'Hermes of the Ways' (one of the three poems Pound initially endorsed), the opening takes the Imagists' much vaunted hardness as a point of departure towards liquidity and flux. The poem does not progress by defining a static image with mounting clarity but through oppositional statements of the pattern 'A but B'. Thus the sea's 'many-foamed ways' is contrasted with the triple ways of Hermes; the metaphorical implications of the trees' twisted boughs are distinguished from a shadow ('of the masthead'), suggesting either shipwreck or arrival from the sea. The setting of the poem is the point where land meets sea, but it is a meeting-place also between the speaker and Hermes. The term 'Hermes' indeed opens up a whole lexicon of possible allusions from which H.D. can select. Primarily the reader would recognise the name of a god, which immediately complicates the specificity of natural description by introducing the *super*natural. The dimension of the poem's reality thus becomes ambiguous, as does the identity of the speaker. If Hermes is coming as psychopomp then the voice of the poem is dead; and if Hermes comes as the guardian of wayfarers then the poem's situation is implicitly located with reference to a hinterland or a future of travelling. A later poem, 'In the Rain', explicitly draws attention to Hermes' intermediary status between two worlds: 'You are a man / feigning the god head'.

'Hermes of the Ways', then, constantly refers beyond itself, destabilising the apparent definiteness of its statements, and in that respect it is not unusual among H.D.'s early poems, which repeatedly evoke essences and beings behind the natural descriptions. 'Oread', for example, implies an identity for its speaker as a mountain nymph and telescopes together the fluidity of the sea and the fixity of a mountain landscape into a perceptual paradox. H.D. gives helpful indications of the way her poetry is moving in her review of John Gould Fletcher's *Goblins and Pagodas* in *The Egoist* for 1916. The qualities she praises in his work reflect back on her own poems: 'it is no static vision that Mr. Fletcher seeks to give us. ... He uses the direct image, it is true, but he seems to use it as a means of evoking other and vaguer images.' His imagery, in other words, does not function as an end in itself but to gain access to further dimensions of meaning; and as her review continues H.D. waxes positively religious over the process of their utterance: 'through it all, it is the soul or mind or inspiration of the poet, knowing within itself its problems, unanswerable. ... Knowing indeed not whence it cometh and whither it goeth, but flaunting in the face of its own ignorance, its own undaunted quest'.[4] The quest of the spirit, as we shall see, becomes a major motif in H.D.'s poetry. Suffice it here to recognise the inspirational dimension she finds in Fletcher's poetry. Having this in mind, the historian of Imagism J. B. Harmer has denied that 'Oread' is an imagistic work at all, preferring instead to see it as a 'perfect example in the Orphic tradition'.[5] And more recently Adalaide Morris has explained the transcendental nature of H.D.'s images: 'Unlike other of the Imagists, H.D. conceived of essence as god-stuff. To her, each intense natural fact is the trace of a spiritual force; each charged landscape enshrines a deity.'[6] Morris argues convincingly that H.D.'s imaginative energies here are projective – addressing, invoking or simply referring to animistic essences behind objects. This attitude to reality must be related to another major aspect of H.D.'s work before her evocation of the transcendental can be properly understood.

From an early stage in her career H.D. tried her hand at translating from Euripides, *Iphigenia in Aulis*, Pausanias and other classical writers. T. S. Eliot was so impressed by the former that he thought they exceeded Gilbert Murray's – which was praise indeed.[7] Many of H.D.'s Grecian poems resemble translations and this similarity offered her an avenue of approach to the transcendental. Rachel Blau DuPlessis has shrewdly identified a twinned purpose in theses poems – 'first, a desire to make meaning as a woman, in part by, second, the desire to supplant dominant meanings in gender depiction'.[8] This is well put and helps to explain how a poem like 'Eurydice' levels an assertive feminine voice against the unnamed male agency of her fate (Orpheus), or how 'Demeter' allows the goddess to declare her identity against male representations of her. Because the reader recognises the mythical nature of these speakers, their relation to the poet is necessarily oblique. Is H.D. simply adopting dramatic personae or offering a free translation from a classical work in order to evoke certain states of mind? The thrust of much feminist criticism of H.D. is to read such poems inwards, to hypothesise the psychic processes at work behind these masks. But they could be taken differently and a comparison with Eliot might help at this point.

In the sequence 'Ash Wednesday' he demonstrates his commitment to the Church of England rhetorically by incorporating sections of the Anglican liturgy so that his own voice merges into a collective voice of prayer. In 'Ash Wednesday' there is no tension between the individual and collective voices, whereas, for H.D., the myths of antiquity offered her narratives which could be re-articulated and revised. Characteristically, then, her texts are palimpsests, superscriptions over known sequences. The poem 'Nossis' dramatises this process as an attempt to call a poet back from the dead. A dialogue takes place between the invoking male voice and a second (female?) voice testing his seriousness. Place takes on the connotations of a shrine ('a shelter / wrought of flame and spirit') and the young poet ('nossis' meaning 'young girl' in classical Greek) is raised in the sense that her words are quoted. This act of quotation amounts to a temporary revivification of the poet and anticipates H.D.'s use of the Egyptian hieroglyphics in her works. There is a constant impulse in her poems to bring these primal texts back to life; indeed it would only be a slight exaggeration to say that H.D. chooses her mythical speakers in order to question the finality of death. One of the most obvious examples in this context would be 'A Dead Priestess Speaks', where contrasts are drawn between the routine religious observations of the living and the visionary experience of the priestess: 'they did not see the reach of purple-wing / that lifted me out of the little room'.[9] But the priestess is no saint. On the contrary, the poem sets up a dialectic between her spirituality and all too human failings, supported by a concentration on her death as a point of transition. H.D. allows for the possibility of speakers from beyond the grave by borrowing the classical notion of underground as the abode of the souls of the dead. Life and death are thus only separated spatially and in that respect there is a clear continuity between her classical poems and 'R.A.F.' (1943), where she is visited by a dead pilot. His wings transform him into a Hermes bringing her a sign of her future and also recalling memories of meeting him before he died. Past, present and future merge in the speaker's recognition of communion with the superhuman: 'we were people who had crossed over'.[10]

The work which most explicitly engages with the notion of re-inscription is H.D.'s novel *Palimpsest* (1926). Here three narrative sections are assembled, each one focusing on a female writer; that of Hipparchia (dated *c.*75 BC), of Raymonde Ransome (dated *c.*1916–26), and that of Helen Fairwood (*c.* 1925). All three are displaced from their native countries. Hipparchia is a Greek in Roman Italy; the second an American in London; and the third an English secretary in Egypt. In each section a triangular love-relationship is adumbrated where a tension emerges between the spirituality of the main female figure and the materialism of the main male character. *Palimpsest* thus sets up triads within triads, pushing repetition to the foreground as one of its main rhetorical devices. But more is involved here than one part of the text echoing an earlier part. Hipparchia, for instance, is repeatedly compared to holy figures; she resembles a 'young Demeter' or 'some Assyrian deity'. These analogies displace the reader simultaneously into a super-human dimension and into a mythical past prior to the narrative itself. In the second section the perspective character of the novel registers a consciousness of duality which questions the primacy of the immediate and the actual: 'Behind the Botticelli, there was another Botticelli, behind London there was another London ... behind a mist and drift of anodyne in an Italian background ... there was another Italy, another Venus, another realm of beauty never to be apprehended with the sends'.[11] No character then is autonomous but in some way each is a re-embodiment of an earlier figure and the refrain which punctuates Part 3, 'James Joyce was right', suggests that *Ulysses* offered H.D. a model of narrative reenactment.

It is essential, however, to recognise that *Palimpsest* anticipates H.D.'s *Trilogy* and later works in investing the past with a spiritual virtue which can only be recaptured by somehow bridging the gap between then and now.[12] In the course of a fine analysis of this novel, Deborah Kelly Kloepfer argues that such connections lie at the centre of the novel's progression: 'H.D. attempts to "close the gap" both within each section and in an intertextual project that appears in early allusions to later textual spheres as she structures a triad that erects boundaries of time and space and then abandons them'.[13] The specification of a dated period for each section and the location of key characters in definite settings both blur as the phenomenal gives ground to the mythic. Egypt has a key role to play in this process ('Egypt ... opened doors. Doors led through').[14] The liminal image is at once internal and external, especially in the third section of the novel, where Helen's nocturnal visit to a burial chamber in a recently opened pyramid has the following effect: 'doors, partitions in herself had been broken in the magic of this atmosphere'.[15] Egypt is the point where all the lines of analogy and spiritual reference converge, without, however, unifying the conclusion to the novel. The dialectic which H.D. makes explicit, in the first section, between the spiritual and the social persists right to the end in the contrasts between sacred locations and the unresponsiveness of most of the European characters.

At one point in *Palimpsest* a character reflects that ' the very names ... of the Greek gods still held virtue' and names do indeed recur throughout H.D.'s works as privileged signifiers, the bearers of special meaning.[16] The poem 'Sea Heroes' commemorates the dead but the very act of listing their names transforms recital into a sacralising utterance: 'and each god-like name spoken / is as a shrine in a godless place.'[17] Naming, then, can take on a quasi-magical significance and it is no coincidence that H.D. chose characters with the same initial as her forename, Hedylus,

Hermione, Hermes, etc.). *Helen in Egypt* (1961) rehearses classical names ('Cypris, Cypria, Amor, / say the words over and over') but refuses to gloss the incantation beyond an exploitation of rhythm and alliteration, perhaps for fear of compromising the performative force of the recital.[18] H.D. is here using names in an occult manner as the repositories of power. Richard Cavendish explains that 'in magical theory the "real" name of a god as an idea contains the essence of that god or idea, and therefore enshrines its power. Using the name turns on this power automatically...'[19] Shortly we shall see other examples of how names figure in H.D.'s works.

Helen in Egypt represents H.D.'s most ambitious attempt at revising a classical myth. It attempts to deflect concentration on Helen's sexual guilt for the Trojan Wars by relocating her, in effect finding another Helen. The story of the Trojan Wars is reduced to 'all this phantasmagoria of Troy' and in its place H.D. posits out a counter-myth expressed by the poet Stesichoros of Sicily and elaborated in Euripides' *Helen*. According to the latter, Paris received in marriage a 'living image compounded of the ether' which resembled Helen.[20] This image desubstantialises the Trojan Helen into a phantasm, whereas the real Helen was transported to Egypt by Hermes and deposited in the palace of Proteus. Where Euripides' play concerns Helen's successful escape from Egypt to return to Greece, H.D. sets up a choric meditation on the nature of the spiritual. In the three books of this sequence we witness Helen in Egypt, then in Greece, where she has been summoned by Thetis, and finally back in Egypt, which functions as a spiritual base. Purpose is articulated through figures of questing as Helen seeks to 're-establish the ancient Mysteries', scrutinising the hieroglyphics (the 'old pictures') for their hidden meaning. But the process of interrogating these images proves to be arduous in the extreme ('indecipherable hieroglyph, ... I can not "read"').[21]

Just as Champollion's decipherment of the Rossetta Stone gave the American Romantics a ready-made analogy for the encoded book of Nature, so these pictograms break down the distinction between script and natural sign.[22] Their refusal to render up meaning paradoxically increases their spiritual force by suggesting a background of unavailable significance. In his study *The Idea of the Holy* (English translation published in 1923), Rudolf Otto links this cryptic quality with the expression of the numinous: 'Nothing can be found in all the world of "natural" feelings bearing so immediate an analogy ... to the religious consciousness of ineffable, unutterable mystery, the "absolute other", as the incomprehensible, unwanted, enigmatic thing, in whatever place or guise it may confront us.'[23]

The exact nature of this hidden meaning is never specified. Instead, as in *Four Quartets*, H.D. articulates the pursuit of that meaning through journeys and figures of penetration ('another portal, another symbol'). *Helen in Egypt* progresses dialogically, establishing its own narrative status in opposition to the non-common Helen myth, pitting a rationalising prose commentary against its poetical voices, and within its choral verses setting up uncompleted dialogues between the speaker and different deities. Their refusal to answer their invocations balances the reluctance of the hieroglyphs to yield up their meanings, and thereby leaves silences in the sequence, semantic gaps which tease the reader's imagination. As early as 1927 the novelist May Sinclair had identified this quality in H.D.'s post-imagistic poems. The obscurities were no accident, she argued. On the contrary, 'the baffling cryptic touch is deliberate, a device for evoking magic, for suggesting the unspeakable mysteries'.[24]

It was these mysteries which linked H.D. to her erstwhile mentor Ezra Pound. She met Pound and William Carlos Williams while they were at the University of Pennsylvania but, of the two, her relationship with Pound was by far the more important. Perhaps because of his commitment to the objectively observable, she declared: 'I thought Williams common-place and banal.'[25] Pound, on the other hand, played a formative role in establishing her career and, to judge from her memoir *End to Torment* (written 1958, published 1979), H.D. saw her destiny as being closely entwined in Pound's. Both poets had a developing interest in ancient religions. In 1911, the same year that H.D. took up residence in London, Pound met the theosophist G. R. S. Mead and wrote a lecture for the latter's Quest Society, 'Psychology and Troubadours', which posits a cult of love in Provencal poetry deriving from the Eleusinian mysteries. This belief persisted, so that in his article 'Terra Italica' (winter 1931) Pound returned to the 'cult of Eleusis' and declared: 'I suggest that students trying to understand the poesy of southern Europe from 1050 to 1400 should try to open it with this key.'[26] Acting on such hints, Leon Surette has presented a case that the Eleusinian mysteries lie at the heart of the *Cantos*. He argues that Pound was fascinated by a cult centred on coition, although he admits that it is often difficult for the reader to decide exactly how Pound is using these mythic references. In spite of his notorious intellectualism these rituals offered Pound a release from thought: 'Eleusis is a cult of the chthonic, uniting in the doubled goddess and god the double process of death and birth ...' The *Raison d'être* of the cults is ' to produce in the faithful a psychic experience, an encounter with the divine, which mystically transforms the lives of the initiates'. Surette drily concludes that 'by going back to Eleusis, Pound no doubt believed himself to be going back to the very rock bed of human religious sensibility'.[27] Surette's analysis locates a whole series of buried references in the *Cantos* and puts into context poems like Cantos 39 and 79. The former conflates references to Roman, Greek and Egyptian fertility goddesses, celebrating sexuality as an apotheosis of the natural; while Canto 79 partly composes a landscape peopled with nymphs and goddesses where the generative energy of nature is expressed as a force embedded in the pomegranate: 'This fruit has a fire within it / Pomona, Pomona'.

Where Pound uses the Eleusinian mysteries to give poetical expression to his own intuitions or to dramatise the sexual dimension to the male creative urge, H.D. devotes a more literal attention to the rites. 'At Eleusis' addresses a novice about to be initiated, maximising the risk of the step she is taking. 'The Mysteries', on the other hand, uses a choric sequence to enact the survival of the spirit. An incantatory repetitive opening sets up a space ('nothing before of mystery, / nothing past, / only the emptiness') which can be filled by a counter-voice asserting the potency of rebirth. The talismanic object enabling the transition from one voice to the other is at once sceptre, flower-shaft, and spear, charged with the magical power of killing the writer. This multiple symbol will be developed in the third part of the war *Trilogy*, 'The Flowering of the Rod'. In 'The Mysteries' the new voice declares a purpose which identifies the poem's ritual as that evoking the resurrection of Adonis.[28]

H.D.'s fire occurs here as a sacralised force not primarily a sexual one, and the voice insists on the permanence of these rites ('the mysteries remain') through the sacramental objects of bread and wine – tactically chosen to straddle the pagan and the Christian. *End to Torment* makes it clear that H.D. read the *Cantos* as they appeared (she even referred to *Helen in Egypt* as her own '*Cantos*') and it is a reasonable inference that she was aware of how her spiritual interests were diverging from Pound's. Both were fascinated by abstruse data but H.D.'s preoccupation with the occult spreads right through her career. Her 1935 novel *Nights* draws on the Arcana of the Tarot to articulate the sexual union of two characters, and, as we shall see, her *Trilogy* makes extensive use of alchemical transformations. H.D. was led by Freud to one interpretation of her preoccupation with secret hidden truths – that it showed a 'suppressed desire for forbidden "signs and wonders" breaking bounds'; but H.D. would never stay satisfied with an interpretation which denied the possibility of transcendental truth.[29]

Both Pound and H.D. were responsive to the growing scholarship on the history of religions, at the centre of which stood Frazer's *Golden Bough*. Frazer applied an evolutionary method to the comparative study of religions, identifying similarities across an enormous range of examples, and arguing that traces of pre-Christian cults could be found in the superstitions and orthodox Christianity of the present. His *magnum opus* directly influenced Jessie L. Weston's *From Ritual to Romance*, a much publicised influence, in turn, on *The Waste Land*. Frazer stands also behind Jane Harrison's pioneering works on the history of Greek religion, which H.D. almost certainly knew, and John B. Vickery has shown how Frazerian motifs appear not only in Pound's *Cantos* but in the novels of H.D.'s first husband Richard Aldington. From a number of different directions, then, H.D. could not have avoided the influence of Frazer, who, Vickery argues, offered the moderns an example of ordering materials, muffling the plot of his 'displaced quest romance' by circling round central motifs and figures.[30] H.D. is also known to have read *The Paganism in Our Christianity* (1928) by the Egyptologist Arthur E. P. B. Weigall, who distinguishes certain areas of the gospels from a basically historical narrative. The descent into Hell is compared to the myths of Osiris, Hermes, etc.; the story of the Magi used in 'The Flowering of the Rod' he identifies as a legend probably from the lost scriptures of Mithras; the cult of which was transferred onto the Virgin Mary, itself of Egyptian origins; and Weigall describes Christmas as the 'birthday of the sun, and of Mithra in particular, and nearly everything about it is purely pagan'.[31] Weigall helped to confirm H.D.'s conviction of the Egyptian origins of much Western religion and gave her further documentation of how religions evolve.

Her religious syncretism is therefore quite different from say Emerson's, where all faiths are taken as equally available, at least intellectually speaking. H.D.'s awareness of how the past can manifest itself in the present is fed by a historical and even

etymological sense of evolution, so that spiritual revitalisation involves for her an investigation of and therefore a return to origins.

Like Eliot's *Four Quartets*, H.D.'s war *Trilogy* responds to cultural
crisis by trying to re-tap spiritual sources and part of this enterprise
involves an investigation of her own Moravian background in *The
Gift* (written in 1941 and 1943). She traces her way through a
'labyrinth of associated memories' back to her realisation that
Count Zinzendorf had headed a band of initiates who had brought
their secret to America. The crucial event for H.D. in her spiritual
inheritance is the discovery that a meeting had taken place between
the Moravians and American Indians, where briefly two religions
had merged. Deciphering a record of this meeting on a 'scroll of
flexible deerskin', H.D. notes her sense of 'strange words spoken,
strange rhythms sung which were prompted, all alike said, by the
power of the Holy Spirit; the Holy Ghost of the Christian ritualists
and the Great Spirit of the Indians poured their grace alike'.[32] By
learning of this meeting H.D. has understood how the 'gift' of the
title (meaning variously spiritual endowment, inheritance, historical object, etc.) can be passed down through generations; and the
event in the past enables the book to end on a prayer from a 'great
choir of strange voices' which takes place in the present – the
London blitz.

In *The Gift* H.D.'s main obstacle was the oblivion of the past, but
in the *Trilogy* the process of recovery can only occur as a struggle
between opposing voices. Where *Four Quartets* will try out forms of
expression and then turn against them ('That was a way of putting
it – not very satisfactory': 'East Coker II') in a prolonged series of
revisions, H.D. sets up a tension between affirming and questioning
voices so that the sequence only arrives at ultimate affirmation after
a dialogue between faith and scepticism. The pronouns in the
Trilogy, therefore, constantly shift as the opposition shift ('we' vs
'they', 'you' vs 'I', etc.) and as the accusations change from charges
of evil to heterodoxy and attacks on H.D.'s method. Poem 38 of
'The Walls Do not Fall' draws on a letter sent to Bryher (H.D.'s
companion Winifred Ellerman) questioning the role of the writer in
reconstruction.[33]

H.D.'s answer, which is crucial to reasserting her method of argument, is to undermine the autonomy of the accusing voice,
tracing back its 'inherited tendencies' to a racial pool where opposing positions meet. A similar clash between voices occurs towards
the end of 'Tribute to the Angels', where an attack on 'facile

reasoning' turns into a debate over representations of feminine spirituality. This debate hinges specifically on qualities of coldness, fixity and abstraction which the affirming voice counters by insisting on vitality, dynamism and simple accessibility. Although the form of these sections (36–9) resembles a theoretical debate ('I grant you her face was innocent') we shall see how H.D. uses different kinds of persuasion – word-play and imagistic transformation, to name only two.

The starting-point for the *Trilogy* is an image of fracture, of bombed-out houses ('ruin everywhere'); but by conflating the London blitz with the opening of the tomb at Karnak H.D. turns destruction into potential discovery. Without losing its initial actuality the house becomes at once tomb, skull, and body – in other words a container. And 'The Walls Do not Fall' proceeds to explore the metaphorical implications of this image. One version of the house is a sea-shell, which Susan Gubar has interpreted partly as echoing the hard objects in H.D.'s early poetry.[34] It is more helpful to consider the shell as a container of internal vitality because one urgency in these poems is to express possibilities of survival.

This H.D. does by shifting the 'flabby, amorphous hermit' within the shell to a proverbial image of the humblest form of life (the worm), which is then transformed into a figure of pride ('So we reveal our status / with twin-horns, disk, erect serpent'). Susan Friedman has rightly spotted a revisionist impulse at work here to change the serpent from a symbol of death back to its pagan connotations of healing.[35] And, in *Tribute to Freud*, H.D. toys with the psychic associations of 'serpent', linking it with Aaron's rod and the letter S ('seal, symbol, serpent').[36] The lines from 'The Walls' just quoted implicitly challenge the reader to dispense with conventional and obvious (and Freudian) suggestions of the phallic in the serpent image, attributing a sacred quality to it as a preliminary step to introducing female spiritual figures.

H.D. never for a moment forgets that she is dealing with language, and accordingly underlines the magic potential of letters by repeating their divine origin from Mercury, Hermes, and Thoth. Playing on the distinction between words and primal logos, she frequently approaches the former as cryptograms where one term is embedded within another. In the section dealing with language ('The Walls' 10) 'Sword' breaks obviously into 'S + word'. If common words carry this potential, names are even more charged with meaning. Thus 'Osiris equates O-sir-is or O-Sire-is' ('The

Walls' 40). The *Trilogy* is riddled (pun intended) with references to enigmas, signs, insignia, all of which are used to imply a vast semantic field ready to be tapped. H.D. is as convinced as the American Puritans that words are 'carriers ... by whose help the thoughts of our minds and savory apprehensions of truth may be communicated', i.e. that words are especially privileged mediators between humanity and spiritual truth.[37] The few 'companions of the flame' who recognise this power of language are potential poets because they therefore recognise how literature and religion overlap. The elite into which H.D. invites the reader, through a collective 'we', reflects what Susan Friedman calls her 'sense of community with the nameless initiates tied to an evolving esoteric tradition'.[38] H.D. becomes a semiotician of the spiritual by finding a permanent significatory quality in all objects, which can only be made articulate through language. The figure of opening up a building thus becomes a trope of semantic dis-covery, and the flowering of a tree within a ruin, which stands at the centre of 'Tribute' (20), becomes a sign of the rebirth of life within a context of death. It is at once literal metonym ('this is no rune nor riddle') and a figural recall of ancient sacred groves, so that a perception of the impression's holy quality becomes a means of apprehending the actual.

H.D.'s focus on names involves etymology as well as lateral identifications. In the typescript of *The Gift* she wrote: 'Under every shrine to Jupiter, to Zeus-pater, or Theus-pater or God-the father ... there is an earlier altar.'[39] 'Tribute to the Angels' redirects such lines of reference on to goddesses and specifically addresses the associations of the name Venus. H.D. explained to Norman Holmes Pearson: 'The Venus name, I believe is Anael but I spelt it Annael; it didn't seem to "work" until I did – it links on too with Anna, Hannah or Grace.[40] The poetical coherence is only achieved once the name can be read as 'Anna-el' and glossed as 'peace of God' ('Tribute' 16). Probably having such names in mind, Robert Duncan has argued that H.D. uses these gods as 'personae of states of mind', although it would be more appropriate to the hermetic and cabbalistic traditions on which H.D. was drawing to see them as the personifications of spiritual essences.[41] Poems 11 and 12 of 'Tribute' attempt to counter the dominant associations between Venus and the flesh ('for venery stands for impurity') by re-inducing a spirit of reverence to this figure. Recapturing these solemn resonances retrospectively reminds us of the significance of the shell as an object holy to Venus or to Aphrodite, her foam-born Greek counterpart; and in this way names can function in the *Trilogy* as key focuses of meaning.

It should be clear by now that one major aim of H.D.'s *Trilogy* is to probe after spiritual sources. This is articulated through a series of injunctions which draw the reader into a common purpose ('let us search the old highways'), into a quest which is at once inner and outer, a journey without maps or familiar markers. In that respect the *Trilogy* continues a declaration of intent which H.D. made in her 1919 prose work *Notes on Thought and Vision*. Here she expresses self-exploration through a familiar American image: 'My sign-posts are not yours, but if I blaze my own trail, it may help to give you confidence and urge you to get out of the murky, dead, old, thousand-times explored old world.'[42] Especially by the time of the second World War this stark antithesis between the old and the new has become complicated into a contrast between the known and the unknown. The latter both terrifies and draws the exploring self – onwards through a series of emergences (from the shell, from the husk of the old self, and so on) to liminal experiences where new spiritual areas are opened up. Now the doctrine of dream becomes anti-Freudian. 'The Walls' 20 stresses the crucial role of dream as a mediator between the self and what she called in 1919 'over-consciousness' ('that way of inspiration / is always open'); whereas Freud, for her, 'shut the door on transcendental specula-tions'.[43] The occult offers H.D. the opposite possibility: 'here is the alchemist's key, / it unlocks secret doors'; but nothing demon-strates the arduous nature of these poems' progression more than the poet's fear at these new possibilities. As Susan Friedman points out, the access to new dimensions of consciousness granted by occult lore threatens to swamp the self out of existence and for this reason H.D. strives for a 'synthesis of intellect and vision, science and religion'.[44] If this is the case, the way a visitation is described during the London bombing takes on a more complex significance: 'The Presence was spectrum-blue, / ultimate blue ray, / rare as radium ...' ('The Walls'). H.D. is not simply using the natural to express the transcendental, which is a frequent device in religious literature, but using the radium analogy to bridge the gap between the rational and the non-rational. It is a cleverly chosen analogy because it appeals to the reader's recognition of one of the most mysterious forces in Nature, and it also anticipates H.D.'s applica-tion of alchemy in the second part of the *Trilogy*.

'Tribute to the Angels' combines two central notions: the apocalyptic destruction of the old order and an institution of the new; and the alchemical concept of transformation whose main agency is fire. As usual, H.D. directs her attention to her own raw materials by 'distilling' words down to a common root. Thus poem & assembles instructions to the apprentice alchemist: 'now polish the crucible ... and change and alter, mer, mere, mére, mater, Maria, Mary'.

The crucible is one form of the sacramental implement the chalice, whose associations H.D. partly identifies in *The Gift* as follows: 'cup, like calix is a word for part of a flower that is like a cup'.[45] 'Tribute' expands these associations since the alchemical process introduces the image of the flowering tree, and looks forward to the final book of the *Trilogy*, 'The Flowering of the Rod'. In the lines quoted above, H.D. at once conflates alchemy, etymology and the litany of the Virgin Mary, tracing terms back to a primal generative matter (or mater). Jung's study *Psychology and Alchemy* identifies the hermetic vessel of such experiments as a 'kind of matrix or uterus' which would be entirely congenial to H.D.'s use of the image.[46] And Adalaide Morris has commented usefully on the 'reverse alchemy' of war (railings being converted into guns), which is countered by H.D.'s re-telling the 'story of the making of the philosopher's stone'.[47]

The descriptions of experiments early in 'Tribute' identify the feminine as a generative matrix out of which can grow another visitation. The abstract 'presence' of 'The Walls' now becomes a personal visit: 'and she was standing there, / actually, at the turn of the stair' ('Tribute' 25). The simple matter-of-fact language insists on the immediacy of this presence, perceived this time by three people; and the following poems in this book are devoted to attempts to explain the feminine principle in opposition to her conventional depictions. This process involves H.D. in one of her most daring applications of the palimpsest – a reworking of the New Testament 'Revelation'. The borrowing of the mystical number seven and the many references to the angels represent two obvious examples of H.D. incorporating biblical elements, but what is more striking is the way she superimposes her new feminine text over the biblical account. Bearing visionary witness is central to this context and H.D.'s personal 'I saw' challenges the textual authority of 'I John saw' (clearly differentiated by appearing in italics) and revises a key episode in 'Revelation' from the masculine to the feminine. In Chapter I: 13–4 John sees 'in the midst of the seven candlesticks one like unto the Son of man, clothed with a garment down to the foot, and girt about the paps with a golden girdle. His head and his hairs were white like wool, and white as snow.' H.D. changes the gender of this figure to associate her with our Lady of the Snow and thus seeks to replace one female archetype, the whore of Babylon, with another whose key attribute of whiteness offers her a climax to 'Tribute' since John's apocalyptic rainbow telescopes together into 'all-colour', a chromatic point where opposites are harmonised.

'The Flowering of the Rod' continues H.D.'s palimpsest of the gospel by presenting a narrative of Mary Magdalene and Kaspar, one of the three magi. The latter legend was identified by Arthur Weigall as Mithraic and an accretion to the main Christian tradition; and Mary Magdalene is chosen, as Susan Gubar suggests, for her social marginality.[48] Once again her name becomes a nexus of association: 'I am Mary – O, there are Mary a-plenty, / (though I am Mara, bitter) I shall be Mary-myrrh' ('The Flowering' 16). Under the guise of Mara she becomes a lamenter of the dead. As myrrh she becomes involved in the cultic use of incense. And as Mary of Magdala ('a tower'. 'I am Mary, a great tower') she challenges the hegemony of the traditional Mary, composing her own litanic statements in place of 'tower of ivory'. The revisionist monologues of H.D.'s earlier poetry now find their culmination in this Mary's assertion of her own dignity. Not only is she a witness to resurrection but she becomes included as another of H.D.'s initiates into secret love, conveying a cryptic message to Kaspar which can only be approached through such metaphors as the opening of a flower.

A conviction of another dimension to experience which can only be glimpsed through revelation lies at the heart of H.D.'s entire oeuvre and explains her interest in the occult and the hermetic as attempts to systematise that conviction. H.D. herself measured her life between mystical experiences she had in Corfu, Egypt, and later, London. As early as 1912 she was experimenting with automatic writing. In the 1920s she turned to the Tarot and numerology, and, about astrology, declared to Bryher: 'I do believe in these things, and think there is a whole other-science of them.'[49] By the time she came to work on the *Trilogy* she was also drawing, as we have seen, on alchemy and religious history. It seems, then, that H.D. clearly belongs in a tradition of American transcendental writing which retains many devices of religious expression quite independent of any body of formal doctrine. She can appear, for example, positively Emersonian in implying that 'every natural act is a symbol of some spiritual fact'. He would exemplify this general truth from the 1836 'Nature' in a poem like 'Two Rivers' where a spiritual river takes over precedence from the Concord River. But although H.D. similarly uses natural objects a signs she refuses to devalue their physical actuality, so that a tension is built up between the natural and the transcendental. From Poe, who was her favourite poet in her teens, H.D. may have taken an interest in dreams giving access to eternity and in dream landscapes peopled by figures taken from Greek mythology (Psyche) or even the Koran (the angel Israel). Her poem 'Egypt' is appropriately dedicated to Poe, as it sets up a dialectic between dream and waking, death and rebirth. Finally, in the 1920s H.D. read Emily Dickinson's poetry, which no doubt encouraged her to indulge in bold spiritual specu-lations. The former's incorporation of contemporary materials into the *Trilogy* enables her, as one critic has written of Dickinson, to mingle 'the matter-of-fact with the visionary'.[50] And for H.D. as for Dickinson, for Poe (in his Helen Poems, for instance) and for Robert Duncan, whose legendary *H.D. Book* was composed alongside his major poetry, the visionary entailed a re-vision of conventional reli-gious tropes and figures.

NOTES

1. D. D. Paige (ed.), *The Selected Letters of Ezra Pound 1907–1941* (London: Faber, 1971) p. 213.
2. T. S. Eliot (ed.), *Literary Essays of Ezra Pound* (London: Faber, 1968) p. 5.
3. Barbara Guest, *Herself Defined: The Poet H.D. and her World* (London: Collins, 1985) p. 42.
4. 'Goblins and Pagodas', *The Egoist*, 3 (1916) pp. 183, 184. The allusion in the quotation is to John 3: viii.
5. J. B. Harmer, *Victory in Limbo: A History of Imagism, 1908–1917* (London: Secker & Warburg, 1975) p. 62.
6. Adalaide Morris, 'The Concept of Projection: H.D.'s Visionary Powers', in Harold Bloom (ed.), *H.D.: Modern Critical Views* (New York: Chelsea House, 1989) p. 105.
7. Guest, op. cit., p. 82.
8. Rachel Blau DuPlessis, *H.D.: The Career of that Struggle* (Brighton: Harvester Press, 1986) pp. 15–16.
9. H.D., *Collected Poems 1912–1944*, ed. Louis L. Martz (Manchester: Carcanet Press, 1984) p. 375.

10. Ibid., p. 491. During the Second World War H.D. shared a keen interest in psychic research with Lord Hugh Downing. In 1945 she began to receive messages from dead pilots in a series of seances. For a full account of these experiences, see Susan Stanford Friedman, *Psyche Reborn: The Emergence of H.D.* (Bloomington: Indiana University Press, 1981) pp. 173–5.

11. H.D., *Palimpsest* (Carbondale, Ill.: Southern Illinois University Press, 1968) p. 104.

12. In his review of *Palimpsest*, Conrad Aiken recognised the originality of this novel, although with misgivings about its 'suggestion of recurring personalities and situations, or even reincarnations' (*A Reviewer's ABC* (London: W. H. Allen, 1961) p. 155.

13. Deborah Kelly Kloepfer, 'Fishing the Murex Up: Sense and Resonance in H.D.'s *Palimpsest*', *Contemporary Literature*, 27, iv (Winter, 1986) p. 558.

14   H.D., ibid., p. 155.

15. Ibid., p. 227.

16. Ibid., p. 72.

17. H.D., *Collected Poems*, p. 129.

18. H.D., *Helen in Egypt* (Manchester: Carcanet Press, 1985) p. 178.

19. Richard Cavendish, *The Black Arts* (London: Pan, 1969) p. 141.

20. Euripides, *The Bacchae and Other Plays*, trans. Philip Vellacott (Harmondsworth: Penguin, 1965) p. 126.

21. H.D.. *Helen in Egypt*, p. 21.

22. This is discussed at length in John T. Irwin's *American Hieroglyphics: The Symbol of the Egyptian Hieroglyphics in the American Renaissance* (New Haven: Yale University Press, 1980).

23. Rudolf Otto, *The Idea of the Holy*, trans. John W. Harvey (Harmondsworth: Penguin, 1959) p. 78.

24. May Sinclair, 'The Poems of "H.D."', *Fortnightly Review*, n.s. 121 (1927) p. 344.

25. Guest, op. cit., p. 163.

26. Ezra Pound, *Selected Prose, 1909–1965*, ed. William Cookson (London: Faber, 1973) p. 59.

27. Leon Surette, *A Light from Eleusis: A Study of Ezra Pound's 'Cantos'* (Oxford: Clarendon Press, 1979) pp. 221–2.

28. H.D., *Collected Poems*, p. 302.

29. H.D., *Tribute to Freud* (Manchester: Carcanet Press, 1985) p. 51.

30. John B. Vickery, *The Literary Impact of 'The Golden Bough'* (Princeton: Princeton University Press, 1973) pp. 136, 140–2, 152–3.

31. Arthur E. P. B. Weigall, *The Paganism in our Christianity* (London: Hutchinson, 1928) p. 238.

32. Griselda Ohannesian (ed.), *The Gift* (London: Virago press, 1984) p. 86.

33. Norman Holmes Pearson, 'Foreword', *Trilogy* (Manchester: Carcanet Press, 1973) p. vii; H.D., *Collected Poems*, p. 539. Subsequent references to the *Trilogy* incorporated into the text.

34. Susan Gubar, 'The Echoing Spell of H.D.'s *Trilogy*', in Bloom, op. cit., pp. 66–7.

35. Friedman, op. cit., p. 217.
36. H.D., *Tribute to Freud*, p. 88.
37. From Thomas Hooker's 'The Application of Redemption', in Roy Harvey Pearce (ed.), *Colonial American Writing* (New York: Holt, Rinehart & Winston, 1969) p. 80.
38. Friedman, op. cit., p. 221.
39. Diana Collecott, 'Introduction', *The Gift*, p. xvii. This line is adapted in 'Tribute' 42.
40. Pearson, p. ix.
41. Robert Duncan, 'Two Chapters from *H.D.*', *Tri-Quarterly*, 12 (1968) p. 97.
42. H.D., *Notes on Thought and Vision* (San Francisco: City Lights Books, 1982) p. 24.
43. H.D., *Tribute to Freud*, p. 102.
44. Friedman, op. cit., pp. 203, 204.
45. H.D., *The Gift*, p. 94.
46. C. J. Jung, *Psychology and Alchemy*, trans. R. F. C. Hull (London: Routledge & Kegan Paul, 1953) p. 227. There are other points of overlap between the two writers. Both were members of the Society for Psychical Research; and H.D.'s notion of overconsciousness could be compared fruitfully with Jung's collective unconscious, which 'contains the whole spiritual heritage of mankind's evolution'.
47. Morris, op. cit., pp. 118–19.
48. Weigall, op. cit., p. 226; Gubar, op. cit., p. 75.
49. Friedman, op. cit., p. 167.
50. David Daiches, *God and the Poets* (Oxford: Clarendon Press, 1985) p. 159.

3

Ezra Pound

IAN F. A. BELL

Melville's Pierre, while 'immaturely' attempting a 'mature work', produces manuscripts where 'chirographical incoherencies' mime the problem of expressing a 'wondrous suggestiveness' that is 'eternally incapable of being translated into words'. The epistemological and creative journey to 'some thoughtful thing of absolute Truth' is, by definition, taxing and one major lesson he fails to recognise in this proto-modernist text is urgent for the modernism Pound begins to explore in *Hugh Selwyn Mauberley*.
Melville comments:

> 'Ten million things were as yet uncovered to Pierre. The old mummy lies buried in cloth on cloth; it takes time to unwrap this Egyptian king. Yet now, forsooth, because Pierre began to see through the superficiality of the world, he fondly weens he has come to the unlayered substance. But, far as any geologist has yet gone down into the world, it is found to consist of nothing but surface stratified on surface. To its axis, the world being nothing but superinduced superficies. By vast pains we mine into the pyramid; by horrible gropings we come to the central room; with joy we espy the sarcophagus; but we lift the lid – and no body is there! – appallingly vacant as vast is the soul of a man![1]

I am not invoking Melville's extraordinary pessimism on behalf of either Pound or modernism generally (even Wyndham Lewis would be wary of gloom to quite such a degree), but the notion of a world of 'surface stratified on surface' is illuminating for both. The notion is determinant for some of the ways in which we may read the structuring of certain modernist practices by commodity forms. These practices find their earliest expression in the *Mauberley* sequence, where the idea of 'surface', crucially freed from its illusory opposition to depth, provides a strategic force.[2] Our object of study, taking

'Medallion', the final poem of the sequence, as exemplary, will be modernism's decentring of the self, or, more accurately, the self's presentation. The 'unlayered substance', the unified subject, that Melville displayed to be illusory, will be seen as both a reflex and a critique of the world of surfaces (the display, the spectacle) constituted by the developing marketplace and the habits of consumption.

It was no accident that Melville chose his initial image from drapery, 'cloth on cloth', or that, in a text published contemporaneously with the composition of *Mauberley*, Henry Adam's establishing of a model of 'self-teaching' rested on the claim that 'the Ego has steadily tended to efface itself' and so become 'a manikin on which the toilet of education is to be draped in order to show the fit or misfit of the clothes. The object of study is the garment, not the figure.'[3] The images chosen by both Melville and Adams, in varying degrees of complexity, rely upon the ludic seriousness of Carlyle's 'Philosophy of Clothes', published in 1831 as *Sartor Resartus*. Henry James, in 1913, experiencing Adam's difficulties with the issues of memory and the past (those bedrock stabilisers of the unified self), again resorted to drapery for articulation: 'The ragbag of memory hung on its nail in my closet. ... I learnt with time to control the habit of bringing it forth.'[4] My point is not to suggest a solely literary history, but to claim that the imagery of clothes in these instances is an agency for the world of appearance and surface, the new 'reality' for the consumptive practices which restructured established notions of a unified or integral self. Such restructuring is not merely a matter for post-modernist theorists, but an issue of material history, of the experiential changes from the social and aesthetic reliance on indices of sincerity and authenticity to those of performance and calculability,[5] changes which parallel the general economic shifts from systems of accumulation to those of production and reproduction.

Pound's own testimony to the restructured self occurs, famously, in his 'Vorticism' essay of 1914:

In the 'search for oneself', in the search for 'sincere self-expression', one gropes, one find some seeming verity. One says 'I am' this, that, or the other, and with the words scarcely uttered one ceases to be that thing.[6]

He excludes the imagery of clothing to register his case, but implicit here is not only Melville's affirmation of the self's illusoriness, but

also an acknowledgement of the self's variousness and hence its liberation from a confining singleness of being,[7] an acknowledgement
sustained by Pound's increasing deployment of those more cere-
monial modes of clothing – masks and personae. The self's variousness depends above all upon its assumptions of roles, its display of
surface, a lesson gleaned most immediately for the tactics of
Mauberley from James and from Wyndham Lewis.[8] In the formal
terms of commentators. Hugh Kenner, for example, has written of
the 'disregard of *up* and *down* and *through*' encouraged by the new
'immediacy of perception' discoverable in the cave paintings which
established such a crucial framework for modernist art, a perception which enables Kenner, rightly, to say of a passage from the
'*Homage to Sextus Propertius*' that 'The words lie flat like the forms
on a Cubist surface.'[9] More recently, Reed Way Dasenbrock has reminded us of Maurice Denis's dictum of 1890 – 'It should be remembered that a picture – before being a warhorse, a nude or an
anecdote of some sort – is essentially a flat surface covered with
colors assembled in a certain order' – to sustain an argument that is
generally true for both Pound and modernism:

> What is significant in a painting is its formal elements, its shapes
> and colors, and what these might represent is unimportant aes-
> thetically. This position was central to nineteenth-century French
> thinking about art long before the coming of abstraction.[10]

Pound knew this from Whistler, as well as from contemporary
painting and sculpture. This new aesthetic attention to surface was
picked up by William Carlos Williams in his 'Vortex', an unpublished essay of 1915 which responded to the 'vortex' of Gaudier-
Brzeska in the second issue of *Blast* and advertisedly redeployed
the sculptor's phrases for its principal axioms:

> I meet in agreement the force that will express its emotional
> content by an arrangement of appearances (of plans).
>   Substance is not considered, for apart from transparency which
> shows nothing, it does not exist aside from surface or plane. [By
> means of] plane [surface] exists in apposition to substance. Plane
> is the appearance. I affirm my existence and perceive its quality
> by apposition of planes. By expressing whatever emotion may
> occur, taking it without choice and putting it surface against

surface, I affirm my independence of all emotions and my denial in time and place of the accident of their appearance.[11]

Williams' position here is not characteristic, and within the conscious avant-gardism of his posture there remains an assumption about expressibility, about representation: although the primary medium for writer, painter and sculptor is agreed as surface, that surface is held still to register its appropriate degree of emotional resonance. The true radicalism of surface in Pound's hands is to suppress such registration as a form of final 'truth' and, in the process, to perform the double function of challenging the world of goods (by opening up the illusion of interiority as a system of signs and, paradoxically, reinvoking that element of manufacture which is always obliterated for the purposes of sale) and missing those very features of display (surfaces) through which that world maintains itself. I assume a direct relation here between the characteristics of goods within the commodity relationship and the experience and presentation of the self under the effects of consumption, and between the formal aesthetic preoccupations of Poundian modernism and the marketplace within which and against which those preoccupations struggled.

The rise of advertising which accompanied the commercial shifts in production and reproduction from the 1870s onwards found clear but seldom documented responses in that literary 'decadence' of the late nineteenth century which provides such strong (and, again, rather neglected) impetus for *Mauberley*. Mallarmé's blank page, with its resistance to language's commercial infections, is but the most familiar and extravagant of such responses. More interesting, and more immediate to my present purpose, is an essay like 'A Defence of Cosmetics' in the *Yellow Book* of 1894. The author is Max Beerbohm, commonly taken to be the 'Brennbaum' of *Mauberley*. It is here that we witness an appreciation of that restructuring of the self through notions of surface newly sanctioned by consumption. Beerbohm chooses cosmetics rather than clothes as a focus presumably because of their greater intimacy with the body. He begins with an ironically serious flourish – 'Artifice must queen it once more in the town. ... The old signs are here and the portents to warn the seer of life that we are ripe for a new epoch of artifice'[12] – and claims that the prejudice against cosmetics is due to a no longer relevant understanding of surface:

Perhaps it savours too much of reason to suggest that the prejudice was due to the tristful confusion man has made of soul and
surface. Through trusting so keenly to the detection of the one by
keeping watch upon the other, and by the force of the thousand
errors following, he has come to think of surface even as the
reverse of soul.   (p. 67)

Beerbohm recognises the complexity of the period which encourages artifice – the terms uses are 'complicated', 'elaborate' and 'sophisticated' (pp. 67, 68, 76) – and recognises also that it is an 'era' of
'range' (p. 68), of variousness. It is precisely such variousness (the
ever more elaborate systems of manners, etiquette and social intercourse produced by the changes in commercial practices) which
enables man to be 'independent of Nature' (in a world viewed as
manufactured rather than as organic) so that 'Artifice is the
strength of the world, and in that same mask of paint and powder,
shadowed with vermeil tint and most trimly pencilled, is woman's
strength' (p. 68). Strength here resides exactly in the breaking up of
the old 'confusion of soul and surface':

And, truly, of all the good things that will happen with the full
renascence of cosmetics, one of the best is that surface will finally
be severed from soul. ... Too long has the face been degraded
from its rank as a thing of beauty to a mere vulgar index of character or emotion.   (p. 71)

Two specific consequences result from this severance. First, the
cleaner, harder prose the following the dispersal of all those aids to
illusion upon which writing has relied:

All those old properties that went to bolster up the ordinary novel
– the trembling lips, the flashing eyes, the determined curve of the
chin, the nervous trick of biting the moustache – aye and the
hectic spot of red on either cheek – will be made spiflicate, as the
puppets were spiflicated by Don Quixote.   (p. 72)

And secondly, the variousness of self that is liberated by these new
notions of surface: the 'nearly numberless' combinations oi line and
colour in cosmetics enable a woman to 'realise her moods in all
their shades and lights and dappledoms, to live many lives and
masquerade through many moments of joy' (p. 78). Beerbohm's

latter point here locates the main thrust of surface's variousness as imaged generally by the line of thought, during the late nineteenth century, that Pound draws upon for his conception of Mauberley's character – the clearest instances are Pater's view of 'La Giaconda' and Wilde's 'The Truth of Masks'. The tone of 'A Defence of Cosmetics' carries strong Wildean echoes, particularly in the claim that 'Artifice's first command to them [women] is that they should repose. With bodily activity their powder will fly, their enamel crack' (p. 70), a claim that is closely in harmony with the 'porcelain revery' which governs Mauberley's imagination: Wilde's 'repose' is a version of the contemplative perception that is essential to the aestheticism he adapted from Pater and transmitted to Mauberley, an aestheticism embedded, as 'The Truth of Masks' tells us, in variousness of self through masks and surfaces.

Variousness gains its potency by its imagination of otherness – this is one of the great lessons imparted by the surfaces which express it, by the 'imaginary portraits' that are so characteristic of both Wilde and Pater. Pater's 'portrait' of Denys L'Auxerrois includes a notion of surface that is usefully applicable to Poundian poetics in general. He begins his portrayal by examining the need for the 'legend of a "golden age"', and notes:

Since we are no longer children, we might well question the advantage of the return to use of a condition of life in which, by the nature of the case, the values of things would, so to speak, lie wholly on their surfaces, unless we could regain also the childish consciousness, or rather unconsciousness, in ourselves, to take all that adroitly and with the appropriate lightness of heart.[13]

This is not the surface of contemporary artifice, the surface of social manners and commercial practices. It is the surface of mythic vision, excellently described by Peter Nicholls as 'the revelation of single numinous objects' based on 'an ideal of artistic production which is anterior to any form of mechanical reproduction',[14] and its role within art's advertised resistance to those displays tellingly, as it displays to the world of consumption – the consumption which preoccupies Pound's art criticism (as it had preoccupied Whistler) during the period he is working on *Mauberley*. The 'Art Notes' he authored as 'B. H. Dias' for the *New Age* between 1917 and 1920 stridently argues 'It would be hypocrisy to consider the Academy as anything save a great market, a stock exchange, a definitely trade

concern', and opposed painting, which 'flourishes as a luxury
trade', to the writer, who 'does not produce an article which can be
bought by the general public to be stored and made a matter of
profit'.[15] Rather later, in an essay on 'The Public Convenience' for
Exile (Spring 1927) which distinguishes between various categories
of goods as 'transient', 'double' and 'permanent', he places works
of art in the last category by employing the schism of consumption
itself: such works are 'permanent' because 'they are always in use
and never consumed; or they are, in jargon, "consumed" but not
destroyed by consumption',[16] by which I understand him to mean
that the works are not paralysed by the abstractions of the commodity relation.

The features of consumption as they are expressed in the literary
history which informs *Mauberley* can be summarised under the
rubric of 'surface', Pound's own term of 1922 for the sequence.[17]
The new acceptability of artifice and social performance, the dis-
ruption of the unified self by the variousness of masks, and the
sheer dazzle of goods on display and the advertisements which
support that display, constitute the main terms of consumption.
They also constitute the major tenets of modernist art: surface, in alliance with the new psychology of the relational, enables the dismantling of those illusions which sustain the aesthetic of opposed
by modernism – the centrality of the subject, the sanction of nature,
and the comfort of origination. Such dismantling has the further
paradoxical function of revealing the world as manufactured, the
very element which is suppressed by the commodity relation in the
interests of exchange. Its great and final lesson is this one of alter-
ability, of imaging other portraits. Poundian modernism both ex-
ploits and falls prey to the world of goods it seeks to combat.

In the *Mauberley* sequence, 'Medallion' is the 'imaginary portrait'
produced by the Mauberleyan temperament. And within the
complex I have been considering, it exhibits also the characteristics
of an advertisement for a female singer: it is simultaneously liberated from conventional presentation and paralysed by the terms of
that liberation. The poem is alert to this paradox and attempts to
negotiate it in pursuit of a portraiture which will open up the issues
of representation. Mauberley's technique of fragmentation produces 'an art / In profile', deliberately resisting 'the full smile', the
unified self of a full-face portrait, as it itemises the form of the
female singer through voice, head, hair, face and finally the eyes,
which always maintain a special expressiveness within Pound's

poetic equipment. Earlier, in poem II of the 'Mauberley 1920' half of the sequence, those eyes had been schematised by Mauberley's quasi-scientific imagination[18] as 'the relation / Of eye-lid and cheek-bone',[19] but in 'Medallion' they provide his portrait's ultimate and most powerful image. The itemising tactics of the poem register clearly the paradox of modernist art under consumption: they function as exploration, seeking to find their subject while refusing the illusory unification of that subject, and they display also those partial presentations which govern the ways we respond to advertisements' focusing of attention upon discrete parts of the human body. Any presumed whole is dispersed in both forms of fragmentation.[20]

Mauberley's complex scientific vocabulary in the 'Mauberley 1920' part of the sequence served as a system of investigation (within clearly defined limits, certainly, but what needs to be emphasised is the labour of that system nevertheless, and not merely the presumed passivity advocated by the bulk of the commentaries) which emerges, finally, as a complicated strategy for self-protection in difficult and uncongenial circumstances.[21] 'Medallion' is innocent of this vocabulary, deriving its major terms and imagery from the artifice of art. But, in a cleverly understated way, the third stanza, devoted to a description of the singer's hair, invokes a specific figure of design. the 'basket-work of braids' seems' Spun in King Minos' half / From metal or intractable amber'. Invoked here is not the artist-figure presented in the first two stanzas as the painter Luini and the historian Reinach, but a figure for ingenious engineering, Dedalus (Pound's imaginative resources were strongly expanded by Joyce during the composition of *Mauberley*), a type for the scientific dexterity of design. The point of the invocation is not, however, to lead us to myth, or even to Joycean experimentalism, but to display the new forms of artifice and design emerging from the issues of consumption. As an index to what is involved here, I want to draw upon the editorial essays on philosophy, science and language written by Dora Marsden for *The Egoist* (one of the great organs for modernist ideas) between 1916 and 1918. Marsden's essays provide illuminating testimony to the battle shared by these forms of knowledge against the abstractions induced by consumptive practices.

Marsden's 'The Science of Signs' of 1916, in negotiating the general problem precision and signification, raises the main effect of forgetfulness:

The mathematician's task of keeping mathematical signs to their deliberately created significations, and keeping in view their purely conventional nature is a simple and straightforward business, and it provides extraordinarily convincing evidence for men's proneness to forget the origins of their own symbolic compacts and to become hypnotized by them, that confusion should have been possible even within the particular "universe of discourse" they themselves have called into being.

This forgetfulness applies equally to numbers, words and figurative symbols derived from both. The hypnosis which follows (Joyce would call it paralysis) is a product of that suppression of labour, of the sense of manufacture which is the characteristic of the commodity form. Since suppression of labour crucially involves a suppression of time, we might usefully recall Pound's portrayal of contemporary culture in poem II of the first half of the *Mauberley* sequence. There, the 'age' demands a 'mould in plaster' to be 'Made with no loss of time', a portrayal which invokes not only the uniformity of mass production but the very obliteration of temporality itself. Furthermore, the monolithic and monotheistic nature of Marsden's equation between sign and signification can be read as a version of that absolutism which sustains the notion of the unified, non-relational self. The abstract world of such forgetfulness makes fresh demands upon the scientist and the philosopher:

If objective science makes especially its won business of discovering new images and new features in old images, philosophy's business is to maintain in adequate condition the body of symbols which keeps custody over all images.[22]

It is very much the business of the artist also, as Pound's own aesthetic continually instructs, and at a strategic moment during the composition of *Mauberley's*, Pound chose a fiscal metaphor to make his point. Writing as B. H. Dias on 'London's first important exhibit of Matisse's work', at the Leicester Gallery in 1919, Pound claimed:

It is not necessary, either in the young or in the mature artist, that all geometry of a painting be tossed up into the consciousness and analysed by the painter before he puts brush to canvas. *The genius can pay in nugget and in lump gold; it is not necessary that he bring up his knowledge into the mint of consciousness, stamp it into either the coin of conscientiously analysed form – detail knowledge or into the paper-money of words, before he transmit it.* A bit of luck for a young man, and the sudden coagulation of bits of knowledge collected here and there during years, need not for the elder artist be re-sorted and arranged into coin. This sort of lump-payment is not mediumistic or psychic-painting; it is mastery.[23]

Paper-money is the most immediate figuration of abstraction. Eliot had used the image for similar purposes in 1917 when he argued 'The majority of mankind live on paper currency: they are terms which are merely good for so much reality, they never see actual coinage,'[24] and both positions derive their most immediate literary impulse from Remy de Gourmont's *'médailles usées'* (an enabling context for Pound's choice of medallions as Mauberley's favoured art-form), the worn coins he compares to clichés and abstractions.[25] Emerson, writing during an earlier period of fiscal uncertainty (the acceleration of America's first industrial revolution and the debates about the banks and the speculation of coined and paper money), found a striking occasion for the image in distinctly Poundian terms when pondering the relationship between words and the world, at the very centre of the chapter on 'Language' in his 1836 treatise, *Nature*:

> The corruption of man is followed by the corruption of language. ... new imagery ceases to be created, and old words are perverted to stand for things which are not; a paper currency is employed when there is no bullion in the vaults. In due time, the fraud is manifest, and words lose all power to stimulate the understanding or the affections.[26]

Emerson's sense of 'fraud', impelled by contemporary commercial changes and the new practices of speculation, anticipates directly Pound's views on language during the next phase of commerce's development, from accumulation to reproduction, where the dangers of abstraction become more stridently experiential. It is tempting to suggest that the 'hard' and 'soft' features of French poetry Pound discerned in 1918[27] may usefully be read in terms of the debate about coined and paper money which continued to have its impact on American political life past the turn of the century. The languages of art and money share a similar epistemological frame here: Emerson, particularly through those subsequent thinkers who were more immediate to Pound – Whitman, Fenollosa and Agassiz (with the 'sensible ideas' of Locke's *An Essay Concerning Human Understanding* informing the entire line) – sought a resolution in the material roots of words and their pictorial expressiveness to resist the abstractive intrusions of the marketplace.

Material picturesqueness engages aesthetic and literary labour; it is a matter of etymological alertness, but nevertheless relies upon dexterous engagement with the notion of things having been made – the very notion that is suppressed by the hypnotism of the commodity relation. Dora Marsden continued her analysis of this hypnotism 'The Constitution of the World and the Character of Our Scientific Knowledge" of 1918 to find the scientist's situation as so 'riveted by the hypnotism of the world-order that he is deaf to the blatantest suggestions regarding the role which his own organisation and activities play in the creation of the panorama which preoccupies him'. Marsden recognises here the suppression of manufacture and maintains the world as manipulable and alterable by scientific hands, by the dexterous design typified in the figuration of Dedalus: 'To be made to know how to manage the world by dint of an acute observation of its changes has come to represent the sum of our scientific expectations.'[28] And Marsden intends those hands as tools for design, for artifice, to be literal, not metaphoric. In a subsequent chapter of her inquiry, later in 1918, on 'The Organic Determination of Our Science of Mechanics', she argues for measurement as the key element in science's description of the world (the majority of Mauberley's scientific terms rely upon measurement), that all instruments of measure derive from the hand, and writes of the compulsion within the scientist's need for measurement:

> *His hand* has compelled him to regard the universe as an increasing flux of displacing forces: made him see everything as movement. Modern physics is a direct product of the increasing intensification of this manually imposed influence.[29]

For Marsden, it is the hand 'as organ and model' that earns man the title of 'fabricator, by right of his physical endowment' and the function of manufacturer.[30] In 'Medallion' the hand of Dedalus measures its subject in the sense that it tests ways of perceiving the singer through the fragmentary images it employs. The poem marks a process of registration and discovery: its fragmentary procedure displays its experimentalism, its trying out of parts where the designer's manual dexterity shows its instruments of measure, its images, not as absolutes but as held within the realm of manufacture and hence the provisory, the alterable. This fragmentation of portraiture is thoroughly in accord with science's resistance to abstraction through its new notions of matter, as Marsden's "Space and Substance' of the following month acknowledges:

> The scientific progress of man can be described as a progress in which the idea of *thinghood* has broadened out from the primitively exclusive one of a solid to the comprehensive one which includes anything capable of making an impress even upon our most exquisitely delicate measuring-instruments. ... the 'containing-vessel' of space primitively regarded as tenanted by comparatively widely separated solid, or partially solidified, blocks comes to be regarded as a closely packed continuum, the formerly recognised solid tenantry being considered as particularly involved, and tightened knots existing in the all-pervasive substance.[31]

The shift Marsden describes is of attention to motion rather than stasis, the dynamism of the knot (another term for the vortex) supplanting the exclusivity of the solid. Proclaimed here is process – 'Sense-forms ... are modes of motion'[32] – and in 'Medallion' what we see is precisely the breaking-up of matter, the singer, into the motion of the several images tested as a means of describing her: or, within the alternative discourse I have been pursuing, the dispersal of the illusory total self into neo-cubist re-alignments – a seeing of things within a variousness of perspective. It is in these senses that the unit of our attention, the fragment, both resists the abstraction of the marketplace and succumbs to its dominant technique – the dismantling tactics of the advertisement. The postmodernist questioning of schisms such as surface/depth, fragment/whole, outside/inside, was already being negotiated by the relational procedures Pound would have discovered in biological method (Agassiz), in transcendentalist anxieties about the developments in commerce (Emerson and Whitman), in the poetics of both China (Fenollosa) and France (Romains and 'Unanimism'), and in novelistic innovations (James): it was not accidental that the *Little Review* published Pound's essays on James and on Romains in 1918. Dismantlement attends above all to fragmentation, and the

ontology of the fragment, as David Murray has so usefully reminded us recently, has a double function in that it 'alerts us both
to its connection with the former context and to its own specificity,
as we try to relate it to its new surrounding'. It is this double function which erodes 'any distinction between inside and outside the
poem'.[33] Such erosion is crucial because it relocates the place of
surface as the arena where things are continually being renegotiated within the variousness of motion. Here, for example, the self is
never allowed to remain static but is always in the process of
redefinition in terms that are predominantly relational. In this
sense, it matters enormously that the portrait in 'Medallion' is of a
singer, a synecdoche for the oral element in literature which necessarily renders illusory any notion of a final version of a text – both
self and text become newly available for the process of understanding as their points of contact are continually re-read through
history.

Perhaps the 'suave bounding-line' which positions the 'face-oval'
in the final stanza of 'Medallion' points us toward what is at stake
here, and to what our activity is in responding to the poem – an activity which recognises the negotiations of form for the portrait (or
the self) and not an authoritative final text. I want to read that
'bounding-line' in Heidegger's sense not of termination or en-
closure but of horizon or commencement:

A boundary is not that at which something stops but, as the
Greeks recognised, the boundary is that from which something
begins its presencing. That is why the concept is that of *horismos*.[34]

To understand boundary in this way is to see how it shares a
similar office to that of surface: presencing is not presence but the
arena where presence is always being renegotiated. Both surface
and presencing depend to a large extent on fragmentary expression, and the fragment always involves delay – the delay of desire
for completion and unity which is precisely the delay of desire organised by the promisory nature of the advertisement. This is also a
version of the delay we experience in language generally (corresponding to the gap between signifier and signified), but it is especially acute within those discourses we designate as mechanical,
artificial, or non-human; for my present purposes, the discourse of
artifice which structures the portrait of the female singer in
'Medallion'. The bulk of the commentaries on the poem, in varying

degrees of positivity and negativity, tend to read it as embodying a refashioning of the human into the terms of art. Both modernist aesthetics (particularly in the formulations of Pound and Lewis) and the practices of consumption reveal stridently that such schisms (along with those of surface/depth, fragment/whole, outside/inside) belong to a much earlier history of artistic, social and commercial intercourse. More locally, as Jo Brantley Berryman has shown in the best exegesis we have on *Mauberley*,[35] it is highly misleading to read the poem in terms of an opposition which the poem itself questions radically. What the poem asks us to do most of all is to recast our notions of the relationship between artifice and the human. This lesson is general to Pound's early poetics, taking its most important cues from the visual arts; from Whistler and Lewis, as the clearest examples, or from Kandinsky, whose *Ueber das Geistige in der Kurst* attracted Edward Wadsworth's attention in the first issue of *Blast*. Wadsworth provided extracts from the commentary upon Kandinsky's text to sustain a major argument that 'Those who perceive no emotional significance in form and colour as such, invariably argue that to avoid human and natural forms is to sterilise one's creative faculties and to rob oneself of all that is noble in art.'[36]

We are not merely at the level of poetic theory here but are concerned with Pound's intellectual and imaginative furniture: the falsity of any simple opposition between the human and the artifice of presentation is strikingly displayed by the language of Pound's early letters of courtship to Dorothy Shakespear, where the beloved female is addressed always in the vocabulary of myth and precious objects.[37] Our recasting of the human within artifice is guided further by Pound's own response in 1920 to Raymonde Collignon herself, the singer for whom 'Medallion' essays its portrayal. Pound's language and perception anticipate closely those employed by the poem:

> No one has a more keen perception than she has of the difference between art and life; of the necessary scale and proportion required in the presentation of a thing which is not the photograph and wax cast, but a re-creation in different and proportional medium. As long as this diseuse was on the stage she was non-human; she was, if you like, a china image; there are Ming porcelains which are respectable; the term 'china' is not in this connection ridiculous. One would like the ability to express

verbally the exact difference between this 'sort of presentation' which is art, and the other sort of presentation, which is just Miss Jones of Peckwell singing a song – being half the time Miss Jones, and half the time something, rather indefinite, but more or less en rapport with the music.[38]

The final, beautiful couplet of 'Medallion' focuses the issues: 'Beneath half-watt rays, / The eyes turn topaz.' Eyes in Pound's early poetry are the site of love and transcendence: arguably, they are the most important organs of the body. Light, through its medieval associations, is always expressive of visionary experience, and jewels provide a dominating halo for Pound's favoured women. In some ways the couplet is a sophisticated re-working of a favourite line from Arnaut Daniel – '*E quel remir contral lums de la lampa*' – which Pound had translated in 1910 as 'she shall disclose to me her fair body, with the glamor of the lamplight about it' and which he argued 'may be taken differentiate Arnault Daniel from all other poets of Provence'.[39] Pound's echoing in itself thus registers acknowledgement of a particularly high point in his hierarchical apprehension of the Western literary tradition. His choice of jewel in 'Medallion' also claims a powerful field of reference – most immediately to Dante's apprehension of Beatrice,[40] to the Intelligence/angels in the *Paradiso*,[41] and to Aphrodite and the transmutational potency of love.[42]

But the striking feature of the couplet is surely its yoking of eyes and topaz within the light of the half-watt rays. Much more is involved here than a reading out of Pound's own literary history, because that light is not only particularly powerful; it is particularly up-to-date, as David Moody has shown.[43] Those rays are aggressively modern, and their modernity is exceptional in a poem which otherwise eschews images of modernity. The only comparable literary moment is perhaps Henry Adams's yoking of the Virgin and the Dynamo in his *Education*. We need to read those rays literary, as part of the concrete scene (the singer on the concert platforms) the poem presents. These powerful modern lights place the female on display, isolate her for the purpose of the occasion from all else: again, in other words, highlight their subject in much the same way as an advertisement highlights its subject for the purpose of sale. The itemisation of features which the poem has constructed so far here achieves its most telling expression, which works a rich literary tradition within the imperative of contemporaneity, the up-to-date forms of artifice. What is seemingly arcane turns out to be entirely appropriate to the age of consumption. It is not accidental that a re-reading of Wilde (the great master of artifice during the early period of consumption) by Alexander S. Kaun in 1916 for the *Little Review* (the time and place, along with the other 'little' magazines, for so much that occurs in the *Mauberley* sequence) provides a clear index to that appropriateness. Kaun is reviewing the Ravenna edition of Wilde's *works*, and his conclusion underlines the special relevance of Wilde's sense of artifice to contemporary conditions:

> He did not mirror his age; but he had realised the potentialities of his age. ... Wilde's paradoxes, *mots*, theories, have proven so appropriate, adaptable, and digestible for our age, that it took only one decade to absorb them into our blood and marrow.[44]

Kaun's re-reading is a telling example of the particular mimesis of Wilde's artifice and performativeness, which are found to be so 'digestible' a decade later because they display so precisely the features of consumption. Kaun applauds also Wilde's lessons of variousness, which preclude singleness and finality of interpretation, and acknowledges his renegotiations of one of the major terms for the single, unified self: 'It is for the style that we accept *De Profundis*, that insincerest attempt for sincerity'.[45] What is especially apposite for the final couplet of 'Medallion' within Kaun's review is its gently ironic pastiche of a presumed preciosity discoverable in a less sophisticated reading of Wilde. The review begins:

> Pull down the shades. Turn out the lights. So. We do not want loud electricity. We shall have a jewelled light. [....] Come, let us recline on Bagdad cushions and Teheran rugs ... and I shall scatter over the fantastic patterns jewels and stones. How softly they illumine the thick dark – these varicoloured glowflies, these streams of wine, emerald wine, and amethyst wine, and wine of topazes 'yellow as the eyes of tigers, and topazes pink as the eyes of wood pigeon, and green topazes that are as the eyes of cats'.[46]

The language here not only mocks Wilde's, but it is also recognisable as the language of much of Pound's early poetry, particularly in its figuration of the female. Kaun's pastiche and jewelled light, the eyes, and, primary amidst its cluster of precious stones, topaz –

and, in the process, registers the scientific perception that is the hallmark of Mauberley's imagination: topaz is usually yellow in colour, but it permits also a range of other colours, a range which is detailed in the account Kaun derives from Wilde. In itself then, topaz ciphers the variousness that is the lesson of Wilde, the practice of the marketplace, and the re-questioning of the unified self. The very artifice of 'Medallion', produced by the scientific temperament catalogued in the preceding poems of the 'Mauberley 1920' half of the sequence, is what simultaneously questions and falls prey to the habits of consumption.

NOTES

1. My quotations are taken from the Library of America edition of *Pierre* (Cambridge: Cambridge University Press, 1984) pp. 329, 330, 332.
2. See Ian F. A. Bell, 'A Mere Surface: Wyndham Lewis, Henry James and the "Latitude" of *Hugh Selwyn Mauberley*', *Paideuma*, xv (Fall and Winter 1986) pp. 53–71.
3. Henry Adams, *The Education of Henry Adams* (Boston and New York: Houghton Mifflin, 1918) pp. ix–x.
4. Henry James, *A Small Boy and Others* (London: Macmillan, 1913) p. 73.
5. The best recent discussion of these changes in the context of nineteenth-century America is Karen Halttunen, *Confidence Men and Painted Women: A Study of Middle-Class Culture in America, 1830–1870* (New Haven and London: Yale University Press, 1982).
6. Ezra Pound, 'Vorticism', *Fortnightly Review* (1914): reprinted in *Gaudier-Brzeska: A Memoir* (New York: New Directions, 1970) p. 85.
7. See Bell, 'A Mere Surface', *passim*.
8. Ibid.
9. Hugh Kenner, *The Pound Ezra* (London: Faber and Faber, 1972) p. 30.
10. Reed Way Dasenbrock, *The Literary Vorticism of Ezra Pound and Wyndham Lewis* (Baltimore and London: The Johns Hopkins University Press, 1985), pp. 246–7, 66.
11. William Carlos Williams, 'Vortex', in Bram Dijkstra (ed.), *A Recognisable Image: William Carlos Williams on Art and Artists* (New York: New Directions, 1978) pp. 57–9.
12. Max Beerbohm, 'A Defence of Cosmetics', *The Yellow Book*, i (April 1894) p. 65. All further references to this essay will be included parenthetically in the main body of the text.
13. Walter Pater, 'Denys L'Auxerrois', *Imaginary Portraits* (London and New York: Macmillan, 1890) p. 51.
14. Peter Nicholls, *Ezra Pound: Politics, Economics and Writing* (London: Macmillan, 1984) p. 9. I am grateful to Peter Nicholls for his perceptive and helpful comments on an earlier draft of the present essay.

15. These quotations are taken from, respectively, 'Art Notes', *The New Age* (20 June 1918) and 'Art and Luxury', *The New Age* (20 February 1920). Both are reprinted in Harriet Zinnes (ed.), *Ezra Pound and the Visual Arts* (New York: New Directions, 1980) pp. 61, 136–7.

16. Reprinted in *Ezra Pound and the Visual Arts*, p. 198.

17. D. D. Paige (ed.), *The Letters of Ezra Pound* (London: Faber and Faber, 1950) p. 248.

18. See Ian F. A. Bell, 'Mauberley's Barrier of Style', in Philip Grover (ed.), *Ezra Pound. The London Years: 1908–1921* (New York: A.M.S. Press, 1978) pp. 89–115, 155–164.

19. The text of *Hugh Selwyn Mauberley* I am using is that given in Ezra Pound, *Collected Shorter Poems* (London: Faber and Faber, 1967).

20. The most recent account of the aesthetic aspect of fragmentation is given in Andrew M. Clearfield, *These Fragments I Have Shored: Collage and Montage in Early Modernist Poetry* (Ann Arbor: UMI Research Press, 1984).

21. See Bell, 'Mauberley's Barrier of Style', *passim*.

22. Dora Marsden, 'The Science of Signs', *The Egoist*, III (August 1916) p. 115.

23. B. H. Dias [Ezra Pound], 'Art Notes', *The New Age* (27 November 1919), reprinted in *Ezra Pound and the Visual Arts*, p. 124.

24. T. S. Eliot, 'Eeldrop and Appleplex', *Little Review*, IV (May 1917) p. 10.

25. See Glenn S. Burne, *Remy de Gourmont: His Ideas and Influence in England and America* (Carbondale: S. Illinois University Press, 1963) p. 117, and Richard Sieburth, *Instigations: Ezra Pound and Remy de Gourmont* (Cambridge, Mass. and London: Harvard University Press, 1978) pp. 67, 115.

26. Ralph Waldo Emerson, *Nature*, in Spiller and Ferguson (eds), *The Collected Works of Ralph Waldo Emerson* (Cambridge, Mass. and London: Harvard University Press, 1971) vol. I, p. 20.

27. Ezra Pound, 'The Hard and Soft in French Poetry', *Poetry*, XI (February 1918), reprinted in T. S. Eliot (ed.), *Literary Essays of Ezra Pound* (London: Faber and Faber, 1963).

28. Dora Marsden, 'The Constitution of the World and the Character of Our Scientific Knowledge', *The Egoist*, V (March 1918) p. 36.

29. Dora Marsden, 'The Organic Determination of Our Science of Mechanics', *The Egoist*, V (August 1918) p. 91.

30. Ibid., p. 93.

31. Dora Marsden, 'Space and Substance', *The Egoist*, V (September 1918) pp. 103–4.

32. Ibid., p. 104.

33. David Murray, 'Unity and Difference: Poetry and Criticism', in David Murray (ed.), *Literary Theory and Poetry: Extending the Canon* (London: Batsford, 1989), pp. 13. 15.

34. Martin Heidegger, *Poetry, Language, Thought*, translated by Albert Hofstadter (New York: Harper and Row, 1971) p. 154.

35. Jo Brantley Berryman, *Circe's Craft: Ezra Pound's 'Hugh Selwyn Mauberley'* (Ann Abor: UMI Research Press, 1983). See particularly chapters 5 and 6.

36.   Edward Wadsworth, 'Inner Necessity', *Blast*, I (June 1914) p. 122.

37.   Omar Pound and A. Walton Litz (eds), *Ezra Pound and Dorothy Shakespear. Their Letters 1909–1914* (London: Faber and Faber, 1984).

38.   William Atheling [Ezra Pound], 'Music', *The New Age* (15 April 1920), reprinted in R. Murray Schafer (ed.), *Ezra Pound and Music* (London: Faber and Faber, 1978) p. 225. Cf. Berryman, *Circe's Craft*, pp. 141–4.

39.   Ezra Pound, *The Spirit of Romance* (London: Peter Owen, 1952) p. 34.

40.   See Karl Malkoff, 'Allusion as Irony: Pound's Use of Dante in *Hugh Selwyn Mauberley*', *Minnesota Review*, VII (1967) p. 88.

41.   See Peter Makin, *Pound's Cantos* (London: George Allen and Unwin, 1985) pp. 277–8.

42.   See Daniel Pearlman, *The Barb of Time: On the Unity of Ezra Pound's Cantos* (New York: Oxford University Press, 1969) p. 61.

43.   In a letter to *Paideuma*, VII (Spring and Fall 1978) pp. 345–6. Cf. Robert G. Eisenhauer, '"Jeweller's Company": Topaz, Half-Light and Bounding-Lines in *The Cantos*', *Paideuma*, XI (Fall 1980) p. 254.

44.   Alexander S. Kaun, 'The Pathos of Proximity', *Little Review*, II (January–February 1916) p. 10.

45.   Ibid., p. 9.

46.   Ibid., p. 8.

4

Hart Crane

GREGORY WOODS

Hart Crane's place in the Modernist pantheon is established by *The Bridge*. Not all of his work is so conspicuously proclaiming itself as modern. He learned from Pound and Eliot that the imperative 'to make it new' was no excuse for a deracinated free-for-all. Modernity looked to the future but depended on the past. Indeed, *The Bridge* itself, whatever else it may be, is largely a meditation on American history. This much is obvious.

The first thing we need to realise about Crane is that he was an *enthusiast* about poetry. He liked to see good poems – and not just his own – in print. In 1928, for instance, he was making efforts to get Gerard Manley Hopkins, to whose work Yvor Winters had introduced him, back into print.[1] Crane was not poetically isolated, despite the provincialism that so worried him as a teenager. He kept himself informed of contemporary literary trends. Throughout his life he made every effort to get hold of inaccessible books, especially new ones, and to help make them available to other readers. He arranged for Gorham Munson to smuggle a copy of *Ulysses* into the United States for him in 1922.[2]

He concentrated his reading in two areas: the American classics and the emergent Modernists in verse and prose. He fully intended, certainly by the time he started work on *The Bridge*, to write his own classic of American Modernism. It was by this criterion, in his own view, that the poem would fail or succeed. I see no reason to think of it otherwise.

America, poetry, Modernism: these three lines converge, inevitably to meet in the figure of Ezra Pound. Crane's relationship with Pound was difficult from the start. When Margaret Anderson published 'In Shadow' (which Crane had written at the age of 18) in the *Little Review*, Pound attacked it. Nevertheless, Crane was a dutiful follower of Pound's career. Joyce and Pound particularly occupied him in 1919, when he asked for his copies of *A Portrait of the*

Artist as a Young Man and Lustra to be sent on to him in New York
from home. (In 1918 he called *A Portrait* 'spiritually the most inspir-
ing book I have ever read', apart from the *Divina Commedia*.[3]

The influence of 'The Dead', in Joyce's *Dubliners*, seeps into
'Legend' as a reference to 'white falling flakes'.[4] And *Ulysses* seems
to have freed him into his later linguistic disruptions.) His reading
lists often included Pound. A 1921 list, for instance, names
Rimbaud, Eliot, William Carlos Williams, Marianne Moore and the
Noh plays of Fenollosa and Pound. He discussed Eliot and Pound,
among others, with William Lescaze in 1921, the year in which he
wrote an article on Pound for a popular magazine. Bill Sommer,
who helped Crane shape the original idea of *The Bridge*, had
studied and made notes on Pound's essay on Gaudier Brzeska.[5]
Pound is present in Crane's poetry, at least as a background figure,
if not as *miglior fabbro*. That role was offered, for the most part, to
Eliot.

Critics seem in disagreement on the extent of Crane's debt to
Imagism. Sure that he fits neatly among other clear debtors, Leslie
Fiedler says that 'all of the ambitious long poems of our time have
been written under Pound's guidance or inspired by his example:
Eliot's *The Waste Land*, for instance, and Hart Crane's *The Bridge*,
and William Carlos Williams' *Paterson*: all of those fragmented, al-
lusion-laden, imagistic portraits of an atomized world which have
so offended the Philistine mind'.[6] K. L. Goodwin, on the other
hand, believes Crane was more obviously shaped by a later stage in
Pound's career. Goodwin says *The Bridge* is 'ideogrammic' but not
'imagistic': 'The completed poem consists of large blocks of quite
distinct material from which a common theme is intended to
emerge; it is, that is to say, ideogrammic. Even within the larger divisions, the same technique of "montage" is applied, though there
is a tendency to revert to a previous block of material for the
purpose of summing up or of balance.' With the exception,
perhaps, of this last characteristic, the above statement would
clearly be as applicable to the *Cantos* as to *The Bridge*. But Goodwin
goes on: 'Attention is never concentrated for long on a particular
object, so that there are no outstanding examples of imagism in the
poem.'[7] As proof, this last remark seems to rely on a mistaken
definition of what Imagism ever sought to do. To 'focus long' is
hardly compatible with the notion of the fleeting glimpse. I see no
reason why we should not agree that the italicised lines in 'The
Harbour Dawn', for instance, owe a heavy debt to Imagism.

Goodwin is right, of course, to draw attention to ideogrammic juxtaposition as a crucial structural procedure which Crane inherited from Pound; but the technique passed to him more fluently from T. S. Eliot.

Crane's complicated indebtedness to *The Waste Land* is often abbreviated by hasty critics. A particularly compact version goes as follows: 'The Waste Land continued to provoke discussion. The poet Hart Crane felt that he had to show up Eliot by writing a big poem about myths and modern life. But unlike *The Waste Land* his poetry would be romantic and optimistic. When *The Bridge* failed he killed himself.'[8] Some of the ingredients of this account are more positively expressed by Robert Martin: 'His poetry might most accurately be called Romantic Modernism, for he resolved the clash of American Romanticism with European Modernism by turning Modernism into a tool with which to rediscover his own poetic heritage.'[9] Perhaps this is a major source of difference from Eliot: Crane believed his heritage could be not only rediscovered and reused, but rebuilt.

Crane's main objection to *The Waste Land* was, indeed, that it was too pessimistic. All of his reactions to it repeat this charge. When he first read it he found it 'good, of course, but so damned dead'. He wrote to Gorham Munson that he felt Eliot's vision ignored 'spiritual events and possibilities'. It quickly became clear, as a letter to Allen Tate shows, that Crane's deep admiration for Eliot's poem would cause problems in the writing of his own poetry, since he wanted to take part in the Modernist experiment that Eliot was shaping, and, as his reading began to follow Eliot's recommendations, to take his own place in the English poetic tradition that Eliot had newly redefined; but he disapproved of the trend Eliot had set in modish pessimism. Crane wrote to Tate, 'I ... would like to leave a few of his "negations" behind.' The same point was repeated in many subsequent conversations with Tate. Most damningly, Hart Crane detected 'a certain narcissism in the voluptuous melancholies of Eliot'. So much for Eliot's much vaunted detachment.[10]

So, while Crane was excited by *The Waste Land* as an experiment in strenuous modernity, he was unconvinced by its depressed view of the modern world. Perhaps one might say he was insufficiently enamoured of European culture to be as loftily pessimistic as Eliot. Crane, after all, still believed in America.

The Waste Land's depression, therefore, became a reference point to which the composition of *The Bridge* would always return, and from which it would purposefully veer. Crane's poem confines its disgust to the debasement of urban physicality that we find in 'The Tunnel' and its portrayal of lost love as 'a burnt match skating in a urinal'. This reference to 'tearoom sex' – or 'cottaging', as British slang would have it – is a pivotal moment in the text's journey through underworlds both literal and figurative. The poem goes no lower than this line. It is not by accident that the line's evocation of a debased sexuality from which all potentially uplifting emotion has been burnt off may well remind us of comparable moments in Eliot's poem: the carbuncular clerk's joyless collision with the typist, the lewd proposition of Mr Eugenides, the listless passivity of the conversation in the pub.

Once individuals appear in the modern world of *The Bridge*, they can seem just as numbed as Eliot's personages. So, for all the poem's hope, there is a good deal of logic in what Roy Harvey Pearce says of *The Bridge*: 'Crane's protagonists, taken all in all, reduce to the American as Prodigal: having wasted his patrimony; now trying somehow to restore it; unable to restore it until he returns to the home, the land, the myth, the language, which he has left behind. The patrimony is simply this: his spontaneous, fully-felt, all-powerful sense of his language as it reveals him as a person.'[11] By this reading, the poem is profoundly nostalgic, and its language is itself both the instrument and the object of that nostalgia. In these respects, the poem reinvokes the tendencies of its main model, *The Waste Land*; and it also, albeit perhaps inadvertently and only occasionally, reflects on the present with a negativism more characteristic of Eliot than of Crane.

It should always be remembered that anyone's relations with Eliot the poet were likely to be complicated by those with Eliot the editor. Crane's poem, 'The Wine Menagerie' was rejected by Eliot for *The Criterion* in 1925; but conditionally accepted – subject to changes – by Marianne Moore for *The Dial*. In the same year, 'Passage' was rejected by both Eliot and Moore.

As an antidote to what he perceived as the negative mood of Eliot's verse, Crane had always kept an eye on the developing career of William Carlos Williams. Throughout his life an indefatigable encourager of young poets, Williams performed this service for Crane as early as 1917, and Crane was later particularly stimulated by reading Williams's *Kora in Hell*. By 1921, Crane was trying to plot a course that led somewhere between the two older men. 'Black Tambourine' is a poem that dates from this uneasy time.

He also kept a close eye on Wallace Stevens, learning from him particular technical stratagems – such as the occasional use of rhyming couplets in otherwise unrhymed sequences – as well as a more general tendency, encouraged by ex-Imagists like Williams and Pound, to build poetry on a foundation of simple, prosaic statements. (At one time Crane was considering writing a critical study of Stevens.[12]) Another important Modernist cross-fertilisation occurred during the writing of 'Ave Maria' and 'Atlantis' in Winter 1926, when Crane was reading Lawrence's *The Plumed Serpent*.[13] Nor should we forget that Crane's reading was further widened, through his admiration for Eliot, to include the Jacobeans and Metaphysicals, as recommended by the master.

I have spoken of how Hart Crane learned from, and shaped himself according to, both classic American literature and transatlantic Modernism. There is a third line of inheritance which must not be – but usually is – ignored. Crane, was, and thought of himself as, a homosexual poet. The first sign of this is that his very first published poem has as its title, wrongly transliterated, the number of Oscar Wilde's cell at Reading Gaol, 'C 33'.

Apart from any other consideration, to ignore Crane's sexuality is to ignore what a number of readers see as the source of his obscurity. For instance, John Logan says that 'the biographical fact of [Crane's 'bisexuality'] in his case helps to account for the difficulty his poetry had in being accepted by an earlier generation, a difficulty which was compounded by an obscurity sometimes present in the language. This obscurity is due in part to the fact that Crane felt compelled to hide and/or to transform his sexuality in his language.'[14] Similarly, R. W. Butterfield says that the obscurity of 'At Melville's Tomb' is caused in part by 'the continual need for the homosexual to disguise the true nature of his passions in an esoteric symbolism'.[15] The irony is, of course, that it is precisely this enforced 'esoteric symbolism' that allows the *canon*-isation of homosexual writers. The supreme pontiff of this approach is Jeffrey Meyers, whose admiration is reserved for homosexual writers who are discreet. 'The clandestine predilections of homosexual novelists are both an obstacle and a stimulus to art, and lead to a creative tension between repression and expression. The novels become a raid on inarticulate feelings, and force the audience to find a language of reticence and evasion, obliqueness and indirection, to convey their theme.' 'If a specifically homosexual tone, sensibility, vision or mode of apprehension exists, then it would be characterized ... by the use of art to conceal rather than to reveal the actual theme of the novel.' 'The emancipation of the homosexual has led, paradoxically, to the decline of his art.'[16]

Be all that as it may (or may not), it is worth noting that a number of Crane's main poetic masters were homosexual or bisexual. The first among these is Walt Whitman.[17] When Crane saw Isadora Duncan dance in Cleveland in 1922, she recommended that all the audience go straight home and read, not some voguish Modernist text, but Walt Whitman's 'Calamus' poems.[18] This was the kind of advice that Crane could most enthusiastically follow: for it combined a distinctly modern concern for physical expression with a seminal American text on comradeship and the future of democracy. You can image Duncan panting as she spoke; you can imagine Hart Crane subsequently panting over 'Calamus'.

One of Crane's inheritances from Whitman – the least attractive, if not the least useful- was poetic ambition. According to Katherine Anne Porter, when Crane was staying with her in 1931 he would get drunk and weep and shout: 'I am Baudelaire, I am Whitman, I am Christopher Marlowe, I am Christ' – but, as Porter commented, 'never once did I hear him say he was Hart Crane'.[19] He wanted to be the next Great American Poet, and it was from Whitman that he learned the rant, even if in Whitman the 'barbaric yawp' was more purposeful and never self-pitying.

Allen Tate also knew Crane in this role: 'Hart had a sort of megalomania: he wanted to be The Great American Poet. I imagine he thought that by getting into the Whitman tradition, he could carry even Whitman further.' However, Tate's reliability as a witness to what Crane wanted to do with Whitman is compromised by the remarks that follow: 'And yet there's another thing we must never forget – there was the homosexual thing, too. … I don't think he was wholly conscious of it, but it must have had some influence. The notion of "comrades," you see, and that sort of business.'[20] This is a characteristic dismissal of gay culture in the guise of recognition. The idea that Crane was not wholly conscious of 'the homosexual thing' that linked him with Whitman is particularly odd. Robert Martin has shown in considerable detail how much of Crane's verse actually relied on such links.[21]

The problem is that Crane did not have the sheer conviction of Whitman. Except, perhaps, when drunk, Crane did not think so much of himself. Roy Harvey Pearce writes that 'Crane utterly lacked Whitman's faith – as he leaned and loafed and took his ease – that all moved toward and away from him.'[22] We may find one reason for this in their respective attitudes to their erotic choice. Whitman's love of men was a constant source of strength and joy, and he brooked no interference in his joy. Crane, on the other hand, while on occasions no less strengthened by sex and love, was frequently on the defensive, and frequently victimised, either physically by queer-bashers or emotionally by acquaintances and 'friends'. The context is crucial: they reflect their respective places in the history of sexuality. Whitman was, as it were, pre-homosexual, loving at a time when, in many of the States, the age of consent between males was as low as 10. Crane lived when sexuality had been pathologised and criminalised. His whole career is marked by this fact, from 'C 33', the poem about Wilde, onwards.[23]

Crane was not temperamentally suited to the free-wheeling, spontaneous nature of Whitman's (and, later, Lawrence's) poetry. Only rarely could he create, by meticulous concentration, the effect of nonchalance. His interest in Whitman is sexual; what he learns from the poetry he does not often imitate but tries to develop. His main aim was to establish a right of succession – partly in pursuance of his poetic ambition, and partly in quest of an atmosphere in which to love. He wanted to believe in adhesiveness and democracy, even in the depths of 'The Tunnel'. He thought he could inherit the mantle of the Good Gray – and gay – Poet himself. Pound and Eliot were already too European; Eliot too strait-laced, Pound too straight.

To return, then, to Eliot, there is a particular reason why Crane followed him more assiduously than Pound. In May 1922 Crane wrote a letter to Allen Tate in which he said, 'I admire Eliot very much too. I've had to work through him, but he's the prime ram of our flock'; which meant, according to Tate, that, along with 'a lot of people', Crane 'had the delusion that Eliot was homosexual'.[24] This leads us to the obvious question of a homosexual tradition; or, at least, to the incontrovertible fact that gay authors often seek out and choose to be influenced by gay authors. As Maurice van Lieshout has said, 'No writer is ever the first to write on homosexuality in literature. Writing on homosexuality often means taking up a position in the homosexual canon of literary texts. A writer can be inspired by and can refer to his predecessors, and he works in a specific literary climate.'[25] Writing on Crane in particular, Robert Martin says: 'The homosexual poet seeks poetic "fathers" who in some sense offer a validation of his sexual nature. Whatever he may learn poetically from the great tradition, he cannot fail to notice that this tradition is, at least on the surface, almost exclusively heterosexual. The choice of a model like Whitman is, therefore, an important element of self-identification, an act of declaring one's sexual identity and of placing oneself in a tradition.'[26]

In terms of the relation between text, critic and the author's biography, Crane will always provide a useful case study for gay critics, if only because his homosexuality, unlike that of so many other writers, is relatively rarely ignored by the critics. But, for the most part, those who do refer to him as homosexual do so, yoking sexuality and alcoholism together, more to account for his suicide than to clarify their readings of his verse.[27] While one may be glad to see so many critics acknowledging what set him apart from the society to which he was writing, one can only deplore the sheer weight of the homophobia he has attracted. Some examples may give pause for thought. 'As to his homosexuality, I am not alone in thinking that his reports exaggerated it.' 'If Hart Crane had chosen to conceal his homosexual inclination, I doubt that even his close friends would have suspected it. He seemed to be a normal male. The reasons for his not concealing it are, to me, obscure and complex.'[28] 'Europe was too old for Rimbaud, and America was too young for Crane, as the homosexual is always too old as a boy and too young as a man.'[29] The 'terrible liability of homosexuality'.[30] 'From the time he first revealed a homosexual proclivity to Gorham Munson … Crane was never able to free himself from this perversion.' Even the news in 1931 that he had been awarded a Guggenheim Fellowship 'did not diminish his vices'.[31] I have tried to give a range of these comments, none of them particularly remarkable in itself. Since literary texts now speak against a hubbub of critical voices – given the nature of what the discipline of 'English' has become – we cannot help but read Crane's poems at the centre of these assertions of hetero superiority. 'Power's script' – the phrase is from 'Cape Hatteras' – is superimposed on Crane's original script, which can be read only through this upper layer.

To theorise his place in the canon, therefore, must involve analysis of the kind of role he is expected to play there – as a dissolute, homosexual suicide. The critical position is succinctly stated in a sentence by D. S. Savage: Hart Crane 'was homosexual and suffered from a deep disharmony of his personal life, lived wildly and wretchedly, and died eventually by his own hand'.[32] The line from homosexuality to suicide is taken as a natural progression, the blame for which lies entirely with the homosexual individual himself ('by his own hand').

It is also instructive to consider how the critics have treated Crane's 1924 relationship with Emil Opffer, in terms of poetic 'inspiration' one of the most productive love affairs in American literary history. Without Opffer there would be no 'Voyages' sequence (though its first poem did date from before the affair) and significant parts of *The Bridge*, notably 'The Harbour Dawn', could not have existed. Vincent Quinn refers to this period, in relation to 'Voyages', as follows: 'The occasion was a homosexual relationship carried on in an apartment overlooking New York harbor and intensified by the intervals when his friend was at sea. It lasted only from the spring to the fall of 1924, but it kept Crane in an ecstasy of tenderness and doubt.'[33] The phrase 'carried on' gives away a lot. The reference to the short span of spring – fall ('only') is made more explicit in a commentary by Paul Friedman: 'But his joy was short-lived, his sense of fulfilment delusive; for the affair, like all his others, was a homosexual one.'[34]

Or take Samuel Hazo's slightly more lengthy account: in 1924, Crane's 'homosexuality asserted itself' and he invited a sailor to share his room overlooking Brooklyn Bridge. But, contrary to those critics (Hazo quotes Philip Horton) who stress how this 'relationship with a sailor' provided 'homosexual excitation to poetic expression' (in a heterosexual poet that 'excitation' would probably be called inspiration), Hazo says:

> Whatever influence Crane's homosexual relationship with a particular sailor may have had upon the composition of 'Voyages' is a point best left to psychological disquisition. There is nothing in the poems that explicitly betrays a perversion of the impulses of love, and there is no thematic reason that would lead a reader to relate the love imagery, where it does exist, to a source homosexual in nature. Consequently, a reasonable reader could find no compelling factors in the six parts of 'Voyages' that would suggest that he consider the impulses of love in any but a heterosexual sense, regardless of the relationship that may have prompted them and regardless of the person to whom they may have been directed.[35]

As Robert K. Martin has shown, even when acknowledged, Opffer appears in supporting material either as a 'young sailor' or as 'E – ', the anonymity of which has an inevitable effect of ashamed secrecy. In fact, Opffer was what Crane called a 'ship's writer', and was 27 when he met the 24-year-old Crane. Far from being a bit of rough trade, he was an intellectual and the publisher of a Danish-language newspaper in New York.[36]

However, not all references to Crane's personal life were negative from the start. An important early commentary on the positive relation of his homosexuality to his verse – and on homosexual writing in general – is Robert Duncan's 1944 essay 'The Homosexual in Society'.[37] This was at once an assertion of homosexuality as a valid and validating creative impulse, central to the fecundity of the homosexual writer, and a refusal to see his affirmation as making homosexuality in any way more special than heterosexuality. As Duncan's own sexual–political manifesto, the essay establishes him as an integrationist, but no apologist. He is determined to claim a place for the homosexual writer on some wider base than that of a queer cult. He despises homosexual readers who seek to set up such cults as much as he despises heterosexual critics who encourage the cultish in order to separate gay art as a distinct and easy target. He uses Crane as *the* example of a poet whose homosexuality has been, not ignored, but used against him – by readers both straight and gay. It is worth nothing that this essay did not go down well with the moguls of the New Critical establishment, and Duncan subsequently found their magazines firmly closed to his importunate poetry. Thus did the New Critics, contrary to all their claimed principles, apply an extrinsic homophobia to the intrinsic homo-eroticism of texts.

Duncan writes: 'Where the Zionists of homosexuality have laid claim to a Palestine of their own,[38] asserting in their miseries their nationality; Crane's suffering, his rebellion, and his love are sources of poetry for him not because they are what make him different from, superior to, mankind, but because he saw in them his link with mankind; he saw in them his sharing of universal human experience.'[39] This universalising tendency, so unfashionable now, has a significant place in the development of gay self-esteem, and should not be lightly dismissed. For much of this century the article of faith, that love itself is universal and universally good, was used with countless refinements to protect homosexual women and men against their detractors. But we must be aware that this use of the *idea* of the universal is itself solidly rooted in the circumstances of the society from which it arose.

Russell Reising has said: 'Future theorists and critics of American literature would do well to address the struggle of American criticism to suppress the social and political significance of American texts.'[40] This is, of course, a response to the powers wielded by the New Criticism through the central period of this century. But nowhere is it more true than in the case of gay texts, which were allowed into the canon at the expense of their gayness. Only *after* the re-sexing of pronouns in Whitman could readers settle down to a literature that safely dealt with the 'universals' of American 'myth', rather than the particulars of social experience.

Not only is the text not autonomous – not isolated from social context – but nor is it isolated from the critical texts which claim its autonomy. To some extent, American Literature as we now see it consists of original texts seen through an overlay of the New Criticism (not to mention the Old). What this means in terms of 'gay literature' is that the gay text must perforce be read through its anti-gay context. As Terry Eagleton has put it, 'All literary works ... are "rewritten", if only unconsciously, by the societies which read them; indeed there is no reading of a work which is not also a "re-writing".'[41]

Crane was rewritten by commentators who sometimes had, at least, the good grace to be open about their revisions and erasures. Samuel Hazo, as quoted above, is the best example: a critic who scrupulously pays attention to Crane's sexuality while claiming there is absolutely no need to do so. His rewritings are unashamedly censorious. He exercises the sheer *power* to choose not to consider important the things which the poet, quite clearly, did consider important.

But what was it Crane was trying to say that needed so securely to be muffled? Nothing particularly alien, surely, to a culture which should already have come to terms with Whitman, albeit a Whitman much tampered with. For Crane's basic vision of America and his place in it is pre-Modernist: it is derived from the so-called American Renaissance, most specifically from Emerson's essay 'The Poet' and Whitman's *Democratic Vistas*. Much of what Crane was trying to reiterate in terms of modern urban life had already been expressed in Whitman's famous footnote:

It is to the development, identification, and general prevalence of that fervid comradeship (the adhesive love, at least rivaling the amative love hitherto possessing imaginative literature if not going beyond it), that I look for the counterbalance and offset of our materialistic and vulgar American democracy, and for the spiritualisation thereof.

In this essay I have not offered any readings (or 're-writings') of Crane's poems. I find they have become, in some important sense, practically unreadable. Too many obstacles to clear reading have been imposed on them, not least by their own author in his understandable fear of the consequences of such clarity.[42] Obscure enough texts in themselves, they have been further obscured by critics unwilling to elucidate them. If we take Modernism as a whole, as comprising both 'primary' and 'secondary' texts – in the present context, both poems and critical apparatus – our impression of the American movement is bound to be of a far more repressed and ill-balanced dialogue between opposed forces than if we were still able to read poems as autonomous verbal patterns transcending the very reality they were trying to describe.

NOTES

1. John Unterecker, *Voyager: A Life of Hart Crane* (New York: Blond, 1970) pp. 526, 528–9.
2. Ibid., π pp. 222, 246.
3. *The Complete Poems and Selected Letters and Prose of Hart Crane* (London: Oxford University Press, 1968) p. 200.
4. Robert K. Martin, *The Homosexual Tradition in American Poetry* (Austin and London: University of Texas Press, 1979) pp. 129–30.
5. Unterecker, pp. 89–90, 133, 173, 209, 211, 267.
6. Leslie Fiedler, 'Traitor or Laureate: The Two Trials of the Poet', in Eva Hesse (ed.), *New Approaches to Ezra Pound: A Co-ordinated Investigation of Pound's Poetry and Ideas* (London: Faber, 1969) p. 371.
7. K. L. Goodwin, *The Influence of Ezra Pound* (London: Oxford University Press, 1966) p. 169.
8. Louis Simpson, *Three on a Tower: The Lives and Works of Ezra Pound, T. S. Eliot and William Carlos Williams* (New York: William Morrow, 1975) p. 152.
9. Martin, p. 133. William Faulkner was putting Modernism to comparable uses in fiction.
10. Unterecker, pp. 260, 270, 272, 241, 242, 431, 434.
11. Roy Harvey Pearce, *The Continuity of American Poetry* (Princeton, NJ: Princeton University Press, 1961) pp. 106–7.
12. Unterecker, p. 703.
13. Brom Weber, *Hart Crane: A Biographical and Critical Study* (New York: Bodley Press, 1948) p. 341.
14. John Logan, 'Foreword' to Hart Crane, *White Buildings* (New York: Liveright, 1972) p. xx.
15. R. W. Butterfield, *The Broken Arc: A Study of Hart Crane* (Edinburgh: Oliver & Boyd, 1969) p. 114.

16. Jeffrey Meyers, *Homosexuality and Literature, 1980–1930* (London: Athlone Press, 1977) pp. 1–2, 3. A similar view is even more bluntly, and recently, expressed by Camille Paglia: 'The more negative homosexual experience, the more it belongs to art.' This is, presumably, because 'Repression makes meaning and purpose' – *Sexual Personae: Art and Decadence from Nefertiti to Emily Dickinson* (New Haven and London: Yale University Press, 1990) pp. 54, 136. I suppose Paglia would have to concede that repression can go too far. How much art emerged from the crematoria to which the Nazis sent the men with the pink triangles?

17. Another important gay master is Rimbaud, whose influence on Crane's poetry is dealt with at some length in Weber, pp. 144–50. For some nastily homophobic readings of Rimbaud and Crane, see Wallace Fowlie, *Love in Literature: Studies in Symbolic Expression* (Bloomington, Indiana: Indiana University Press, 1965). Let the following serve as a taster: 'Rimbaud and Crane were riveted to homosexuality in much the same way that a convict is riveted to his chain. They could look at the river and the sea and discover there a kind of poetic freedom, but only after the contemplation of their own hearts had drugged them with bitterness and frustration' (p. 134).

18. Unterecker, p. 264.

19. Unterecker, p. 659.

20. Unterecker, p. 431. It is not unlikely that Crane read Emory Holloway's essay on the homo-erotic element in Whitman's work, 'Walt Whitman's Love Affairs', *The Dial*, November 1920; see Jonathan Ned Katz, *Gay/Lesbian Almanac: A New Documentary* (New York: Harper & Row, 1983) pp. 388–91. Crane probably soon became aware, also, of D. H. Lawrence's essay on Whitman in *The Nation* (London), reviewed in the *New York Times Book Review*, 28 August 1921, p. 27; see Katz, pp. 400–1.

21. Martin, pp. 136–63. Harold Norse offers a revealing anecdote about Tate's 'friendship' with Crane: 'Tate, who'd been a close friend of Hart Crane's but who made nasty remarks behind his back about his homosexuality, received the news of Crane's suicide by getting drunk with his wife, the writer Caroline Gordon, and repeating jubilantly, with thigh-slapping glee, "Well, what do you know, the sharks ate 'im!"' – *Memoirs of a Bastard Angel* (London: Bloomsbury, 1990) p. 194.

22. Pearce, p. 108.

23. Crane was more a follower than a shaper of a specifically gay culture. So the lack of any reference to him in a book like Michael Bronski's *Culture Clash: The Making of Gay Sensibility* (Boston: South End Press, 1984) is unsurprising and leaves no great gap. Far more of an omission is his absence from Stephen Coote (ed.), *The Penguin Book of Homosexual Verse* (London: Penguin, 1983).

    Crane does, however, take his place in the family tree of gay American poets. In a typical moment of identification, Harold Norse remembers: 'Right next door to Crane's old apartment I lost my cherry to a college professor and learned about homosexual love, with Whitman and Crane nodding sadly and mellowly over us' – Winston Leyland (ed.), *Gay Sunshine Interviews, Volume 1* (San Francisco: Gay Sunshine Press, 1978) p. 210. Crane frequently crops up as an orphic gay victim, elegised and eulogised by even more gay poets than have been significantly influenced by his poetry. Allen Ginsberg is a particular fan; see 'Death to Van Gogh's Ear', 'Kansas City to Saint Louis' and 'Cleveland, the Flats' – *Collected Poems 1947–1980* (Harmondsworth: Viking, 1985) pp. 167, 413, 429. In a bizarre moment of identification, James Baldwin once imagined he looked like Hart Crane – Norse, *Memoirs of a Bastard Angel*, p. 175.

24. Unterecker, p. 240. If we ignore the possibility that Tate was wrong, and that Crane's 'our' included, with himself and Eliot, the heterosexual Tate – as being all *poets* – it is easy to see how such a 'delusion' might have materialised. The relevant material is on display in John Peter, 'A New Interpretation of *The Waste Land*', *Essays in Criticism*, xix, 2 (April 1969) pp. 140–75. Eliot himself got his solicitors to suppress the earlier version of this essay.

25. Maurice van Lieshout, 'The Context of Gay Writing and Reading', in Dennis Altman et al., *Homosexuality, Which Homosexuality? International Conference on Gay and Lesbian Studies* (London: GMP, 1989) p. 117.

26. Martin, p. 148.

27. See Gregory Woods, *Articulate Flesh: Male Homo-eroticism and Modern Poetry* (New Haven and London: Yale University Press, 1987) pp. 140–1. To me it seems more reasonable to assume that it was less Crane's homosexuality that drove him to drink, and then to suicide, than the consistent homophobia not only of the society he lived in, but also of so many of his 'friends'.

28. Susan Jenkins Brown, *Robber Rocks: Letters and Memories of Hart Crane, 1923–1932* (Middletown, Connecticut: Wesleyan University Press) pp. 14, 15.

29. Fowlie, p. 136.

30. Philip Horton, *Hart Crane: The Life of an American Poet* (New York: Viking, 1957) p. 92.

31. Samuel Hazo, *Hart Crane: An Introduction and Interpretation* (New York: Barnes and Noble, 1963) pp. 7, 14.

32. D. S. Savage, 'The Americanism of Hart Crane', *The Personal Principle: Studies in Modern Poetry* (London: Routledge, 1944) p. 113.

33. Vincent Quinn, *Hart Crane* (New York: Twayne, 1963) p. 106.

34. Paul Friedman. 'The Bridge: A Study in Symbolism', *The Psychoanalytic Quarterly*, xxi, 1 (1952) p. 77. Friedman comments further: 'The archetype of Oneness is the act of [hetero]sexual intercourse, which was beyond Crane's capacity' (p. 78). Anyone who knows about Crane's relationship with Peggy Baird immediately before his suicide will know (a) that 'sexual intercourse' was not beyond Crane's 'capacity', but (b) that it led to nothing like that pompously capitalised 'Oneness'.

35. Hazo, pp. 10, 55, 56.

36.   Robert K. Martin, 'Reclaiming Our Lives', in Michael Denneny, Charles Ortleb and Thomas Steele (eds), *The View from Christopher Street* (London: Chatto & Windus/The Hogarth Press, 1984) p. 25.

37.   *Politics*, i, 7 (August 1944) pp. 209–11. Reprinted in Ekbert Faas, *Young Robert Duncan: Portrait of the Poet as Homosexual in Society* (Santa Barbara, Cal.: Black Sparrow Press, 1983) pp. 319–22.

38.   This is clearly a figure which Duncan inherits from Marcel Proust.

39.   Faas, p. 321.

40.   Russell Reising, *The Unusable Past: Theory and the Study of American Literature* (New York and London: Methuen, 1986) p. 237.

41.   Terry Eagleton, *Literary Theory: An Introduction* (Oxford: Blackwell, 1983) p. 12. Note that Eagleton, in the course of this book, shows no awareness of important re-readings by lesbian and gay theorists.

42.   For some lively and powerful readings of the poems in relation to homosexuality and the homophobia in which it was ensnared, see Paul Giles, *Hart Crane: The Contexts of The Bridge* (Cambridge: Cambridge University Press, 1986) pp. 163–182. Giles bases his interpretations on the judicious assumption that 'the repressed puns in *The Bridge* mirror the agonised repression of Crane's own homosexuality' (p. 181).

5

William Carlos Williams

ALISTAIR WISKER

William Carlos Williams described *Kora in Hell: Improvisations* as the one book he had enjoyed referring to more than any of his others. It was a unique book, unlike any other by him, and it realised something which he did not have in mind when he started it. Uniquity was guaranteed by experience. The title came from a conversation with Ezra Pound about Kora, the Greek parallel to Persephone, the legend of springtime captured and taken to Hades. Williams thought of himself as springtime and felt he was a little along the way to Hell. He treats this book in a very personal way, saying, for instance: 'It reveals myself to me and perhaps that is why I have kept it to myself.'[1] When the book was complete Williams thought of the Prologue – which is really, therefore, more of an epilogue – because he wanted to give an indication of himself to the people he knew:[2]

> sound off, tell the world – especially my intimate friends – how I felt about them. All my gripes to other poets, all my loyalties to other poets, are here in the Prologue. It has been referred to many times because it includes extracts of important letters from people who influenced me in my career.

Williams attended assiduously to what he was told, and these loyalties which he mentions, of his and to him, are very important in a career during which he generated many creative relationships, oppositions, and allegiances. He weighed things and made up his own mind. There is a central example of this which occurred when Williams was halfway through the Prologue to Kora:[3]

> 'Prufrock' appeared. I had a violent feeling that Eliot had betrayed what I believed in. He was looking backward; I was looking forward. He was a conformist with wit, learning which I

did not possess. He knew French, Latin, Arabic, God knows what. I was interested in that. But I felt he had rejected America and I refused to be rejected and so my reaction was violent. I realized the responsibility I must accept. I knew he would influence all subsequent American poets and take them out of my sphere. I had envisaged a new form of poetic composition, a form for the future. It was a shock to me that he was so tremendously successful; my contemporaries flocked to him – away from what I wanted. It forced me to be successful.

So here we have the ground rules, the responsibility which Williams felt, based on an intense literary opposition. Williams gave such a hostile reception to *Prufrock and Other Observations* because he believed that Eliot had rejected America and therefore himself and the new form of poetic composition which he had created for the future. The betrayal inscribed in Eliot's poems was that they returned the art to the classroom just when:[4]

> I felt that we were on the point of an escape much closer to the essence of a new art form itself – rooted in the locality which should give it fruit.

This is the key assertion with which to fight the betrayal, the attack from the centre out, distinguishing between the national or international in letters and the preeminent importance of the locality. As Williams wrote about Poe:[5]

> What he wanted was connected with no particular
> place; therefore it *must* be where he *was* ... The
> strong sense of a beginning in Poe is in *no one*
> else before him. What he says, being thoroughly
> local in origin, has some chance of being universal
> in application, a thing they never dared conceive.
> Made to fit *a place* it will have that actual quality
> of *things* anti-metaphysical —
>
>   About Poe there is—
> No supernatural mystery—
> No extraordinary eccentricity of fate—
> He is American, understandable by a simple exercise of
> reason; a light in the morass.

In writing about Poe in this way, Williams is announcing himself and mapping his own territory – as he is in so much of *In the American Grain*. Just as in his comments on Eliot, he is taking an opportunity to discover and define his own poetic identity. Williams set himself firmly and consistently against a literature which breeds on literature, dedicated himself to developing a literature discovered in the human barnyard:

> I wanted to write a poem
> that you would understand.

He writes this to an old woman in 'January Morning' and is careful to add admonishingly 'But you got to try hard'. So it won't be an easy poetry, this poetry of the local rather than of the classroom. It will be an aggressively modern poetry of vivid observation, inclusive, often celebrating seemingly unpoetic and sometimes arbitrary items like 'the broken / pieces of a green / bottle' in 'Between Walls', the list of ice-cream prices in 'April', or someone's market shopping in 'Elena'.

The poem 'Pastoral' appeared in the volume *Al Que Quiere!*, published in the same year as Eliot's 'Prufrock', 1917. Williams often observed the potentially emblematic ingeniousness of sparrows, and 'Pastoral' opens with the sharp voices of the little birds quarrelling 'over those things / that interest them' juxtaposed with people who shut themselves in, not revealing their thoughts to anyone. The poem moves on through the transitional 'meanwhile' to seemingly unconnected assertions. What brings this series of observations to life, organising the experience and validating the poem, is the closure:

> These things
> astonish me beyond words.

The poem is a montage and, in its construction, language is treated as a series of ready-mades found in the community environment – an activity which no doubt reveals the influence on Williams of new developments in painting. 'Pastoral' also demonstrates the basis of his poetry in things, in locality, in the modern, and anticipates the effort which Williams relentlessly made to create 'somehow by an intense, individual effort, a new – an American – poetic language'. His opposition to Eliot serves to emphasise the complex and extraordinarily compound nature of Modernism, of which they can be identified as equal proponents. What a poem like 'Pastoral' does is to discover and reveal a poetry that is actually there, 'in the life before us, every moment that we are listening, a rarest element – not in our imagination but there, there in fact'.[6]

This is what Williams is all about, paying attention to the particularity of things and moments, homing in on what is and checking the too-easy slither into abstraction as well as the tendency to be taken in by the backward pull of the English tradition. Henry James described this as the complex fate of being an American, and Whitman, of course, had explored the notion in 'Starting from Paumanok':

Dead poets, philosophs, priests,
Martyrs, artists, inventors, governments long since,
Language-shapers, on other shores,
Nations once powerful, now reduced, withdrawn, or desolate,
I dare not proceed till I respectfully credit what you have left,
    wafted hither:
I have perused it – own it as admirable, (moving awhile among it)
Think nothing can ever be greater – nothing can ever deserve
    more than it deserves;
Regarding it all intently a long while – then dismissing it,
I stand in my place, with my own day, here.

This concern to credit what has gone before and then to inhabit his own day, his own place, is to the fore in Carlos Williams, whose work was once described as 'a sort of spiritual prolongation of the voyages of Columbus'.[7] The effort to rescue the everyday matter of modern American life and make it the material of his poetry, Williams saw as the business of the poet: 'Not to talk in vague categories but to write particularly, as a physician works upon a patient, upon the thing before him, in the particular to discover the universal.'[8] These concerns, as we have seen, come through in the subjects of his poems. Williams was also increasingly concerned with structure and ways of creating aural designs. As a result, he necessarily rejected the dead moulds from the English tradition and sought the right measure for the indigenous American idiom: 'it came to me that the concept of the foot itself would have to be altered in our new relativistic world'.[9] Williams wanted to be able to follow the unique pattern of speech and thereby to counter the levelling assumptions of print. He spent a lot of time exploring the relationships between speech and silence, white space and print, and as a result of these explorations he developed the concept of the variable foot, which occupied a lot of his thinking time in his later years.[10]

Williams was schooled in Rutherford, New Jersey, and at Horace Mann High School in New York City. One day at Horace Mann he had a heart attack or murmur, as a result of which he had to give up running and baseball: 'I was forced back on myself. I had to think about myself, look into myself. And I began to read.'[11]

From 1902 to 1906 Williams studied medicine at the University of Pennsylvania and from 1906 to 1909 he was an intern at the Old French Hospital and at Nursery and Child's Hospital back in New York City. It was in 1910 that Williams began general practice in Rutherford, the work which he continued until 1951 when he retired after suffering one of several heart attacks. In training he met Ezra Pound, who was to become a lifelong friend, sounding-board, contestant, and mutual standard-bearer. It was in a letter to Williams that Pound first outlined his ideas about poetry, which were:[12]

1. To paint the thing as I see it.
2. Beauty.
3. Freedom from didacticism.
4. It is only good manners if you repeat a few other men to at least do it better or more briefly.

It is not difficult to see likenesses between these objectives, which were to be further refined in order to express the aims of Imagism, and the interests of the young Carlos Williams. And Pound was instrumental in the appearance of Williams in the first Imagist Anthology in 1914, alongside work by H. D. and Richard Aldington, Amy Lowell, F. S. Flint and Ford Maddox Hueffer. Williams enjoins us to remember that 'Before meeting Ezra Pound is like B.C. and A.D.' and that it was to Pound he first showed the new 'quick spontaneous' poems which he had written when he moved on from bad imitations of Keats:[13]

My quick spontaneous poems, as opposed to my studied Keatsian sonnets, were written down in thick, stiff-covered copybooks. I can see them still, bound in marbelized paper. There were eighteen of them, full. I was tremendously impressed with them and kept them above my bed. They looked very serious and important. The point is I had something to show when I met Ezra Pound. He was not impressed. He was impressed with his own poetry; but then, I was impressed with my own poetry, too, so we got along all right.

Again we see Williams measuring himself against another poet, making his own decisions. He tells a story[14] about Pound meeting his father and mother, and arguing seriously with the outspoken, hard-headed Englishman about one of his poems concerning a collection of jewels. Williams senior said the poem was all right but asked what it meant. Pound explained that the jewels, the rubies, sapphires, amethysts and whatnot were the backs of the books on his bookcase, and received the rejoinder: 'If you mean that, why don't you say it?' Thus, one imagines, saving his son the trouble. Anyway, this incident commenced the funny feeling which Williams had about Pound, not knowing what kind of animal he was, liking him but not wanting to be like him.

During the same years Williams was friendly with the still un- dervalued H. D. (Hilda Doolittle), who followed Pound to London and then, albeit briefly, was married to Richard Aldington. Williams images their relationship in this way: 'When I was with her my feet always seemed to be sticking to the ground while she would be walking on the tips of the grass stems.'[15] A decade later she wrote to him about his poem 'March', which had appeared in *The Egoist*, of which she was assistant editor:[16]

I don't know what you think but I consider this business of writing a very sacred thing! – I think you have the 'spark' – am sure of it, and when you speak *direct* are a poet. I feel in the hey-ding-ding touch running through your poem a derivative tendency which, to me, is not *you* – not your very self. It is as if you were *ashamed* of your Spirit, ashamed of your inspiration! – as if you mocked at your own song. It's very well to *mock* at yourself – it is a spiritual sin to mock at your inspiration –

This gets her dear Bill going. It is one of the spurs to self and artistic definition which he quotes in the *Prologue to Kora in Hell*, preceding the response from Wallace Stevens to *Al Que Quiere!* H. D. causes Williams to think some things through:

There is nothing sacred about literature, it is damned from one end to the other. There is nothing in literature but change and change is mockery. I'll write whatever I damn please, whenever I damn please and as I damn please and it'll be good if the authentic spirit of change is on it.

   But in any case H. D. misses the entire intent of what I am doing no matter how just her remarks concerning that particular poem happen to have been. The hey-ding-ding touch *was* derivative, but it filled a gap that I did not know how better to fill at the time. It might be said that that touch is the prototype of the improvisations.

So we have Williams identifying himself through his responses to Eliot, Pound, and H. D. He also met the painter Charles Demuth in the early years. Cézanne and Sheeler were influences on Williams and direct touchpoints for poetry, but Demuth became a friend and Williams owned one of his temperas titled 'End of the Parade: Coatsville, Pa.' as well as two watercolours – 'The Gossips' and 'Tuberoses'. The volume *Sour Grapes*, published in 1921, contained a remarkable poem, a city syncopation enigmatically titled 'The Great Figure'. In 1928 Demuth produced a painting in tribute to a line in the poem, 'I saw the figure 5 in Gold'.

   Williams returned the compliment on the death of Demuth in 1935 by dedicating one of his finest poems to the painter, 'The Crimson Cyclamen'. The inclusion of the title, only to deny its accuracy ('more rose than crimson', 'crimson's a dull word'), implies the inadequacy of language to describe such a unique phenomenon. Yet language is the tool we have to try with, we use it to enfold and to pierce a subject in the way that light enfolds and pierces. Words, light and, of course, paint depict their subjects as best they can. In this poem Williams shows how they share and even exchange characteristics: The poem focusing on and slowly revealing the structure of a petal. 'The Crimson Cyclamen' is based on the inter-relationship between painting and poetry, the way both are created from raw potentiality. Of the flowers,

   silence holds them –
   in that space. And
   colour has been construed
   from emptiness

Colour and language terms are exchanged (colour construed, and silence in a space), painting and poem are both likewise construed from an emptiness.

There is more to this than mutual title-swapping between artists, although interrelating the arts in this way has its significance. As well as the title-swapping and the exchange of terms, there is a new understanding of form which is shared by the painters and poets of the Williams generation. In *I Wanted to Write a Poem* Williams discusses the frontispiece for *Kora in Hell*:[17]

> I had seen a drawing by Stuart Davis, a young artist I had never met, which I wanted reproduced in my book because it was as close as possible to my idea of the Improvisations. It was, graphically, exactly what I was trying to do in words, put the Improvisations down as a unit on the page. You must remember I had a strong inclination all my life to be a painter. Under different circumstances I would rather have been a painter than to bother with these god-dam words.

This announcement by Williams is revealing about his personal development and significant as a way of understanding his work. He and Floss (he had married Flossie Herman, who he described as the rock on which he built, in December 1912) got permission from Stuart Davis to use his art work. Williams reveals that his entire book occurred backwards. The improvisations came first, then the interpretations below the dividing line, then the title, then the Stuart Davis drawing, and finally the prologue. Here the theorising not only postdates the practice but is a part of it – as in the case of so many post-Romantic poets, truth lies *in* the search, which is not perceived as coming to an end. It is not surprising that his critical vocabulary reveals Williams as concerned with possibility, variability, and neither shutout nor shutdown.

Williams is explicit about what he felt the painters had done, and his work, from *The Tempers* to *Spring and All*,[18] indeed his entire output as a poet, can be related to painters and painting. As he says himself, 'it was the work of the painters following Cézanne and the Impressionists that, critically, opened up the age of Stein, Joyce and a good many others'. Williams brought what he wanted of the new painting, of Paris, into the American scene; he introduced Walt Whitman to Gris and Cézanne and aligned Cubist fragmentation with American photography. With his inclination to be a painter, he saw that the painters had been opening gates, and when he reflected on the early decades of the century he was convinced that:[19]

> it was the French painters rather than the writers who influenced us, and their influence was very great. They created an atmosphere of release, color release, release from stereotyped forms, trite subjects.

Williams was fascinated by the ways in which influence occurs: the ways in which Columbus, Daniel Boone, George Washington and Edgar Allan Poe, for instance, influenced and shaped the American grain. Mutual influence, a mingling of characteristics, also becomes the fulcrum of a number of his poems – as, for example, happens in 'Flowers By the Sea'. Here the sea becomes a plant and the plants become a seascape, the idea comes from the things brought into a new juxtaposition. Since a poem is an object, thought Williams, 'it must be the purpose of the poet to make of his work a new form: to invent, that is, an object consonant with his day'. It is in his inventiveness and his attempts to make new forms that Williams can be associated, as he associated himself, with the painters of his day. At different times his work can be likened to the 'Ash Can' school, with its stress on the vitality of American city life, to the imported European movements centred on Cubism, with its new apprehension of structure and form, or, as when, in *Paterson*, Williams takes energy released as a theme and a technique, to the 'action' painters like Jackson Pollock. Williams once wrote:[20]

> There had been a break somewhere, we were all streaming through, each thinking his own thoughts, driving his own design towards his self's objectives. Whether the Armory Show in painting did it or whether that was also no more than a facet – the poetic line, the way the image was to lie on the page, was our immediate concern. For myself all that implied, in the materials, respecting the place I knew best, was finding a local assertion – to my everlasting relief.

This bringing together of his local assertion with the influence of painters and painting helps to trace the development of his poetry. The influence of painting can be seen from the impact of the Armory Show all the way through to the exceptional *Pictures from Brueghel* or the late poem 'Tribute to the Painters', which appeared in *Journey to Love* in 1955.

The imaginative recreation of *Pictures from Brueghel* results in poems which have all the dizziness and immediacy of being *there*. Take, for instance, 'The Hunters in the Snow', in which the hill becomes a pattern of skaters brought to life by the artist. Then there are the children's horrific toys which many of us both remember and become reintroduced to by our own children – in awe. The words are released with all the apparently innocent malevolence of children at unsupervised play: Reading *Pictures from Brueghel* one understands the strong inclination to painting and the extent of its influence on the poet(ry). Sometimes Williams seems to have adopted a Fauvist frenzy of colour, sometimes there is a Dadaist quirkiness. In his *Autobiography* he asserted that 'impressionism, dadaism, surrealism applied to both painting and the poem'. But the influence of painting on his poetry centres on Cubism. Williams was driven to unravel the structural implications which Cubism held for poetry because:

> the imagination for Williams was identified with the cubist re-structuring of reality: modern poetry with its ellipses, its confrontation of disparates, its use of verbal collages provided direct analogies.[21]

It is possible, for instance, to view a poem like 'Spring Strains' as an example of the attempt to transcribe pictorial structure into a poem. The mixture of the painterly terms, 'monotone' and 'drawing', and the 'blue-grey' colour of the buds and twigs, which turns out to be the same colour as that of the 'blue-grey' local birds as they chase each other – lines on a plane, colour into colour – create something close to a cubist poem. 'It had been part of the Cubist programme to renounce the illusion of infinite distance, and to exploit the formal potentialities inherent in the medium', and that is part of what Williams is doing here – producing lines like 'in a tissue-thin monotone of blue-grey buds' which could only be reconstituted as the things in which Williams found the ideas.[22]

An early poem illustrates many of the points I have been making:[23]

> No one
> will believe this
> of vast import to the nation.

Despite what the last lines say, the poem represents an intimate report on the state of the nation. It is also a series of notations for or

from a painting – 'roof out of the line with sides', 'a bluish green /
that properly weathered / please me best / of all colors'. A
painterly perception sets out in words the endless merging of pastoral and urban squalor. It arises from a focus on place, generating
a tension between the apparently inconsequential yet endlessly
significant. What is revealed here is an aggressive modernism, the
emphasis which Williams gave to observation rendered vividly in
words, his effort to create a new, an American poetic language, and
his belief that poetry is to be found in fact, that there are no ideas
but in things. All this is given to us in words layed on paper with a
painter's eye and unswerving originality.

Whether he is writing of trees, flowers, the poor, the sick, the
seasons, months, cities or streetscenes, or city individuals, the
subject matter and method of Williams reveal 'a certain rustic un-
couthness whose end is a celebration and which wears the stamp of
locality'.[24] In all of his work place is the focus:[25]

> Not only is 'locality' (a sticking to New Jersey when Pound and
> Eliot had chosen European exile) the geographic source of
> William's poetry, but 'locality', seen as the jerks and outblurts of
> speech rendered on to the here and now of the page, is the source
> of his lineation.

It is this sense of locality which permeates the work of Carlos
Williams and gives a startling clarity to poems like 'Proletarian
Portrait', 'The Lonely Street', 'To a Poor Old Woman', 'A Women in
Front of a Bank' or either of the poems titled 'Pastoral', which we
have explored. It is in these precise and vivid street scenes particularly that we can see just how Williams retrieves local everyday experience and makes it viable for verse. Deceptively simple, these
poems are totally committed to the distinctiveness of the people, the
moment, the object, the feeling, the whatever is the focus of their attention. This, for me, is the stuff of great poetry. A favourite poem of
mine, which comes from the middle of the 1930s, is 'Fine Work with
Pitch and Copper'. A gang of workmen are resting 'separately in
unison' before they start work after lunch – the occasion of the rest.
The intrinsic movement of the poem centres on the verbs – 'resting',
'stacked', 'strewn', 'beaten', 'lies', 'chewing', and 'runs'. What they
are going to work on is, of course, part of the scene, visually at right
/ angles' – the eye bringing the meaning, as it does at the end of
this poem and so many others by Williams, to life.

The reputation of Williams grew steadily in the late 1940s and the 1950s, partly through the gradual publication of *Paterson*, his long poem in five parts which, in a characteristically contentious headnote, describes its function as poetry to be 'a reply to Greek and Latin with the bare hands'. This work is an unfinished American epic, in which Paterson the city and Paterson the man are one, for, as the Author's Note says, 'a man in himself is a city, beginning, seeking, achieving and concluding his life in ways which the various aspects of a city may embody'. *Book One* was published in 1946 and opens with some justly famous lines:

> To make a start,
> out of particulars
> and make them general

which accrue more resonance once the reader discovers that not only is there Paterson the man and Paterson the city. Paterson is also the poet himself, necessarily standing for all people. Williams was still working on his epic (Book 6) when he died in 1963. He had become increasingly more known through the little magazines which supported him and, without any doubt, brought him to and kept him in the public eye. We have observed the influence on him of painters, both met contemporaries and revered masters, but there is no doubt that Williams also owed a lot to a number of editors. In his early writing days he had poems accepted by many little (and one rushes to say, big) magazines, including the *Glebe*, *Poetry*, *Others*, the *Little Review*, *The Egoist*, *The Dial*, and *Broom*. It was the world of the little magazines in his day which brought Williams, personally, together with many writers of his day. His work for *Contact*, as an instance, meant working with Robert McAlmon and, of course, Nathaniel West, who became an associate editor in 1932 – early versions of West's *Miss Lonelyhearts* appeared in *Contact* and one of the episodes in *Paterson* (IV, 3) recounts a story about West during his hotel management days.[26] The headnote to the magazine helps to place the artistic identity of the editors, and especially Williams himself – '*Contact* will attempt to cut a trail through the American jungle without the use of a European compass.'

It was during the 1960s that the real impact of his work was felt. In 1965 *Cambridge Opinion* devoted an issue to 'Carlos Williams in England', in which a number of writers whose reputations have subsequently grown or been confirmed (Hugh Kenner, Michael Weaver, Gael Turnbull, Jim Burns, Andrew Crozier, Anselm Hollo, Roy Fisher, Tom Pickard) demonstrated their allegiance to Williams. In the same year, Thom Gunn wrote in *Encounter* that Williams was somebody 'from whom it is time we started taking lessons'. Williams had constructed himself as an underdog ever since Eliot's success with 'Prufrock'. He became a subculture and, although we need to ask the extent to which this was forced on him, there is no doubt that he enjoyed the struggle even if it was forced on him. He had identified Eliot as the enemy, rightly it seems. Eliot dominated poetry until the early 1950s:[27]

> such is literary fashion that apparently Williams could not but suffer – being misunderstood or, more commonly, disregarded under such dominance ... What must be stressed, at this late date, is that he offers a valid alternative of style and attitude to the others available. It is offered not in his theory, which is fragmentary, sometimes inconsistent, and often poorly expressed, but in his poetry, which is among the best of our time.

I can remember, as a sixth-former, the publication of a then representative collection of works of Gregory Corso, Lawrence Ferlinghetti, and Allen Ginsberg – and penning a poem to the cafe where I and my friends met to talk about life, literature, and the fleeting hand of time.[28] It wasn't until I was at the University of Essex that I encountered the poetry of William Carlos Williams. I listened to Gabriel Pearson, Donald Wesling, Andrew Crozier, Donald Davie, and Ed Dorn, and knew that, not far away, at the University of East Anglia, there was Jonathan Raban. Here was a generation, or rather, to do them service, a sometimes embattled gathering of people, who I felt were persuaded by the validity of the Williams subculture – determined to acknowledge and either follow or expose it. At the beginning of this chapter I quoted Williams's response to Eliot's 'Prufrock'. His view of *The Waste Land* was then even more direct and troubled. He saw Eliot's work as a catastrophe which gave the poem back to the academics: 'out of the blue *The Dial* brought out *The Waste Land* and all our hilarity ended. It wiped out our world as if an atom bomb had been dropped upon it and our brave sallies into the unknown were turned to dust.'[29] Gabriel Pearson ended an essay on Eliot, somewhat perversely, by quoting this passage from Williams's

Autobiography and intimating that his devastations had not been as permanent as he feared:[30]

> he elected to play it very patient and very cool, to look and to listen, to work and to love among the common noises and sights of his obdurately real city. It is too early to say, but it looks possible that at the end of the game the practising doctor and not the displaced priest may have held the winning card all along.

Many would now agree that the practising doctor did indeed hold the winning hand in the art of poetry, the mug's game.

It was in the 1970s that his reputation was secured. Charles Tomlinson, more than anyone else, was responsible for introducing Williams over here. In 1972 his critical anthology appeared, displaying a breadth of analysis and critical respect from many of the century's greatest critical and creative writers; in 1976 came Tomlinson's edition of Williams's *Selected Poems*, which restores a number of poems to their chronological order and presents a representative, balanced selection of Williams which is as accessible as the comparable selected Eliot.[31] It is now clear that the effort of some British writers was at least as necessary in constructing and maintaining a deserved place for Williams as were the American advocates – as Hugh Kenner recently put it: 'two of the best critics of William Carlos Williams, two sure guides to his saliences, are Mike Weaver and Charles Tomlinson, both Englishmen. Weaver's book (*William Carlos Williams: The American Background*) best explains the complex fate with which America confronted Williams; Tomlinson's choice of a *Selected Poems* has defined a Williams canon'.[32] Tomlinson's selection from Williams appeared twenty years after his own 'Letter to Dr Williams'.[33]

Along with his great predecessor, Walt Whitman, Williams is 'the finest American celebrant of the democratic impulse'[34] and the politics of his poetic structures concern the democratisation of the poem itself. His poetry gives the reader direct access to a created place made of some bits and pieces of other places and hand-welded into a new linguistic event; an event which without this expression would have been obliterated. An event in which the following exchange:

How long can you stay?

Six-thirty   .   I've got
to meet the boy friend

    Take off your clothes

    No. I'm good at saying that.

          She stood
    quietly to be undressed

leads on to the likely situation:

    – on the couch, kissing and talking while his
    hands explored her body, slowly   .
    courteously   .   persistent   .

All of this results in conversation which is both itself and a part of
Paterson, Book 4; poetry which is conterminous with the actuality
from which it is created:

    Be careful   .
    I've got an awful cold

    It's the first
    this year. We went
    fishing in all
    that rain last week

    Who? Your father?
    – and my boy friend

    Fly fishing?
    No. Bass. But it isn't

    the season. I know that
    but nobody saw us

    I got soaked to the skin
    Can you fish?

    Oh I have a pole and a
    line and just fish along

    We caught quite a few

Here we have a poetry that retrieves as it recreates experience, a
poetry of futurity, a poetry which our century has been unable to
ignore, which has played its own hand. The effort which Williams

made has been made several times in the history of poetry but was particularly necessary following the position of unprecedented elitism occupied by some of the new generation of the early twentieth century, on whose behalf the term Modernism is sometimes hijacked in a single-minded act of possession. We are now in a position to realise that the situation is more complex, more diverse, and that the Modernist years produced a multiple and essentially paradoxical compounds of talents – 'the futuristic and the nihilistic, the revolutionary and the conservative, the naturalistic and the symbolistic, the romantic and the classical.'[35] The adjectives which best apply to Williams are futuristic, revolutionary, naturalistic, and romantic.

The poet's role as defined by Eliot and Pound, 'craggily isolated visionary standing in the detritus of a fallen world', is balanced by the force and ability of the poem itself to 'assimilate all the bits and pieces of language that happens to lie around it'.[36] Returning to the *Prologue to Kora in Hell*, Williams underscores this process of assimilation:[37]

> a poem is tough ... solely from that attenuated power which draws perhaps many broken things into a dance giving them thus a full being.

Williams is on the side of the poem, he wanted to write a poem. He was disturbed by the view of the poet as isolated visionary and soothsayer, which leads to a rejection of continuity and inevitably a wrangle about ends and beginnings – in its greatest expressions it is clear that there will be a holocaust necessitating a second coming. Inevitably poetry underpinned by this view produces events and wisdoms, every poem the end of an era. Eliot's *Four Quartets*, for instance, represents 'a stage of such subtlety and intricacy in the post-symbolist tradition that it is impossible to think of its ever being taken a stage further'.[38] Williams always proposed a poetry based on assimilation rather than prohibition, which makes of the future a priority and seeks to create 'a new form of poetic composition, a form for the future' – a poetry full of the freshness, the hum and buzz of everyday life in which truly 'so much depends / upon / a red wheel / barrow / glazed with rain / water / beside the white / chickens'. He drew a number of proletarian, portraits, in one of which we see a 'big young bareheaded woman / in an apron'.[39] The field of poetry is an open and active one in Williams's expression, the essential features of the poem are recreated by the verbs, the doing words, on which the intrinsic movement of the poetry depends – 'slicked', 'standing', 'toeing', 'Looking', 'pulls', 'find' and 'hurting'. When you think about it, that particular nail must have hurt lots of people.

NOTES

1.   Williams Carlos Williams, *I Wanted to Write a Poem* (London: Jonathan Cape, 1967) p. 38.
2.   Ibid., p. 42.
3.   Ibid.
4.   William Carlos Williams, *Autobiography* (London: MacGibbon & Kee, 1969) quoted in Alistair Wisker, 'William Carlos Williams', *Stand*, vol. 18, no. 4 (1977), pp. 30–3.
5.   William Carlos Williams, *In the American Grain* (New York: New Directions, 1956) pp. 220 and 222.
6.   Williams, *Autobiography*, quoted in Wisker, 'William Carlos Williams', pp. 30–3.
7.   Paul Rosenfeld, 'A Sort of Spiritual Prolongation of the Voyages of Columbus', *Nation*, 23 November 1940, quoted in Charles Doyle (ed.), *William Carlos Williams: The Critical Heritage* (London: Routledge & Kegan Paul, 1980) p. 166.
8.   Williams, *Autobiography*, p. 391.
9.   Williams, *I Wanted to Write a Poem*, p. 86.
10.   Williams was always fascinated by line and measures – Kenneth Rexroth, in a review of *The Desert Music*, described Williams's line as 'welded to American speech like muscle to bone'. In his own comment on writing *The Desert Music*, in 1954, Williams said 'There is something special about this book... . My whole interest in poetry now was in developing the concept I had discovered – the variable foot – based on the model of the poem in *Paterson* Book Two, section three. Now, consciously, I knew what I wanted to do.' This is recorded in *I Wanted to Write a Poem*, p. 98. In the summer of 1958 Williams planned a work on measure, which remained incomplete because of the state of his health. This was published as a loosely assembled essay, with an introduction by Hugh Kenner, in *Cambridge Opinion*, 41, 1965. Although the essay 'Measure' is incomplete, it reveals the enthusiasm which Williams has for reconsidering fixed measure, which 'regularly counted, has dominated all prosody in all languages, except the Hebrew, certainly all the classic languages taught in our academies in recent times'. Williams sketches in some topics he would have further developed and commences the exploration of his own ideas on measure. It is clearly the habitual, predictive aspect of the fixed foot which troubles Williams, together with the need for form – thus: 'We are finished with the aberration of free verse, but we have to learn to

recount, taking our idiom as a constant.' The loosely assembled essay ends with an understanding of precisely how the concept of the variable foot relates to the poetry of Williams and those who have followed him: 'It is not easy to teach. It is not even easy to apprehend. But the incentive it gives to a choice of words not out of a book leads to surprising assemblies and turns of phrases which are sometimes rewarding in succinctness and vivid interplays when the poet does not feel constrained by the habitual.' I have constrained all of this in a note because it was becoming another chapter – and perhaps it will.

11. Williams, *I Wanted to Write a Poem*, p. 13.
12. Ezra Pound to William Carlos Williams, 21 October 1908. Quoted in Noel Stock, *The Life of Ezra Pound* (Harmondsworth: Penguin, 1974) p. 69.
13. Williams, *I Wanted to Write a Poem*, p. 17.
14. Ibid., p. 20. Williams also recounts this story in the *Prologue to Kora in Hell*.
15. William Carlos Williams, *Prologue to Kora in Hell*, in Charles Tomlinson (ed.), *William Carlos Williams: A Critical Anthology* (Harmondsworth: Penguin, 1972) p. 42.
16. Ibid., pp. 42–3.
17. Williams, *I Wanted to Write a Poem*, pp. 40–1.
18. Discussed in Wisker, 'William Carlos Williams', pp. 30–3. See also Bram Dijkstra (ed.), *A Recognizable Image: William Carlos Williams on Art and Artists* (New York: New Directions, 1978). A book which was new to me, but I found a first edition of it whilst writing this chapter and recommend it highly.
19. Wisker, 'William Carlos Williams', p. 32.
20. Williams, *Autobiography*, p. 138.
21. Charles Tomlinson (ed.), *William Carlos Williams: Selected Poems* (Harmondsworth: Penguin, 1976) p. 150.
22. Ruth Grogan, 'Williams and Painting', in Tomlinson (ed.), *William Carlos Williams: A Critical Anthology*, p. 270.
23. William Carlos Williams, 'Pastoral' , in *The Collected Earlier Poems* (London: MacGibbon & Kee, 1967) p. 121.
24. Tomlinson (ed.), *William Carlos Williams*, p. 11.
25. 'Place is the focus' is the first line of the poem 'In Defence of Metaphysics' by Charles Tomlinson. It is this aspect of the work of Williams which has underscored Tomlinson's admiration of it and which is tackled and emphasised in his critical anthology. See Wisker, 'William Carlos Williams', pp. 30–3. In commenting on the 'jerks and outblurts of speech' rendered in a page of Williams, Tomlinson is picking up from Pound's early, instinctive approbation of *Al Que Quiere!*: 'Distinct and as different as possible from the orderly statements of an Eliot … are the poems of Carlos Williams. I do not pretend to follow all of his volts, jerks, sulks, balks, outblurts and jump-overs; but for all this roughness there remains with me the conviction that there is nothing meaningless in his book, *Al que Quiere*, not a line.'

26. For an account of this passage in *Paterson*, IV, 3, see Alistair Wisker, *The Writing of Nathaniel West* (London: Macmillan, 1990) p. 105.

27. Thom Gunn, 'William Carlos Williams', *Encounter*, XXV, 1 July 1965, reprinted in Thom Gunn, *The Occasions of Poetry* (London: Faber and Faber, 1982) p. 32.

28. *Penguin Modern Poets 5* (Harmondsworth: Penguin, 1963). 'In the Fleeting Hand of Time' is the title of one of Gregory Corso's poems.

29. Williams, *Autobiography*, p. 174.

30. Gabriel Pearson, 'Eliot: An American Use of Symbolism', in Graham Martin (ed.), *Eliot in Perspective* (London: Macmillan, 1970) p. 101.

31. Wisker, 'William Carlos Williams', p. 31.

32. Hugh Kenner, *A Sinking Island: The Modern English Writers* (London: Barrie & Jenkins, 1988) p. 5.

33. Charles Tomlinson, 'Letter to Dr Williams', *Spectrum*, vol. 1, no. 3 (1957) in *William Carlos Williams: A Critical Anthology*, p. 364.

34. Richard Gray, *American Poetry of the Twentieth Century* (London: Longman, 1990) p. 88.

35. Wisker, *The Writing of Nathaniel West*, p. 122.

36. Jonathan Raban, *The Society of the Poem* (London: Harrap, 1971), pp. 64 and 44.

37. William Carlos Williams, quoted in Charles Tomlinson (ed.), *William Carlos Williams: A Critical Anthology*, p. 35.

38. Donald Davie, 'T. S. Eliot: The End of an Era', in Hugh Kenner (ed.), *T. S. Eliot: A Collection of Critical Essays* (Englewood Cliffs, NJ: Prentice Hall, 1963) p. 205.

39. William Carlos Williams, 'Proletarian Portrait', *The Collected Earlier Poems* (London: MacGibbon & Kee, 1967) p. 101.

6

Wallace Stevens

PAT RIGHELATO

Wallace Stevens is, at times, the exemplary figure of the austere Modernist, shorn of Transcendental excess, wary of its expansionist programme for consciousness: 'Anecdote of the Jar' has been mined by generations of students teasing out its seemingly endless self-referentiality to demonstrate that 'less is more'. The poem is, of course, an ironic critique of the Romantic yearning for the creative interfusion of consciousness and nature as the basis of art. Its circular self-enclosing form seems an austere rebuke to Emerson's more expansive solipsism. Emerson wrote, 'The eye is the first circle; the horizon which it forms is the second; and throughout nature this primary figure is repeated without end',[1] but Steven's circling is a demarcation line, an exclusion zone. Similarly the poem cheats the reader's desire for narrative lift-off; this is an anecdote which leads nowhere, which fends off chatty familiarity, and in which there is no significant joining that transcends its constitutive elements.

These refusals are particularly evident when comparing the poem with its famous Romantic precursor, Keats's 'Ode on a Grecian Urn'. The heated imagination of the narrator of Keats's Ode desperately interrogates the 'cold' and 'silent' Urn about the narrative significance of its figures; this is frustrating for the questioner, but at least the Urn bears signs of nature to which consciousness can respond. Stevens's jar, more exigently, has no trace of nature, human or otherwise, and the 'I' of the poem does not attempt to read the jar or to express feeling, but merely notes its regulatory effect with a punctilious disinterestedness. The poem itself jars, repels the reader's consciousness. Keats's poem concludes in enigmatic utterance, yet the very ambiguity as to whose voice the final words are to be attributed is a kind of merger:

Thou shalt remain, in midst of other woe
Than ours, a friend to man, to whom thou say'st,

'Beauty is truth, truth beauty' – that is all
Ye know on earth, and all ye need to know.[2]

The voice is rhetorically identified as the voice of art, whose utterance has been achieved by the coming together of passionate
warmth and cold silence; *together* they have produced the epigram
(literally 'an inscription') which, although circular, seems to suggest
something beyond its apparent limited prescription.

Most strikingly and consolingly, the reader of Keats's poem is
aligned with nature, with 'breathing human passion'; the reader
and the poet share the intensities of transience, whereas the bald
statements of Stevens's poem are indifferent to such intensities. The
jar is a visual surveillance point, not teasingly enigmatic but blank,
without cordial allusions to illustrious urn forebears and implicitly
a rebuff to Keats's expression of ardent longing for a consummate
reciprocity between art and nature. Stevens's own Keatsian procliv-
ities are being kept well in check in this self-admonitory anecdote –
an anecdote *for* the artist.

But Stevens's modernist austerity nakedly reveals that his theme
is power. In an American context the poem engages with
Emerson's Transcendentalist emphasis on the possessive power of
the eye. The genteel tradition, of which Emerson was the principal
representative, might seem to have existed in rarefied seclusion
from the commercial energies of the age, but it underwrote the expansionist energy of the era by transforming its power into an aesthetic of consciousness. In his essay 'Nature', Emerson comments
on property:

> The charming landscape which I saw this morning is indubitably
> made up of some twenty or thirty farms. Miller owns this field,
> Locke that, and Manning the woodland beyond. But none of
> them owns the landscape. There is a property in the horizon
> which no man has but he whose eye can integrate all the parts,
> that is, the poet.[3]

What is significant here is that this is not a rejection of ownership –
indeed it expresses land-hunger – but a relinquishment of an infe-
rior category of ownership for a superior, more active one.
Similarly, Emerson's 'transparent eyeball' utterance is the expression of a colonising consciousness – there is space which the eye
can acquire:

Standing on the bare ground – my head bathed by the blithe air and uplifted into infinite space, – all mean egotism vanishes. I become a transparent eyeball; I am nothing: I see all; the currents of the Universal Being circulate through me; I am part or parcel of God ... I am the lover of uncontained and immortal beauty.[4]

The disclaimer, 'I am nothing' is disingenuous within the overall context of the egotistical sublime in which 'I' becomes 'eye', infinitely expansive, capable of encircling nature. Consciousness is prehensile and invasive, its transports masking its annexations.

In 'Anecdote of the Jar', Stevens's curious use of the word 'slovenly'[5] to describe the 'wilderness' converts the traditional meaning of the expression to a positive rather than a pejorative sense, as well as drawing on the more recent and more neutral American meaning of 'uncultivated'. Indeed, in 'Anecdote of the Jar' the Tennessee wilderness is less satisfactorily assimilated by the power of the colonising consciousness: the jar may take 'dominion', but the wilderness is not internalised as an active source of creative power; it does not give its energy and fecundity to the jar. Emerson, 'crossing a bare common', is exhilarated by the winter landscape and the initial bleakness is suffused with a rhetoric of euphoric exchange; however, when Stevens's starting point in the *Harmonium* volume is an Emersonian one, the bleakness is not the occasion of rapturous interfusion. In a poem like 'The Snow Man' the exacting eye registers not merging but a precise equivalence; consciousness must cut back, not expand. 'The Snow Man' is a rejection of the idea that nature is the vehicle of human splendours and miseries; rather, the creative consciousness must discipline itself to a condition of wintriness in order to apprehend without embellishment: 'One must have a mind of winter'.[6]

The condition of having 'been cold a long time' is not really a deprivation, although it involves depriving oneself of easy ecstasies, but is rather a condition of acutest, clearest perception:

> For the listener, who listens in the snow,
> And, nothing himself, beholds
> Nothing that is not there and the nothing that is.

The listener does not confuse his own moods with the sound of the wind, and in the recognition that the landscape is not there to inflate his consciousness, he is thus enabled to 'behold' (a

significant verb in Stevens, denoting privileged insight) 'Nothing
that is not there', i.e. the scene without embellishment, with
nothing extraneous, and 'the nothing that is', i.e. with an understanding of its essential bareness, its irreducible reality. This is not a
grandiose claim for the infinite extent of consciousness, but it is
nevertheless a heroic effort of perception, a Modernist reassessment
of Transcendentalist vision, a revision of Emerson's ecstatic
merging in the more sustained awareness of the separation of consciousness and nature. Stevens is trying to make 'a new intelligence
prevail',[7] an intelligence which understands the strategies of consciousness as fictions rather than religious truths.

Reductiveness was not the only mode in which Stevens meditated
on the relationship of consciousness and nature. 'The Comedian as
the Letter C'[8] is the most attractive of the longer poems in which the
theme is addressed. It is a comic epic of consciousness: Crispin is
conscious with a large C, not surprising when one considers that he
is a kind of conglomerate of his literary predecessors of heroic consciousness. Like Ishmael/Ahab he learns a thing or two about the
awesome sublimity of nature when he goes to sea, but he has
Whitmanesque powers of elaboration and extension, he is consciousness on the loose, free to adopt an infinite variety of personae
and attitudes. But this was never a fair contest: Crispin is 'at sea',
overwhelmed by nature's vastness, 'washed away by magnitude'.
He is mesmerised by the 'hallucinating horn' of the faded myths of
the European tradition, plagued by the 'oracular rockings' of
Whitman and, in struggling to create a 'mythology of self', veers
between introspection and assiduous note-taking. He even relapses
into bluster, appalled by the monotonous 'brunt' of the sea. And all
the time, 'Against his pipping sounds a trumpet cried / Celestial
sneering boisterously'; nature mocks his efforts.

Each successive stance of the poem is an exploration of possible
relationships with nature, but every effort is doomed to self-
consciousness: no authentic 'Song of Myself' emerges. Constant
exposure to nature's effortless sublimity reduces Crispin to 'moody
rucks', an unheroic retreat into introspection or to the role of
'connoisseur ... Aware of exquisite thought', a mere 'fagot in the
lunar fire', deluded with the dream of a 'blissful liaison, / Between
himself and his environment'.

It hardly even seems possible for Crispin to be a Snow Man, for
there is considerable irony in the poem at the expense of the desire
for a 'mind of winter'. Indeed, the spring 'Was gemmy marionette to

him that sought / A sinewy nakedness'. Thrown back repeatedly
upon himself, Crispin's only chance is to colonise his own consciousness – a nice twist to the Emersonian programme. Crispin's colony
has a Whitmanesque variety and indeed seems staked out by illustrious predecessors – in section V of the poem, Crispin is discovered as
hermit in Thoreau-like seclusion. However, his solitude does not en-
gender distilled wisdom, but rather spawns endless seductive linguistic progeny, as indicated in the ironic title of section VI, 'And
Daughters with Curls'. This is self defeating not only in its own re-
dundance, but more overwhelmingly in being brought up against
Whitman:

Effective coloniser sharply stopped
In the dooryard by his own capacious bloom.

The lines are arrestingly evocative, poignant tribute, wry self-
assessment. But even this is something which Crispin must fan-
tastically elaborate. Crispin is condemned to verbosity, to endless
efflorescence and the only way to muzzle him is to bring the
poem to an arbitrary stop which is curiously deflating, in the rueful
observation, 'So may the relation of each man be clipped.'

'The Comedian as the Letter C' is a sprawling comic antithesis to
the frigidity of poems like 'The Snow Man' and 'Anecdote of the
Jar'. Although Crispin is everywhere outdone by nature, the poem
is not a 'sustained nightmare'[9] but a celebration of the capacious-
ness, resilience and elasticity of American consciousness. Stevens
exposes the sublime to comic scrutiny, not in order to reject it, but
to naturalise himself into its mythology. Crispin is a comic
Malvolio figure, but his creator is urbanely at ease with a Jamesian
sense of incongruities. And, in spite of his local difficulties, in the
broader topography of the poem Crispin is voyager to his America,
his New Found Land of poetry, everywhere in the exuberance and
hyperbole of his language, in his desire to position himself in the
sublime, an expression of the 'optative mood' which Emerson saw
as the keynote of 'Our American literature and spiritual history'.[10]

Nowhere is Stevens more Transcendental in his expression of the
'optative mood' than in 'The Paltry Nude Starts on a Spring
Voyage'.[11] Botticelli's Venus is wafted by the zephyrs towards
Cytherea, but Stevens's Venus cannot stay to pose on a shell as a
delectable vision for connoisseurs of beauty: it is Venus herself who
desires; she is not an object of desire.

With Whitmanesque zest and appetite she steps on 'the first-found weed' (the marine equivalent of grass, the most common form of nature) for her own adventures of the spirit, 'eager for the brine and bellowing' of a correspondingly voracious ocean; she is not intimidated by its 'brunt'. The energy and brashness of this Venus who 'scuds the glitters' is not an image of completed perfection, but of restless aspiration. Her crudities will, in the course of time, be transcended, will seem 'meagre play' in the light of future transformations of desire into beauty. But this is not a Jamesian lament for the thin medium of American life: she heralds, she is preliminary to the more queenly progress of the 'goldener nude' and 'sea-green pomp' of a later day which will itself, as comparative rather than superlative, be ceaselessly in process of change. Any aristocratic, Yeatsian implications of 'goldener nude' are robustly subverted by the forward momentum of the poem (there is no Yeatsian longing for Byzantine fixity here) and by the use of the baser term 'scullion'. To be the kitchen wench of fate suggests resilience, and indeed the ambiguity of the expression 'scullion of fate' leaves it open as to whether the paltry nude propels or is propelled by fate. Whichever it is, there is no passivity but concentrated momentum: 'spick' is a brilliantly chosen colloquialism which condenses meaning, suggesting the pristine state of earliness and also speed, rapid transit. Her course is 'irretrievable' in that there is no turning back, no recovery of her experience – she is ahead of the game. The word 'paltry' means worthless, or the verb 'palter' to speak indistinctly, without trappings, and these meanings are converted to positives in the sense of being unencumbered, incipient, self-creating, the 'purple stuff' which she desires vigorously undefined.

The paltry nude is the Emersonian active soul in the theatre of nature. She has a more than Emersonian freedom in that the 'circle of her traverse' is not a prehensile colonisation but a fictive voyage. The ambiguity as to whether the voyage is surface or depth, centre of circumference expressed in the phrase 'high interiors of the sea', shows a pleasure in metamorphosis. Power and *potentia*, the Transcendental imperatives, are radiantly productive in this poem. Harold Bloom has eloquently identified the affinity in Emerson and Stevens's sense of *potentia*:

Emerson rightly sees that form, in nature or in poems is itself only one trope or another. The metamorphosis or interplay of forms is victory, surprise, joy, when seen from the perspective of Power rather than Fate. Freedom or 'the free spirit' makes form into *potentia*, into the strength that Emerson defines as eloquence. So, in the late essay 'Eloquence', he gives this as his final word on the most desired of gifts: 'It is a triumph of pure power, and it has a beautiful and prodigious surprise in it.' Power, in Emerson as in his American descendants, means to be of *capable* imagination, not so much to have the lordship as to have the ability. ... I have been describing Emerson, yet any deep reader of Stevens will be aware that I am describing Stevens also.[12]

Indeed, in the ability to express *potentia*, an unforced intimacy with the sublime in consciousness and nature, Stevens was to prove more 'capable' than Emerson. He worked through the problem of the discrepancy of scale between consciousness and nature in 'The Idea of Order at Key West'.[13] It is a *key* poem in that its engagement with the sublime is schematic, yet lyrical.

In the first verse the girl singer (symbol of the lyric poet), who walks beside the sea, sings *beyond* the sea because the sea is incapable of expressive utterance; the sea is empty rhetoric – (what Crispin called 'the brunt'): the sea is at once presence and absence.

In the second verse the problematic relationship between humanity and nature is stated: 'The song and water were not medleyed sound'. The elements might *seem* to be 'gasping' for utterance but utterance is *human*. The decisiveness of the statement 'But it was she' affirms human significance but also bleakly acknowledges the autonomy of the created world of art – beside and beyond but not *with* the sea.

In verse four, the empty rhetoric of nature is only *potentially* sublime and meaningful: 'the heaving speech of air', 'the meaningless plunges of water' need the human voice to give them significance. There is moreover a discrepancy of scale in this theatre – the small figure of the girl and the huge ocean – but it is the girl who brings it all to bear:

It was her voice that made
The sky acutest at its vanishing

This line again suggests intensity given by poetic expression but also nature's escape – 'vanishing' – a poignant expression of the separation of humanity and nature.

In verse five, the poet addresses a fellow human being, asking why it is that artistic expression (the song of the girl) has the magical effect of intensifying consciousness, seeming to order nature. In moonlight (the imagination's symbol) the human lights seem to localise the cosmos: they 'mastered the night and portioned out the sea'. It is an *idea* of order; it is the imagination's power to communicate an idea of order.

The last verse is a celebratory chant, a celebration of the powers of language and of creative desire. In the last line the 'ghostlier demarcations' in moonlight, the imagination's light, are 'ghostlier' because creations of the spirit creating its territory, its 'demarcations'; the 'keener sounds' are the utterance of poetry, 'keener', more intense, sharper than the impotent 'heaving' rhetoric of nature. The final image is at once removed, shadowy and closer to us.

In "The Idea of Order at Key West' Stevens overcomes Crispin's ineffectuality before the vast theatre of nature. Crispin's verbosity is redundant and his rhetoric tempered into an ordered belief in the created world of poetry. The imagination creates what is merely an *idea* of order, that is, what Stevens calls a 'fiction'; indeed, the 'supreme fiction'.[14]

'The Comedian as the Letter C', 'The Snow Man', 'The Idea of Order at Key West', are concerned with the poet's struggle to encompass the world of nature in its intimidating sublimity. The consciousness of the poet awed by the phenomena of nature recognises that the ordering power of the imagination, the desire to create significance, is a fiction, but it is this desire which is human, which is democratic and which we can share with other humans in a sense of wonder, 'Ramon Fernandez tell me if you know ...' the poet asks the question in a spirit of marvelling.

Stevens's last poems have a visionary, dreamlike power; they are distilled meditations in which the imagination accepts the provisional nature of its own propositions. What the imagination proposes is 'enough'.[15] Stevens now no longer needs to discard the European mythic heritage; rather it can be woven into his own American myth of consciousness, of desire.

In 'The World as Meditation'[16] Stevens invokes the great classical myth of Homer, 'The Odyssey'. Homer's story of the vicissitudes of Ulysses concludes with the return of Ulysses to his homeland, to his wife, Penelope. Stevens's poem is concerned with imminence – and the state of readiness for Ulysses' return is like the state of readiness for the coming of spring in nature's cycle.

> Someone is moving
> On the horizon and lifting himself up above it.

The 'someone' is the sun and also the resourceful figure of Ulysses in Homer's myth. As well as these two interwoven strands of meaning – the cycle of nature and the Homeric myth – there is also a third: the effort involved in Ulysses 'lifting himself' into sight suggests the effort of inception – the coming into being of a poem.

In the world of heroic myth the returning Ulysses is a sexual force, the male coming to reclaim his woman, and we can see that they might both have readjustments to make as Ulysses approaches the domestic realm symbolised by Penelope's bourgeois curtains:

> A form of fire approaches the cretonnes of Penelope

The line also, of course, suggests the morning sunlight which will come flooding in through the curtains. This comic discrepancy of scale between the sun, the 'form of fire' and the cosy domesticity of Penelope's abode is not quite bathos, is not an inversion of the sublime, although it might be seen momentarily as a witty domestication of the sublime. It is not dissimilar in its discrepancy of scale to 'The Idea of Order at Key West', in which the vast power of the ocean seems to gasp for utterance which only the girl can express. The power of expression is like a haven, the harbour lights of Key West give a reassuring idea of order, but it is an order which is a refuge projected beyond an insentient universe.

Similarly, in 'The World as Meditation', in Stevens's mythology – what I have called the third strand of meaning – the sun symbolises the non-human world of nature, the reality in which humans find themselves precariously located. This large non-human cycle has its own rhythms. And consciousness, or as we might say, Penelope, seeks to embrace this reality, this power outside herself, to create her own mythology of the desire of consciousness to incorporate reality. The poem asks: is the myth that consciousness weaves about itself and reality true or not? Is Ulysses really coming? 'But was it 'Ulysses?' The answer given in the poem is

> It was Ulysses and it was not.

It is true and it is not. Perhaps then, the epic encounter of consciousness and nature is the imagination's fictive imagining, is provisional in status, is desire rather than realisation. However, we might say that, if Penelope is in one sense the receptive aspect of consciousness, yet in another sense the power to lift Ulysses above the horizon is the creative power of consciousness to bring its imagining, its desire into being – what has been aptly named 'Transcendentalist eros'.[17] This is its coming consummated in the act of the poem, in the act of creating a poem. The creative imagination has faith in its own power to bring into being.

Walt Whitman, in 'Song of Myself', wrote

Dazzling and tremendous how quick the sun-rise would kill me,
If I could not now and always send sun-rise out of me

Similarly Penelope, as meditative consciousness, creates the reality of Ulysses.

In his final poems, Wallace Stevens, a poet in his seventies, celebrates the influx of creative power. This can be seen in his poem, 'Not Ideas about the Thing but the Thing Itself'.[18] The title tells us that a poem is not descriptive of reality but is itself the signifying. The poem is not so much an Idea of Order but seeks to express the state of alertness which precedes creativity and which imperceptibly becomes the act of creating. Stevens wrote in another poem,

The poem is the cry of its occasion
Part of the res itself and not about it[19]

The beauty of 'Not Ideas About the Thing but the Thing Itself' is in its expression of the condition of bareness which precedes spring (a reminder of the wintry world of 'The Snow Man'), a bareness, a nothingness which trembles upon the verge of a becoming. The expression of the coming of spring is also the coming of the expression of the poem, 'The poem is the cry of its occasion'. At the moment of suspension between winter and spring, in the paradox of 'earliest ending', 'a scrawny cry' of the bird is an annunciator, a herald of what is coming, 'a chorister whose c preceded the choir'. It is also the poem's utterance of itself, its coming from nothing. It is the imagination's act of birth, the poem hatching into distinct and autonomous being and thus attaining an outside status, detached, 'it would have been outside'. This imminence, this intensifying sound is not a dream, it is not 'sleep's faded papier-mâché' – it is not the vague memory of a dream's fabrications; this imaginative act has the authority of external revelation and it seems in its power of inception to announce and summon the vast forces of reality. The phrasing is very scrupulous,

> *It was like*
> A new knowledge of reality.

'A chorister whose c preceded the choir' takes us back to the poem 'The Comedian as the Letter C', in which Crispin the capricious American coloniser of the world cries for a voice amidst the over-whelming 'brunt' of nature. In 'Not Ideas about the Thing but the Thing Itself', Crispin as chorister with small 'c' draws the reader into his conception, summoning the sun to his cretonne, now at home in the sublime. But Stevens's domestication of the sublime is not an egotistical inflation of consciousness – where Emerson's con-sciousness is inflated, but merely receptive – a receptacle, Stevens's is inceptive and potentiating; for Stevens, consciousness is the portal of desire, is the small c for coming, and there can be both awe and intimacy in its revelations.

NOTES

1. Ralph Waldo Emerson, 'Circles', *The Complete Works of Ralph Waldo Emerson* (London: Bell and Duldy, 1866) vol. I, p. 125.
2. Miriam Allott (ed.), *The Poems of John Keats* (London: Longman, 1970) p. 537.
3. Emerson, 'Nature', *The Complete Works*, vol. II, p. 142.
4. Ibid.
5. Wallace Stevens, *The Collected Poems of Wallace Stevens* (New York: Alfred A. Knopf, 1954; London, 1955) p. 76.
6. Ibid., p. 9.
7. Stevens, 'The Comedian as the Letter C', *Collected Poems*, p. 37.
8. Stevens, *Collected Poems*, p. 27.
9. Frank Kermode, *Wallace Stevens* (London, 1960; London: Faber and Faber, 1989) p. 41.
10. Emerson, 'The Transcendentalist', *The Complete Works*, vol. II, p. 284.
11. Stevens, *Collected Poems*, p. 5.
12. Harold Bloom, *Wallace Stevens: The Poems of Our Climate* (Ithaca and London: Cornell University Press, 1976) p. 7.
13. Stevens, *Collected Poems*, p. 128.
14. As in Stevens, 'A High-Toned Old Christian Woman', *Collected Poems*, p. 59.

15.   Stevens, 'Final Soliloquy of the Interior Paramour', *Collected Poems*,
       p. 524.
16.   Stevens, *Collected Poems*, p. 520.
17.   Bloom, *Wallace Stevens: The Poems of Our Climate*, p. 198.
18.   Stevens, *Collected Poems*, p. 534.
19.   Stevens, 'An Ordinary Evening in New Haven', *Collected Poems*,
       p. 473.

7

Kenneth Rexroth

THOMAS EVANS

Kenneth Rexroth should be remembered, primarily, for his contemplative verse; but this was by no means the extent of his best work. By the end of the Second World War he was already well known on the West Coast as a discerning critic, an essayist who covered an encyclopedic range of subjects, an accomplished painter, and a long-time political activist; and, throughout the later part of his life, for his translations from French, Swedish, Greek, Latin, Spanish, Chinese and Japanese, which drew attention to previously unacknowledged European and Oriental poets.

He was born in Indiana in 1905, and raised by parents who held liberal views. From the beginning, his mother encouraged him to develop his artistic abilities and to allow no-one to compel him to choose a career other than that of writer and artist. In *An Autobiographical Novel* he mentions that, from earliest memory, he had experienced an 'awareness, not a feeling, of timeless, spaceless, total bliss'.[1] Such experiences gave him the determinative philosophy to achieve his ambitions. When he was orphaned, at the age of thirteen, he set out resolutely to fulfil his aspirations. Often finding himself well in advance of his classmates, he took to educating himself with dedication, and was soon influenced by the works of H. G. Wells, the French 'literary Cubists', various Christian mystics, and classical Chinese poetry; he also met D. H. Lawrence, G. K. Chesterton, the Loeb family, Louis Aragon, Tristan Tzara and many other luminaries of the 1920s. And it was throughout the Twenties and Thirties that he developed his profound love of the countryside, mainly by exploring the mountains of the North West. At the same time he became actively involved with such movements as the John Reed Club and the International Workers of the World (IWW). He visited Sacco and Vanzetti in their prison cells, and the memory of this encounter – and their subsequent executions – was

93

instrumental in directing his political tendencies. His early activities shaped a lifelong belief in anarcho-pacifism.

Rexroth had a turbulent personal life. He had an adoring mother, and the psychological damage of being orphaned at an early age may have affected his marriages. His wives had to compete with the idealised memory of Delia Rexroth.[2] He was married four times, and, whenever a marriage ran into trouble, seemed unable to accept that his misdemeanours were a cause of friction. Yet, in contrast to this domestic instability, his verse reflects a poetic identity of one searching with contemplative detachment for a means of coming to terms with his existence.

In the last twenty or so years of his life, Rexroth became increasingly attracted to Chinese and Japanese culture – the subject of numerous essays, poems and translations. His knowledge was extraordinarily wide (his favourite reading was the seven volumes of Joseph Needham's *Science and Civilisation in China*, but he was selective in what he chose to introduce into his own verse. He identified strongly with the basic principles of Mahayana Buddhism, which imbued his later poetry with an enhanced spirituality. Indeed, it is curious that Rexroth did not come earlier to Buddhism, since it advocates a lifestyle similar to the one he had aspired to. Although there are allusions to Buddhist beliefs in, for example, 'The Dragon and the Unicorn' (1944–50), it is not until we come to a poem like 'On Flower Wreath Hill' (1974) that we can observe him embracing Buddhist principles, after time spent in intense study to acquire an integrated understanding of the faith. It is this understanding which illuminates the contemplative aspect of such poems.

Analysed from a Buddhist point of view, much of Kenneth Rexroth's poetry can be seen as a meditation on the impermanence of all substance – the Mahayana concept of Sunyata. His love for the natural world does not present a contradiction since it is by intense contemplation on its wonders and beauty that one arrives at a realisation of this concept. In a sense, many of his poems become gateways to an understanding of that which lies beyond all changing substance, Sunyata, or Voidness (Sunya is Void, Sunyata Voidness), through their visionary evocation of this impermanence in nature, and the doctrine of Sunyata is manifest in their transcendental imagery. In later works it is also addressed directly as an explicit theme.

There are further Buddhist perspectives when Rexroth's poetry incorporates his political convictions. His anarcho-pacifism merged naturally with an actively compassionate form of Buddhism; it engendered a poet-narrator as a Bodhisattva figure. The Bodhisattva postpones Nirvana in order to serve mankind; Rexroth, the contemplative, retains his belief in political activism and participation in self-governing community.

I

It was in *An Autobiographical Novel* that Kenneth Rexroth affirmed his faith in the Noble Eightfold Path of Buddha which culminates in Nirvana.[3] The Noble Eightfold Path is a highly disciplined way of life for those who would conquer desire, since the second of the Four Noble Truths teaches that the cause of suffering in the world is desire.

To some, it is a way of life which rejects responsibility for social problems; this is, of course, not so. Those who transcend suffering and desire do not transcend compassion, and for a Buddhist the issue of social responsibility and participation is one of major importance; for a Mahayana Buddhist it is an ideal embodied in the Bodhisattva, who dedicates his life to it. The ideal influences and informs Rexroth's work at least from 1944, when he began writing the long didactic poem, 'The Dragon and the Unicorn', and later in 'The Heart's Garden, the Garden's Heart': 'I will not enter Nirvana / Until all sentient creatures are saved';[4] and it is a belief which fuses with his anarcho-pacifist assertion that patriarchal, hierarchical society represses man's natural forms of communication (concurring on this point with the Marxist concept of 'human self-alienation'), and that the individual has the capability to take on more responsibility for the sustenance of his existence than he is given by a capitalist society; in this he endorses George Woodcock's theory of 'individual capability'[5] and introduces it into 'The Dragon and the Unicorn' where he states that love can only exist as a kind of Gnostic cult 'Until men learn / To administer things ...'.[6]

It follows, he maintains, that society functions more effectively without government when it is replaced by hitherto repressed, natural co-operation and voluntary organisation within the community. Rexroth has explored the implications of this with great faith in its practicability, and in the possibility of a 'community of contemplatives',[7] motivated by Agape (brotherly love),[8] which a Bodhisattva would practice on principle. Sir Herbert Read, whose political writings influenced Rexroth from his youth, claims, in his essay 'Anarchism and the Religious Impulse'[9] that 'a religion is a necessary element in any organic society' since it represents a natural authority which effectively counters the artificial authority of government. Therefore, a religion that is itself hierarchical cannot accommodate the needs of an anarchist society; but the Bodhisattva principle encourages the individual to take an active part in the 'religion' of the community and excludes a hierarchical structure. 'Buddhist Agape', so to speak, becomes the religion, and compassion becomes instinctive instead of a tiresome necessity.

There is a further, more spiritual level on which this 'symbiosis' of Buddhism and anarcho-pacifism exists in Rexroth's poetry. In the Avatamsaka Sutra (Avatamsaka means 'flower wreath', the inspiration for Rexroth's poem 'On Flower Wreath Hill') occurs the image of the 'Jewel Net of Indra', in which reality is likened to a net, each knot of which can be compared to a 'jewel' or the perspective of an individual human being, which is reflected in all the other 'jewels' or perspectives. Our separate perspectives are thus bound together by a single infinite law. By contemplation on the interdependence of all the other 'jewels', rather than by selfish introspection, one becomes bound to them on an intuitive level; in Rexroth's words, everything is 'in its place, the ecology / Of infinity'.[10] In the poem 'Hapax', from which this line is taken, the Net is a feature of the organic world; the closer a community is to such an organic world, the closer it comes to perpetuating a fully integrated existence in a substantial universe – as far as this is possible in Buddhism, where all substance is impermanent.

Rexroth also uses the image of the Net in 'On Flower Wreath Hill', to create the peace that spreads in Nature when the Net is no longer shaken or disturbed by human disharmony; even the 'Spider's net of jewels has ceased / to tremble'.[11] His perception of the Net becomes a sustaining religious experience in this poem. Although it is true that he perceives this net in the architecture of nature rather than in the 'architecture' of community, the Net has a social function, as a subsidiary part of its universal purpose, since it binds together mutually supportive human beings. Significantly, Rexroth told an interviewer, 'A life lived according to the Buddha law will not need much from politics.'[12] In the same interview, Rexroth maintained that 'the religious experience is self-sufficient'. This takes on a broader significance in the context of his desire for an organic community: the impetus provided by the experience is a compelling but intuitive force, and is the ultimate affirmation of man's link with mankind. The community is bound by the experience to work for its own health and Agape becomes instinctive.

The religious experience sustains the health of the Buddhist anarcho-pacifist community, while war preserves the health of the hierarchical capitalist state – a sentiment expressed in 'The Dragon and the Unicorn': 'War is the health of the State? / War against its own members'.[13] 'War is the Health of the State' is the title of an essay by Randolph Bourne, in which he observes that man was always fundamentally and naturally gregarious, and that individualism came later. As he travels through Chicago in 'The Dragon and the Unicorn', Rexroth witnesses the products of 'self-alienated man' in the drastically commercialised cityscape, and understands 'What Marvell meant by desarts / Of vast eternitie. Man / Gets daily sicker and his Ugliness knots his bowels'.[14] The industrial panorama is the result of a social system which functions by pitting man against man and by denying the gregarious instinct.

Having absorbed an IWW antipathy towards organisations which prosper through the destruction of workers' solidarity, Rexroth frequently felt morally obliged to introduce a didacticism into his poetry (typically in 'Thou Shalt Not Kill', 1956). But in much of his later poetry he excludes an overt political stance, since by its very nature it functions as a catalyst for Mahakaruna, 'great compassion'. It evokes a powerful, unifying religious experience which, as Rexroth has said, transcends politics.

In his lifetime, Rexroth came close to witnessing something approaching his ideal in movements on the post-war West Coast, an area with a strong tradition of oriental awareness and anarcho-pacifism. The dynamism may have been lost, but its spirit remains in his verse.

II

I referred earlier to Rexroth's poetry as being a gateway to a perception of what lies beyond all transient matter: Sunya, the Void. This Mahayana doctrine permeates his later work; most notably in 'On Flower Wreath Hill'. It is worth concentrating on this poem; but before doing so, a fuller explanation of Sunya is necessary.

Sunyata (Voidness) is basic to the Mahayana school of Buddhism, although it has roots in the earlier school of Hinayana.

It is the belief that what we know as reality is only comparatively real to us, but what exists as comparative reality is a component part of ultimate reality: 'The One is all things, and is incomplete without the least of them.'[15] All things which exist in our comparative reality are impermanent and possess no real content, i.e. they are Void of content. They are manifestations of the Void, ultimate reality, which lies beyond them. For a Buddhist to fulfil the essence of this Void is enlightenment, the only absolute. This is the doctrine of Mind Only or Void Only: Sunyata.

This is the ultimate theme of 'On Flower Wreath Hill' but the poem is also laden with references to Japanese and Buddhist mythology, and bears the powerful influence of the Late T'ang poet Tu Fu, particularly in the way Rexroth intersperses descriptive passages with personal meditations. Buddhism was at a peak in China throughout the T'ang dynasty, and the poetry of this period that is not political often contemplates the world of nature. (Ezra Pound and Arthur Waley were dissatisfied with their translations of Tu Fu, whereas Rexroth translated many of Tu Fu's poems with great sensitivity.)

Parts One and Two of the poem introduce the theme of transience by establishing links between the ancient past and the present, demonstrating the cyclical nature of time. As the narrator walks through the forest, he considers the fallen leaves and the burial mound beneath them which contains a long-dead princess; he is concerned not only with the change of tangible matter (Anicca) but with the nature even of abstract concepts such as honour and beauty: 'Who was this princess under / This mound overgrown with trees / Now almost bare of leaves?'[16] The imagery of leaves is extended when Rexroth very probably refers to an episode in the life of the Buddha, when he grasped a handful of leaves from the ground, and asked his disciples which were more numerous, the leaves in his hand or those on the trees of the forest, (the former being the truths he had told them and the latter being the ones he had not revealed).

And now, for Rexroth, on the brink of religious revelation, 'There are more leaves on / The ground than grew on the trees'.[17] In the lines that follow this quotation, Rexroth considers the paradox that nostalgic memory perpetuates delusions of immortality, despite earlier intuition of impermanence. After expanding on the theme of the silence and natural glory of Autumn, in Parts Three and Four, he returns in Part Five to yet another distraction from complete knowledge of Sunyata: memories of suffering, painful memories reverberate through his consciousness like a temple bell. Each part of the poem, in sequence, depicts inner conflict or comparatively serene contemplation; for, in Part Six, he reflects with equanimity on the royal dead beneath their shattered gravestones, whom no-one remembers.

The penultimate section abandons the influence of Tu Fu upon the structure of the poem (description followed by reflection), in favour of a not entirely satisfactory combination of Buddhist mythology, and ultimately an emphatic affirmation of Annica: 'Change rules the world forever. / And man but a little while'.[18] These lines bid farewell to doubt, and clear the way for the confident tone of the final section.

In the first verse of Part Eight, the narrator generates an anticipatory tension with images of the world being 'alive', and of his body being penetrated with electric life. He sits in the darkness on a 'Sotoba', a grave marked by symbolic stones representing earth, water, air, fire and ether. These remind him of impermanence, which for the first time leads him to contemplate directly what lies beyond, in emptiness: 'The heart's mirror hangs in the void.'[19] (In his essay 'Poetry and Mysticism', Colin Wilson sees man as becoming 'an enormous mirror that reflects reality'.[20] Again we return to the Avatamsaka Sutra and the Jewel Net of Indra. The imagery of the Net is handled with consummate skill; initially it is only referred to obliquely, in terms of silver and pearls that gleam on a young girl's sleeves, an image which is transposed to a mist of silver and pearls (Interestingly, Rexroth has suggested that one should approach illumination 'as though an invisible mist was coming up behind you and enveloping you'.[21] These oblique references reflect the poet's gradual progression towards full realisation of the Net.

The fifth verse of this final section reflects on Annica, change, in the organic world, in the pattern of the seasons, and acts as a precursor to the harmony of the last verse; here the Net of Indra has ceased to tremble. It prepares us for a kind of frozen tableau of a mist whose every drop is lit by moonlight – transcendental architecture in which each part is a component of a harmonious whole.

In the last fifteen lines, Rexroth experiences Absolute Reality, a revelation of Void Only. In the forest, the mist and the moon, he sees the Net of Indra, linking partial reality to Absolute Reality. The sense of perfect harmony between the temporal world and infinity is strengthened by the soundless music of Krishna's flute which summons the Gopis, or milkmaids, to dance and become Real.

'On Flower Wreath Hill' is Rexroth's most significant exposition of Buddhist philosophy. His shorter poem, 'Void Only' is less artistically impressive, but it is an explicit statement of Sunyata which is at least effective in its concrete language, paring down his viewpoint to an Absolute: 'Only emptiness / No limits'[22] (there is an erotic version of this poem in 'The Silver Swan'[23]). What 'On Flower Wreath Hill' and 'Void Only' have in common is their handling of Sunyata, which is direct and explicit. But, in 'On Flower Wreath Hill', the reader is prepared gradually for the experience, which occurs in the last verse, whereas in *'Void Only'*, the poet (and by implication, the reader) is almost surprised by it, as he wakens from a dream.

In other poems, such as 'Towards an Organic Philosophy' and 'A Spark in the Tinder of Knowing', Rexroth implies Voidness, rather than addressing it directly, and through this method creates the style of poetry for which he is best known. Richard Eberhart once said of Rexroth's poetry that it achieved a 'calmness and grandeur, as if something eternal in the natural world has been mastered'. In Buddhist terms, the Net of Indra provides that 'something eternal', a successful image for the inter-relationship of all things. In 'Towards an Organic Philosophy', he describes three landscapes which have been subjected to different kinds of change, such as glaciation in the Sierras, and finds a common factor in 'The chain of dependence which runs through creation'[24] (a quotation from Tyndall). As in 'The Dragon and the Unicorn', shift of scene leaves an impression of constant change, the gentle motion of Annica.

'The Spark in the Tinder of Knowing' takes a single scene in which man communes with nature and finds in himself the peace which stills the landscape, a suggestion of the Void beyond Annica. But, just as 'Towards an Organic Philosophy' attempts to create no more than the impression of Sunyata, through an expression of nature's part in Oneness, so this poem stops short of probing the implications of Annica. In this Rexroth is putting into effect Keats's Negative Capability, thus relying on the power of transcendence.

When he came to write 'On Flower Wreath Hill', Rexroth did not abandon his transcendental descriptiveness, for it was a technique which had made him original and influential, but he combined it with explicit statements. Later poems such as 'Confusion of the Senses', 'Privacy', or 'Red Maple Leaves' show that he retained his ability to sensualise his mystical organic philosophy without needing to define it. But it would be reckless to categorise his poems rigidly, since there is a reflective, contemplative element in so many of them.

It is also important to realise that, despite the depth and breadth of his erudition, Rexroth was unwilling to give unconditional allegiance to any one school of Buddhism, preferring to absorb those teachings which confirmed and broadened his own intuitive and intellectual concepts. He found them in Jakob Boehme, A. N. Whitehead, Tu Fu, Whitman and many others, but it was most demonstrably in the fundamental beliefs of the Mahayana school – above all in the doctrine of Sunyata – that he encountered the consummate vision of reality that he had sought.

III

Rexroth wrote contemplative verse, based on an organic philosophy strongly influenced by Mahayana Buddhism. The two poets he influenced above all, William Everson and Gary Snyder, preserved the essence of his belief in an organic Reality, but other religious influences broadened their vision. William Everson's loosely contemplative poetry was affected by his conversion to Catholicism. Gary Snyder felt an active kinship with nature and propounded a work ethic within that particular environment; and his beliefs were complemented by his formal Zen education in Japan.

Snyder was of a younger generation of poets; it was Rexroth and Everson who planted the seeds of organic philosophy in the San Francisco Renaissance, for it was they who had turned to religion to sustain their pacifist integrity throughout the Second World War. The War ended the era described in *An Autobiographical Novel*, and Michael Davidson writes of a subsequent elegiac mode in much of Rexroth's and Everson's work.[25] In his collection of poems *The Signature of All Things* (1949), Rexroth finds it hard to shake off his sense of utter loss and the futility of human endeavour: 'Finally you say, "I am not / Weeping for our own Troubles / But for the general chaos / Of the world"'.[26] In Everson's 'October Tragedy' there is the same sentiment: 'Do not sing those old songs here tonight.'[27]

Rexroth and Everson may share this elegiac mood, but they have different emphases. In the organic world, Rexroth finds equanimity (see for example, 'Hojoki' or 'Advent' which is dedicated to Everson), whereas Everson almost succumbs to the pathetic fallacy:

'Bitter is the quiet singing of the cricket, / And the silent pools lie black beneath still reeds'.[28]

Although poets of Snyder's generation maintained the religious impulse, it took a more dynamic, exuberant form under the influence of Zen Buddhism. There was a determination to renew society and banish the stupor of the late Forties and the Fifties. However, only Snyder retained a dedicated organic sensibility from Rexroth's and Everson's lead (although Rexroth was by far the more influential of the two). Much to Rexroth's distaste, Snyder's poetry also showed the influence of Ezra Pound in its form and method. Under these influences, Snyder evolved his own approach to nature, which was as distinct from Rexroth's as his Buddhism.

Although Rexroth was by no means aloof from the natural world, his poetic stance is far more passive than Snyder's. His search is always for what points to the eternal in nature, while Snyder, following the more dynamic Zen philosophy, involves himself with nature viewed as a friend who is generally the stronger, supportive partner, but who is currently subjective to the same abuse as exploited people. In 'Revolution in The Revolution in The Revolution', the landscape is personified as being 'Among the most ruthlessly exploited classes: / Animals, trees, water, air, grasses'.[29]

Despite their differences, Rexroth and Snyder share the conviction that urban life contains little that is energising and revitalising, an opinion which is encapsulated in Snyder's 'Before the Stuff Comes Down', in which he leaves the consumerism of suburbia and greets the Californian landscape as if it were a gust of fresh air: 'Suddenly it's California: / Live oak, brown grasses'.[30] As the title implies, it is a vulnerable resource.

In his essay 'Buddhism and the Possibilities of a Planetary Culture',[31] Snyder refers to the Avatamsaka Sutra and the interdependence of all things, but he sees it as having more value as a reason for practical effort than as a basis for contemplation. Rexroth's emphasis is on the latter as the basis of a supportive community. Different schools of Buddhism affected the work of Rexroth and Snyder, but they were united in their belief in anarcho-pacifism and in Buddhism's contribution to an autonomous American poetry.

What, then, are the influences on the San Francisco Renaissance which are traceable to Rexroth? For Everson, they are the values of solitary contemplation, which he saw in terms of Catholicism and

Jungian psychology; for Snyder, Rexroth provided an exemplar, in the preceding generation, as one who had fused Buddhism and anarcho-pacifist attitudes. His view of the landscape in terms of his organic philosophy served as a model for Everson and Snyder, and perhaps even for poets like Richard Eberhart, whose work reflects a similar sense of decay and regeneration (as in Eberhart's 'Rumination'[32]).

Oriental literature and mythology, and much else, were all sources for Kenneth Rexroth, but he created a mature American poetry which William Carlos Williams quickly acknowledged. He is ultimately an American contemplative whose vision was given shape by Buddhism. These lines of his were inscribed on his gravestone:

As the full moon rises ...
The swan sings
In sleep
On the lake of the mind.[33]

NOTES

1. Kenneth Rexroth, *An Autobiographical Novel* (Surrey: Whittet Books, 1977) p. 338.
2. Kenneth Rexroth, 'Delia Rexroth', *Collected Shorter Poems* (New York: New Directions, 1966) pp. 153 and 186. (There are two poems with the same title.)
3. Rexroth, *An Autobiographical Novel*.
4. Kenneth Rexroth, 'The Heart's Garden, the Garden's Heart', *Collected Longer Poems* (New York: New Directions, 1968) p. 292.
5. George Woodcock, 'Anarchism: a Historical Introduction', in *The Anarchist Reader*, ed. George Woodcock (Glasgow: Fontana, 1977) p. 21.
6. Kenneth Rexroth, 'The Dragon and the Unicorn', *Collected Longer Poems* (New York: New Directions, 1968) p. 191.
7. See interview in *Zero*, vol. 2, ed. Eric Lerner (Los Angeles: Zero Press, 1979) p. 34.
8. See interview in *The San Francisco Poets*, ed. David Meltzer (New York: Ballantine, 1971) p. 40.
9. Herbert Read, 'Anarchism and the Religious Impulse', in *The Anarchist Reader*, ed. George Woodcock, p. 74.
10. Kenneth Rexroth, 'Hapax', *Flower Wreath Hill* (New York: New Directions, 1991) p. 7.
11. Kenneth Rexroth, 'On Flower Wreath Hill', *Flower Wreath Hill*, p. 100.
12. Interview in *Zero*, vol. 2, p. 28.
13. Rexroth, 'The Dragon and the Unicorn', p. 209.

14. Ibid., p. 87.
15. Christmas Humphreys, *Buddhism* (London: Penguin, 1951) p. 17.
16. Rexroth, 'On Flower Wreath Hill', p. 92.
17. Ibid., p. 92.
18. Ibid., p. 97.
19. Ibid., p. 99.
20. Colin Wilson, *Poetry and Mysticism* (San Francisco: City Lights, 1969) p. 22.
21. See interview in *Zero*, vol. 2, p. 33.
22. Kenneth Rexroth, 'Void Only', *Flower Wreath Hill*, p. 22.
23. Ibid., p. 70.
24. Kenneth Rexroth, 'Towards an Organic Philosophy', *Collected Shorter Poems*, p. 101.
25. Michael Davidson, *The San Francisco Renaissance* (Cambridge, Cambridge University Press, 1989) ch. 1.
26. Kenneth Rexroth 'Maximian Elegy V', *Collected Shorter Poems*, p. 195.
27. William Everson, 'October Tragedy', *The Residual Years* (New York: New Directions, 1948) p. 3.
28. Ibid.
29. Gary Snyder, 'Revolution in The Revolution in The Revolution', *Regarding Wave* (New York: New Directions, 1970) p. 39.
30. Gary Snyder, 'Before the Stuff Comes Down', *Regarding Wave*, p. 61.
31. Gary Snyder, 'Buddhism and the Possibilities of a Planetary Culture', in *The Path of Compassion: Writings on Socially Engaged Buddhism*, ed. Fred Eppsteiner (Berkeley, Buddhist Peace Fellowship, 1985) p. 82.
32. Richard Eberhart, 'Rumination', *Selected Poems 1930–1965* (New York: New Directions, 1965) p. 20.
33. Kenneth Rexroth, 'The Silver Swan', *Flower Wreath Hill*, p. 67.

8

Marianne Moore

LORRAYNE CARROLL

The belief that 'one is a woman' is almost as absurd and obscurantist as the belief that 'one is a man'.[1]

And there is one final, and 'magnificent' compliment: Miss Moore's poetry is as 'feminine' as Christina Rossetti's, one never forgets that it is written by a woman; but with both one never thinks of this particularity as anything but a positive virtue.[2]

T. S. Eliot's discovery of the 'positive virtue' in Marianne Moore's poetry is at best cryptic, at worst patronising. Why enclose 'magnificent' and 'feminine' within quotations? What are the constant reminders which define the poetry as written by a woman? Eliot's avuncular appreciation subverts and trivialises 'feminine' – female – poetry while marking its difference. The distinctions Eliot finds, the 'particularity' – one almost reads 'peculiarity' – open a reading of Moore's poems which assert her difference from the tradition in which Eliot had ensconced himself with *The Waste Land*, published only the year before Moore's longest poem, 'Marriage'.

Those shored fragments in Eliot's poem, propping the ruins of a blasted literary inheritance, adumbrate the multifarious quotations in 'Marriage'. Moore's poetic contraption is disparate and eclectic, an array of linguistic pieces, not shored but careening off one another. Syntactically tortuous, 'Marriage' almost defies reading, although Moore provided 'Notes', ostensibly to guide the reader through the dense jungle of citations and tangled locutions. Unlike Moore's earlier syllabic poems, 'Marriage' is not anchored to a visual or aural pattern. In fact, those neat patterns which characterise 'The Fish' or 'To a Prize Bird' are exploded in this 'colloquy'.

While considering the predominant cultural institution, 'Marriage' talks and talks. It is Moore's longest, and most loquacious, poem.

The voices in the poem play with the public/private dichotomy represented by sentimental (especially Victorian) notions of marriage as refuge. Traditional images construct marriage as a private retreat, a locus of respite for the world-weary husband. They posit a (culturally sanctioned) heterosexual union as the venue for revelations of the 'real' personality, the (male) identity not encumbered by public 'self-fashioning'. Although the field and space tropes in Moore's poem mark marriage as some kind of locus, they do not emblematise a haven where male desires are fulfilled. Rather, the spaces represent the emptiness which characterise a wife's allotment in the arrangement. Moore's carefully constructed versions of male and female domains, however, are not stable. They point up the difficulties either sex encounters in attempting to delineate a space that can define identity.

The discourse of 'Marriage' is not confined to a male/female dialogue. Indeed, dialogue may be as inappropriate a term for the discursive adventures of the poem as 'narrative' or 'lyric'.[3] The interplay of direct quotation and Moore's own ground – the unattributed language – juxtapose assumptions about gender roles, sexual identity, and the manipulation of the power inherent in writing. Moore subverts the dialectic of marriage by inserting several voices. A cacophony of sexual rejoinders, tired platitudes, and angry accusations paradoxically generate a sense of emptiness; silences threaten domestic tranquility. Reading 'Marriage' in the shadow of Eliot's fragments, one finds that Moore's peculiarity derives from her refusal to shore up any of the conventional, sentimentalised beliefs investing marriage or gender roles. Instead, she assembles a poem whose construction both denies a haven and reveals the ruinous assumptions at the heart of this central institution of heterosexual relations.

Moore's elaborate poetic apparatus plays with the inside/outside, public/private device of notes. As with many of Moore's notes, the heuristic devices that accompany 'Marriage' are as obfuscatory as illuminating. Moore offers them as 'Statements that took my fancy which I tried to arrange plausibly'.[4] Apparently random citations follow each other, strange bedfellows in this baffling arrangement. 'Everything to do with love is a mystery' according to 'F. C. Tilney' (272), and a reader may well assume that mystery is the basis of 'Marriage'. The play of voices, the direct discourse of 'he said/she said' and the marginalised notes subvert any one-to-one correspondence which romantics, literary and sexual, seek to perpetuate as models for the relationships between people and between words. The binary model, whether male/female, signifier/signified, connotation/denotation, or symbol/reality disintegrates (if indeed it ever existed) under the persistent pressure of an exorbitant clamour.

'Marriage' counters the implicit critical hegemony of a male Modernist poetic according to Pound or Eliot. That is, in Moore's 1923 milieu, poetic authority remains vested in the mandarins of Modernism: they make the rules, they interpret the texts, they theorise, they *talk* about the writing. Men, then, are the speaking subjects of modernism (although not always the publishers). Or at least they try to be. Dominating the critical discourse, Pound and Eliot 'make' modernism with their responses to the tradition erected by previous spoke*men* of Western literary culture. 'Marriage' also addresses this model of the speaking man, whose presence asserts power, the power of representation. Moore's position in the early Modernist movement is *a priori* suspicious because she cannot inherit the mantle of the spokes*man*.

Her experience as a relatively poor, unmarried woman who writes for a living informs 'Marriage''s convoluted presentation of relationships. Moore's own negotiations with the culture are quite evidently grounded in her *otherness*. As Jeanne Kammer states:

The situation is complicated for the woman poet by a cultural hierarchy of vocal strength: the male voice carries more 'universal' authority than the female. In diaphoric poetry, where (as [Hugh] Kenner points out in Moore) the voice is not the universal 'we' of bard of orator, but an individual quality as distinctly *other* as the objects of experience it describes, the sex of the sayer is unimportant: male and female speech has equal validity.[5]

I agree with Kammer's estimation of the cultural authority of the male voice, and I concur in her reading of the female 'we' as distinct from the universal 'we' of oratory ('We the [white, male, propertied] people'). However, Kammer constructs a gendered episteme which I think 'Marriage' destabilises. That is, she sees diaphoric forms – juxtaposition without connectives – as the rhetoric of contraction and, ultimately, female identity. Thus, for Kammer, T. S. Eliot's use of diaphor differs from Emily Dickinson's in this manner:

The effect of 'Sweeney Among the Nightingales' is of an accumulation of images and archetypal associations which together
suggest a condition of the collective modern temper; the effect of
'After Great Pain' is of a group of images and associations gathered in to a singular, interior nerve center.[6]

Both versions offer an identity, one collective and 'archetypal', the
other 'singular'. This identity, gathered and generated by a speaking subject, is exactly what 'Marriage' defers and, I think, finally re-
pudiates. The idea of one generative voice, ordering and arranging,
is abandoned. In the face of traditional male author-ity, Moore
pieces together an allegory of the impossibility of identity, of a
writing 'presence' in the poem. There can be no one authoritative
writing subject, just as no 'one' is a 'woman'. Subjectivity, in its
sense as a personal, individualised expression of the artist, cannot
be rendered in a world where 'the strange experience of beauty /
... tears one to pieces' (37–39).

As I have said, 'Marriage' defies reading. By this I mean it is an
example of that 'incomprehensible' poetry to which Julia Kristeva
refers in *Revolution in Poetic Language*.[7] This kind of language calls
attention to itself as a *process* of signifying rather than as a product
(signification). For Kristeva, marginalised systems reveal a methodology of meaning:

> Magic, shamanism, esoterism, the carnival and 'incomprehensi-
> ble' poetry all underscore the limits of socially useful discourse
> and attest to what it represses: the *process* that exceeds the subject
> and his communicative structure.[8]

Accordingly, 'Marriage' may be read as a revelatory moment in the
history of Modernism. The repressions implicit in Eliot's
Modernism – not the least of which is the constitution of *the* subject
as white, Western, and male – surface in Moore's poem. An encounter with 'Marriage' compels the reader to negotiate a series of
subjects, none of which can be consistently identified. Even the familiar signs 'Adam' and 'Eve' disintegrate under the pressures of
an intricate syntactical and graphic apparatus. 'Marriage' presumes
no one authoritative voice, no one ordering provenance that generates the poem.

Syntactical intricacies combine with quotation and 'quotation' to
assemble a kaleidoscopic text. Even the term 'kaleidoscopic' cannot

adequately describe the flux of the text, because it assumes a single focus for the reader, and the discontinuities and juxtapositions which form the poem push the reader into various parallactic movements, adjusting his or her interpretive positioning with each shifting fragment of quotation or phrase. Quotations and their 'contextualizing' 'Notes' seem less to explain than to complicate.

Turning to the 'Notes' provides no relief from the baffling accumulation of citations. Rather, the 'Notes' appear to be a random sampling of Marianne Moore's eclectic reading tastes. And their status in relation to the poem proper is never quite articulated. Quotation functions as predominant rhetorical strategy within 'Marriage', although not every phrase enclosed within quotation marks results in a note. Some 'quotes' derive from speaking subjects which only exist in the text of the poem, and, as such, the poem is itself a series of imaginary conversations (significantly *not* the Pateresque vehicles for the pronouncements of the Great Men of Letters). So, Adam appropriates not only Hazlitt's words, but 'quotes' himself:

> he has prophesied correctly –
> the industrious waterfall,
> 'the speedy stream which violently bears all before it,
> at one time silent as the air
> and now as powerful as the wind.'   (76–83)

'[T]he speedy stream ... the wind' is not attributed in the 'Notes'. Adam invokes the past and then prophesies from it. Only Adam has the authority to quote himself; Eve's speech throughout the poem is direct discourse, always prefaced by 'She says' or, in one case, a colon. Later, I will discuss the significance of oratory to a male stance. For now, I am arguing that the appearance of this 'imaginary' quotation undermines the authority of the actual notes. If the poem can quote itself, positing a prior 'language' from its speakers which can be recapitulated as readily as the language of different texts, then the poem refuses to mark any interiority/exteriority distinction. In deferring that distinction, 'Marriage' violates authorial sanctity: if the parameters of the poem itself are not defined, if there are no clear demarcations between the poet's poem and its sources, then poetic 'self' as arranger and progenitor of the poem is questioned.

The question of Moore's quotations is addressed by various critics and is not confined to a discussion of 'Marriage'. John Slatin sees quotation as Moore's acknowledgement of 'the creative power wielded by other writers' and of her 'experience' of reading them.[9] His estimation presumes a community of creativity which Moore taps in order to represent the orderliness of her experience. Tess Gallagher's evaluation of Moore's 'picking and choosing' is closer to what I see as a vital recognition of the multiplicity of the speaking subject that writes. But Gallagher, too, wishes to retrieve collectivity rather than dispersal in the quotations:

> I prefer to see quotations as proof of Moore's ambition not to write simply in the isolation of the ego, but to write as if she were a team, or an orchestra. ... She was willing to take responsibility to a new enlarged arena, then, to present and credit views other than her own, and to provide a context for hearing a concert of voices.[10]

I agree that Moore provided a forum for a 'concert' of voices', but not in the sense that Gallagher intends. Moore's constitution of herself as not 'ego' but 'team' relies on the collectivity, and ultimately, the identity of that 'team'. Indeed, the image of the orchestra perpetuates the notion that, however different the music on the stands in front of the individual musicians, they are still playing the same piece.

Rather, I see the 'concert' as a disparate mob, shattering with its cacophony the unity presumed in the poetic voice, the voice of the author. Moore may want to be a team player – baseball was a favourite of hers – but the act of writing denies the kind of collective identity implied in shoring up fragments. Here I return to Kristeva for a reading of the dialectic produced by the multifarious quotations of 'Marriage'. That dialectic, which is figured in the *pretence* of an inside/outside (poem/notes), defers any combinatory process which will yield a unity. Kristeva's process of arriving at a dialectical model to understand 'a theory of signification based on the subject, his formation, and his corporeal, linguistic, and social dialectic' is akin to the dialectical impetus of 'Marriage':

> At least indicates its own position, and renounces both the totalizing fragmentation characteristic of positivist discourse, which reduces all signifying practices to a formalism, and a reductive identification with other (discursive, ideological, economic) islands of the social aggregate. ... From this position, it seems

possible to perceive a signifying practice which, although produced in language, is only intelligible *through* it.[11]

I offer this reading as an interpretive entry into the quotations. Several critics want to view them as a basic 'democratising' gesture on Moore's part, but I think her use of quotation exceeds that formulation, while it includes it. That is, although Hugh Kenner discusses the 'richness of found phrases' whose effect is 'to democratize "tradition" very considerably',[12] the effect goes beyond a sense of community and collectivity. Moore's 'Marriage' opens the language to an inspection not only of the presuppositions about the institution of marriage, but also of the ideological assumptions implicit in the notion of a coherent subject.

Helen Vendler approaches this interpretation when she says of Moore: 'Perhaps her work is in fact more "feminine" than it may appear to a woman reader, to whom Moore's angle of vision may seem more congenial.'[13] The return of the term 'feminine' to a critical appraisal of Moore's work recalls the (rather patronising) description offered by Eliot in his 1923 review.[14] Although I do not want to argue that Vendler's is a conscious or unconscious recapitulation of that review, I am interested in her assertion that women may find Moore's 'angle of vision' more 'congenial' than men would. Both Eliot and Vendler want to mark that angle as 'feminine'. Both read a difference in Moore which they want to attribute to a biological fact rather than a linguistic effect. Moore's strategy of convolution and eclecticism, particularly that found in 'Marriage', may be traced to her experiences as a woman living and writing in a patriarchy. But I find the poem to be most compelling as a critique of the coherent subject presumed in literary models up to and including Modernist works like Eliot's. While I agree that this subject is gendered (male), I think that the evasive discourse of 'Marriage' is not merely an indictment of that gendered 'authority'. Rather, it questions the possibility for any intact subject, gender notwithstanding.

As I noted above, quotations prevent the definition of an authorising subject in 'Marriage'. In doing so, they also subvert the representation of a public/private dichotomy: the public domain figured in the 'Notes' (product of many) and the private space of the 'personal' poem (product of the one poet). The description of marriage as 'This institution ... requiring public promises ... to fulfil a private obligation' (1–8) inscribes it as a transgressive 'enterprise',

violating the domains of public and private selves. Marriage functions here as the trope of emptiness, an interstice, the space where
either party to the institution dissolves into its 'circular traditions and
impostures' (14). There can be no privacy in that putatively most
private of arrangements because there is no private self to assent to
the arrangement *ab initio*. Marriage, then, is a futility, since no stable
identity is available to merge with – or diverge from – another.

The 'criminal ingenuity' required to avoid marriage is the same
wily process practised by a poet who must (impossibly) posit a coherent authorising voice in order to write. 'Criminal ingenuity' thus
is the hallmark of writing subjects in 'Marriage'. The emptiness
figured by marriage is the space of writing itself, the possibility for
inscription. Filling that space with language, with signification, the
writing is an 'imposture', because it transgresses any boundaries
erected by a putatively discrete, distinctive self. This is one reason
for the difficulty of interpreting 'Marriage'. The poem refuses to
display a dichotomous rhetoric. It is not a dramatic dialogue, although there are aspects of the dialogic in the exchange between
Adam and Eve. But their voices are not purely oppositional; they
babble past each other, careening off shards of discourse generated
by the 'noted' sources and the 'I's and 'we's scattered throughout
the poem. These various subjects produce the (written) text of
'Marriage' through their 'speech', the language enclosed within
quotation marks.

The tensions which characterise the highly ambiguous language
of the poem reflect the internal split of these subjects, a split represented by the opposition of 'speech' and 'writing'. The speaking
subjects of 'Marriage' lack any identity to which authority can be
attributed: authority itself is in question, in the sense that it is able
to vest in a subject. Subjectivity, rather than identity, is only constituted as an effect of speech. Because 'Marriage' represents an explo-
sion of quotation and speech, that subjectivity disseminates
throughout the text. An example of the subjects' dispersal across
the poem is in the shift of the first person singular 'I' to 'we' and to
'use'.[15] Significantly, the poem begins with the starkly impersonal
'one' as a grammatical subject. From there on, the reader encounters a succession of pronominal metamorphoses.

Initially, 'I' appears to be the mark of the (traditional) subject that
arranges, that tells the story of Adams and Eve: 'I wonder what
Adam and Eve / think of it by this time.' (9–10). Then the 'I'
remarks of Eve: 'I have seen her / when she was so handsome /

she gave me a start' (22–4). So Eve does give this 'I' a start – as an object against which to oppose/compose itself as the seeing 'I'.[16] That is, the speaking subject is only provisionally constituted against the object with which it has a relationship, in this case, a relationship of specularity. Shortly after 'I' sees Eve, Eve emphatically appropriates 'I' for herself: '"*I* should like to be alone"; / to which the visitor replies, / "I should like to be alone; why not be alone together?"' (31–4). The subjectivity in both these instances results from both Eve's and the visitor's lack of solitude. Indeed, the visitor, sounding much like Groucho Marx, posits the very paradox of subjectivity, the fact that it can only be 'alone together'.

The (or an) 'I' returns with a linguistic vengeance near the end of the poem. There, it emerges from the most syntactically occluded passage in 'Marriage' into a seven-line 'quotation' set apart from the text by the spaces on either end:

'I am such a cow,
if I had a sorrow
I should feel it a long time;
I am not one of those
who have a great sorrow
in the morning
and a great joy at noon'   (275–81)

The reiteration of 'I' and its difference from 'one of those' indicates that, here again, subjectivity can only be produced by its opposition to some *other* object. The insistent 'I' is a function of 'that striking grasp of opposites / opposed each to the other, not to unity' (265–6).[17] I read this last line as another figure of paradox, a recapitulation of the 'alone together' figure of subjectivity that operates throughout 'Marriage'. The series of speaking subjects in the poem rely on oppositions – objects – in order to posit (ion) themselves as speakers. I would like to turn now from a discussion of how subjectivity is constituted and dispersed throughout the poem to the effect that oscillation has on the status of speech and writing.

The invocation of 'the debater', 'that orator reminding you', and 'Daniel Webster' at the end of 'Marriage' calls to mind the several versions of oratorical posturing which recur throughout 'Marriage'.

Many of these instances involve Adam, the most verbose of the poem's speakers. Indeed, Adam is 'Alive with words, / vibrating like a cymbal / touched before it has been struck' (74–6). This oratorical positioning, then, is generally a male prerogative, as far as one wants to read 'Adam' and 'Eve' as gendered images. When Eve speaks, she either addresses Adam or, in one notorious case, she talks and writes at the same time, 'equally positive in demanding a commotion / and in stipulating quiet' (29–30). Although Adam does most of the talking, Eve, too, speaks, but she also writes.

The binary speech/writing does not fracture across a clearly gendered line, then because the poem is full of speaking subjects – 'I', 'he', 'she', 'we'. But in all this chatter, different kinds of speech do not carry the same valence, and the powerful speech that holds an entire audience captive is obviously vested in Adam. His oratorical presentations seem to be more authoritative and universal than Eve's utterances. The exchanges give Adam more to say, and he assumes an authority never attributed to Eve. Adam is not only the speaking subject, but the orating subject, whose authority and ascendancy over Eve depends on the immanence of the speech act. Thus, Adam's status as the figure of a privileged speaker derives from his asserting presence, the presumption of an orator. Eve's voice, conversely, is subdued, 'constrained in speaking of the serpent' (56), and she 'speaks' fewer lines than Adam.

There is one instance in the poem, however, where Adam's oratorical power is disrupted. '[H]e stumbles over marriage' (124) because he is

> Plagued by the nightingale
> in the new leaves,
> with its silence –
> not its silence but its silences, ...   (103–6)[18]

Although oratory appears to be the privileged mode of speech, 'silences' shift the register of power, and Eve controls these oratorical absences: 'equally positive in demanding a commotion / and in stipulating quiet.' Eve talks 'in the meantime' while she is exhibiting her most startling capability 'to write simultaneously / in three languages' (25–6). Eve writes and talks, and Adam only speaks. Adam is plagued and 'Unnerved' by silences because they oppose the preeminence of his loquacity. John Slatin supposes this to be Moore's answer to patriarchal presumptions when he says, 'Thus

Moore uses silence itself with "criminal ingenuity" to circumvent the father's authority and appropriate it to herself.'[19] Most recent interpretations of 'Marriage' seem to assert, as Slatin does here, that the poem is an antidote to patriarchy because, in the end, Eve/Marianne takes back the power appropriated by the fathers.

In considering this observation, I return now to the discussion in the beginning of this chapter, of a public/private split. There I stated that Moore's constructions of male and female domains are not stable, because subjectivity – whether gendered male or female – is itself split and dispersed over the poem. So, although I have been reading 'Adam' and 'Eve' as conventional signs of different genders, I am not interpreting them as markers for either a male or a female identity. Rather, they are, like 'marriage; and 'space', tropes that operate in various ways across the text. I align Adam with oratory and Eve with writing, not because I think the poem wants to gender speech and writing, but because the text uses the metaphor of gender difference to mark a distinction between these two functions of language. The sexual aspects of the trope are, of course, charged by the context of 'Marriage' itself: a poem written by a woman immersed in the Modernist milieu dominated by men. But 'Marriage''s critique of patriarchy does not derive from a simple inversion of conventional power models or the rigid ascription of discursive modes along sexual lines.

One last observation may serve to clarify this distinction. The strategy of citation in 'Marriage', which denies an inside/outside reading of the poem, also undermines a writing/speech distinction. 'Speech' is represented by inscription: the quotation 'marks'. All the speaking subjects and their speeches are products of writing, the writing that 'write[s] simultaneously / in three languages' and 'talks in the meantime.' The oratorical privilege is thus subsumed under this writing because the 'speech' of the orator is in this sense the *text* of the speech, the words on paper that govern the oratory. So the orator, near the end of the poem, states, 'I am yours to command' (260).

If speech, then, is a function of writing, there would seem to be a totalising power girding the poem. Opposed to the dispersal figured by the constructions of subjectivity, writing *per se* might be deemed the gathering, generating force that produces the poem, a 'universal' subject as dominant as any model of male hegemony. However, writing itself is dispersed by the only writer in the poem, who writes in 'three languages' and intersperses the writing with 'talk'. Even writing is split; its representations of identity and unity are pretences, attempts toward 'cycloid inclusiveness'. The critique of Western concepts of identity, signalled by dispersed subjectivity, is explicit:

> We Occidentals are so unemotional,
> self lost, the irony preserved, ...   (184–5)

And the final image of the poem explodes the notion of an essential writing, produced by a masterful transcendent subject. I interpret the 'it' of this passage as the mark of that unity and essentialism (erroneously) assumed to be characteristic of the writing subject of Western poetry:

>   'I have encountered it
> among those unpretentious
> protégés of wisdom,
> where seeming to parade
> as the debater and the Roman,
> the statesmanship
> of an archaic Daniel Webster
> persists to their simplicity of temper
> as the essence of the matter' ...   (282–90)

This essence, 'Liberty and union / now and forever', symbolises the Procrustean effort to collapse heterogeneity to a homogeneous mass: it is the complete denial of 'the strange experience of beauty' whose 'existence is too much; / it tears one to pieces.'

The impulse to deny the splits and disseminations attendant upon writing is the impulse to diminish writing's energetic play into static objectification. Working through the marriage metaphor, this is akin to an institutional model which constrains difference for the greater good of the marriage, the 'union'. The poem deflates the possibility of that 'union' ('this amalgamation which can never be more / than an interesting impossibility') and parodies those who support marriage as a verity. The last lines of 'Marriage' figure the intolerance and absurdity of that position, even as they inscribe its dominance. All writing has been reduced to 'the Book' and the 'universal' subject, the orator,[20] looms smugly over it, 'the hand in the breast-pocket', a figure of unyielding convention.

NOTES

1. Julia Kristeva, 'Women Can Never Be Defined', in Elaine Marks and Isabelle de Courtivron (eds), *New French Feminisms* (New York: Schocken Books, 1981) p. 137.
2. T. S. Eliot, 'Marianne Moore', *The Dial*, 75 (July–Dec., 1923) 594.
3. T. S. Eliot, 'Introduction', in Marianne Moore, *Selected Poems* (New York: Macmillan, 1935) p. x.
4. Marianne Moore, '"Notes" (for "Marriage")', in *The Complete Poems of Marianne Moore* (New York: Penguin, 1981) p. 271. All references to the poem and the 'Notes' are from this edition and will be cited in the text by line number and page respectively.
5. Jeanne Kammer, 'The Art of Silence and the Forms of Women's Poetry', in *Shakespeare's Sisters: Feminist Essays on Women Poets*, ed. Sandra Gilbert and Susan Gubar (Bloomington and London: Indiana University Press, 1979) p. 159.
6. Ibid., p. 158.
7. Julia Kristeva, *Revolution in Poetic Language*, trans. Margaret Waller (New York: Columbia University Press, 1984) p. 16.
8. Ibid. See Margaret Waller's 'Translator's Preface' for her explanation of the choice to use the male pronoun as a universal.
9. John Slatin, *The Savage's Romance: The Poetry of Marianne Moore* (University Park and London: The Pennsylvania State University Press, 1986) p. 102. Slatin argues that the strict economy of syllabics cannot accommodate the quotation which is necessary to Moore's 'search for community', itself in turn dependent on an experience of 'creative power'. 'Collectively, they [the quotations in free verse] reveal Moore's effort to open up her work, both to her readers and to those manifestations of "creative power" (to quote "The Labors of Hercules" again) that were appearing all around her, and to which her association with *The Dial* in particular demanded that she pay heed' (102).
10. Tess Gallagher, 'Throwing the Scarecrows from the Garden', *Parnassus*, 12: 2/13: 1 (1985): 50.
11. Kristeva, *Revolution*, p. 15.
12. Hugh Kenner, *A Homemade World* (New York: Alfred A. Knopf, 1975) p. 111.
13. Helen Vendler, *Part of Nature, Part of Us* (Cambridge and London: Harvard University Press, 1980) p. 74.
14. Interestingly, Moore herself uses the term in a review of H.D.'s *Hymen*: 'Woman tends unconsciously to be the aesthetic norm of intellectual home life and preeminently in the case of H.D., we have the intellectual social woman; non-public and "feminine." ' The fact that 'feminine', when used by Moore, Eliot, and Vendler as a critical description, appears in quotation marks is itself an indication of the problematical status of woman writers. The dispersal of meanings for the term, its instability as a critical term (evident in the quotation marks), calls for a closer inspection of 'feminine' *per se* in the critical

discourse of Modernism. As I argue here, the term is used (provisionally) to name the disquieting aspects of reading figurations of the incoherent subject within a critical atmosphere that assumes a universalist, unified male subjectivity.

15. Barbara Johnson observes this same move in Zora Neale Hurston's *Their Eyes Were Watching God*: 'The narrative voice in this novel expresses its own self-division by shifting between the first and third person, standard English and dialect. This self-division culminates in the frequent use of free indirect discourse, in which, as Henry Louis Gates, Jr. points out, the inside/outside boundaries between narrative and character, between standard and individual, are both transgressed and preserved, making it impossible to identify and totalize either the subject or the nature of discourse.' See *A World of Difference* (Baltimore: The Johns Hopkins University Press, 1987) p. 171.

16. Even the absent subject of the imperative is invoked with a specular model: 'See her, see her in this common world ...' (42).

17. 'This positionality, which Husserlian phenomenology orchestrates through the concepts of *doxa*, *position*, and *thesis*, is structured as a break in the signifying process, establishing the identification of the subject and its object as preconditions of propositionality. We shall call this break, which produces the positing of signification, a *thetic* phase. All enunciation, whether of a word or of a sentence, is thetic. It requires an identification; in other words, the subject must separate from and through his image, from and through his objects. This image and objects must first be posited in space, that becomes symbolic because it connects the two separated positions, recording them or redistributing them in an open combinatorial system.' Kristeva, *Revolution*, p. 43. So, for the purposes of interpreting 'Marriage', one can read the images produced in this subject–object construction – for example, 'I have seen her' – as the process whereby the speaking subject ('I') positions itself in relation to an object ('her') in order to posit signification – that is, 'write' the poem. This signifying process is not, of course, confined to the first person pronoun. Indeed an excessive instance of this relational propositioning occurs in the second person construction referring to Adam:

>   – the O thou
>   to whom from whom,
>   without whom nothing – Adam   (62–4)

This parallactic pronominal shifting in regard to Adam produces his ambiguous status as '"something feline, / something colubrine"' (65–6), even as it marks this objectification as the venue of signification: 'without whom nothing'.

18. This passage recalls Eliot's use of the Philomela myth in *The Waste Land*. However, Moore invests the nightingale with the power to disturb, to 'plague' Adam with silence, choosing to grant that

absence of speech with a greater power than that which has been
accorded to Adam as orator. Eliot's passage on the nightingale is
followed by an equally provoked speaker:

'My nerves are bad to-night. Yes, bad. Stay with me.
Speak to me. Why do you never speak? Speak.'   (111–12).

As I have noted in other sections of this essay, the shadow of Eliot
hangs over 'Marriage'. There may be ways to read the poem as an
answer to/supplement of/antidote for *The Waste Land* (and I think a
good place to begin that interpretation would be 'The Game of
Chess'), but that discussion is beyond the scope of this chapter's
specific concern with subjectivity.

19.   Slatin, *The Savage's Romance*, p. 151.
20.   Helen Vendler proposes that Moore is positioning herself within the
American canon with a rejection of oratory's imprecision: 'Moore
sets herself firmly against one sort of American writing – the breezy
rhetoric of native oratory, the afflatus of romantic sentiment, the optimism of self-help – and just as firmly placed herself in alliance with
another American attitude toward words: our pragmatic, taxonomic,
realistic conviction that words are useful, practical, and exact. ... To
write so that no single word can be misunderstood is a mark of the
American pride in accuracy, punctual speech, and laconic completeness; the abstractions of metaphysical dispute are as foreign to this
sort of American as are the pleasures of mystification in the service of
sentiment' (61). I agree that rhetoric itself is being critiqued within
'Marriage', but I do not think there is an antidote to its sentimentality
offered by precision, taxonomising, and exactitude. Rather, the mys-
tifying syntax and dispersed subjectivity displayed throughout the
poem undermine the possibility for a linguistic 'accuracy'.

9

e. e. cummings

BRIAN DOCHERTY

e. e. cummings is at once the most modern of traditionalists and the most traditional of Modernists. This ironic paradox runs through both his life and his poetry. Born in 1894 to a family of impeccably New England Puritan stock, his life as a writer was to some extent a negation of his background. Like Ezra Pound, cummings never held a 'normal' job, but lived true to his principles, devoted to his art even at the expense of so-called material success. His father was both an academic, who became America's first Professor of Sociology, and a Unitarian minister at Boston's fashionable Back Bay Church. Two conspicuous features of cummings's work are a hatred of rationalising intellectual types and a virtual absence of orthodox Christian faith, Puritan or otherwise. This is not to imply that he was in any way estranged from his family. It was his father who secured his release from a French prison in 1917 (this adventure is related in *The Enormous Room*), and there are some beautiful poems to his parents, obviously written out of a deep love, notably 'my father moved through dooms of love'. (Most of cummings's poems are untitled, so first lines have been taken as titles in this chapter.)

Like Pound, cummings enjoyed the benefits of a sound classical education, studying Greek and Latin at high school before going on to Harvard in 1911. cummings was part of probably the last generation to be educated in precisely this manner, and his training shows through in the poetic strategies he adopted. He shared Pound's desire to 'make it new', but not the obsession with the Provençal troubadours and the Eleusinian mystery religion. His interest in classical language is also different from that of, say, H.D., who valued those qualities we think of as 'classical': clarity, hardness and precision. cummings set out to write a vernacular American, and succeeded as well as William Carlos Williams in capturing the true vulgarity of American speech. He did it by treating English as if it

120

were a foreign language, full of wonder and freshness, and by writing English as if it were an inflected language like Greek or Latin. Some of the perceived characteristics his detractors have objected to can possibly be blamed on his Harvard education. Harvard is, of course, one of the world's great universities, but it is fair to say that nobody there at that time had any conception of literary theory. 'English Literature', as an academic discipline in its own right, was the invention of F. R. Leavis, William Empson and I. A. Richards in England, and the 'New Critics' in America.

cummings was largely taught by classics scholars, a body of men who often believed that reading and criticising modern literature was the sort of thing any intelligent man could do in his bath. Although cummings believed in self-discipline in an Emersonian sense (and rejected all external standards), he never learnt self-criticism as a writer, although he worked hard, being a careful and meticulous craftsman. Perhaps a dose of Leavis-style 'close reading' would have helped him to distinguish between successful and unsuccessful poems. A published output of some 800 poems would seem to mark a determination to get everything into print, rather than the 'distillation' or 'essence' theory favoured by other poets. This is characteristic both of the Puritan obsession to save and use every scrap, in any activity, and of cummings's own temperament. He is primarily a poet of spring, overflowing with life and vitality.

Like Walt Whitman, cummings has sometimes been accused of lacking a sufficient sense of evil or a tragic vision of the world. This view ignores the fact that cummings perceives certain aspects of the modern world as tragedy in the making, or more accurately, as grotesque farce. His perception of the world as it is, and not as he would like it to be, either by a reconstitution of past order and wholeness, or as the stage for a revolution of visionary utopia, makes cummings a poet of hate as well as a poet of love. (And it serves to distinguish him from, on the one hand, Pound and Eliot, and on the other hand, Whitman and Ginsberg.) Even in his hates, however, cummings is a generous poet, willing to say some things other poets shied away from, with a kind of stiff-necked New England honesty. Since cummings took his Emersonian transcendentalism seriously and conscientiously, his concept of love was not determined by Christianity of the 'gentle Jesus meek and mild' variety. For cummings, an honest man could only be a good lover if he was a good hater. His hatred is reserved for political tyranny, of both left and right, for the ill-treatment or torture of individuals, for bureaucrats, politicians, salesmen, people unable to think for themselves, and bigots. By his willingness to take up the stones of castigation, cummings confronts his readers with the follies, abuses and evils of the modern world, and most people's willingness to close their eyes, turn their back, or cross the street.

'Humanity i love you' (CP, 53) is an example of his technique of paradox. After five stanzas of wry acceptance of the compromises people employ in their daily lives, the last line, 'i hate you', is a shock the reader is not prepared for. cummings appears to suggest that while acceptance of such compromises keeps the world turning, intelligent consideration would lead to rejection of such attitudes and practices. The implication is that if we all start to hate compromise, a more honest society might be possible. 'a man who had fallen among thieves' (CP, 256) is a version of the biblical story of the Good Samaritan, condemning the hypocritical upright citizens who refuse to help this unfortunate man, robbed of both his money and his dignity by whoever sold him drink. cummings's contempt for the by-passer is coupled with a love for the individual strong enough to let him help the fallen man even though he is 'banged with terror' (CP, 256).

'next to of course god america i' (CP, 267) is a satire on both the cliché-spouting patriot and the gullibility of his audience. cummings includes most of the clichés politicians mouth at election time, and his point is that while anyone who dared to criticise any of these concepts would be labelled un-American and a commie subversive, it is politicians like this who have muted the voice of liberty. His general attitude to politicians is expressed succinctly in 'a politician is an arse upon' (CP, 550), a two-line epigram in the best classical tradition. Politicians of the liberal, compromising variety are condemned in 'THANKSGIVING (1956)' (CP, 711), one of his relatively new titled poems. It is a disciplined exercise in rhymed four-line stanzas designed to be heard loud and clear. The Russian state is stigmatised as a 'monstering horror', and the Soviet leadership as 'a which that walks like a who'. Hungary is praised for having the bravery to stand up for freedom and liberty, while both the United Nations and the United States are criticised for failing to come to Hungary's aid when it is invaded by the forces of Communism which 'Western democracy' professes to oppose. Individuals in Europe and America who failed to condemn the invasion are included in his critique, and liberal democracy is shown to be impotent in the face of Stalinist aggression.

uncle sam shrugs his pretty
pink shoulders you know how
and he twitches a liberal titty
and lisps 'i'm busy right now'   (CP, 711)

The implication is that America is run by homosexuals, whom cummings regarded as decadent perverts who were probably fellow travellers anyway. The persona in the poem echoes the rantings of the crazed bigot Senator McCarthy, who ruined many people's lives in the 1950s with his anti-communist witch-hunts.

Homosexuals feature in another hate poem, 'flotsam and fetsam' (CP, 492). This little gem is perhaps aimed at W. H. Auden and Christopher Isherwood, who arrived in America in early 1939, some months before the outbreak of the Second World War. The poem criticises gays, middle-class intellectuals fleeing the coming war, and left-wingers with the means to insulate themselves from the economic realities of life. While advocating the principles of communism, they are themselves insured by Lloyd's. Left-wing dogma is also condemned in 'kumrads die because they're told' (CP, 413), an attack on what cummings views as the de-individualising effects of collectivist philosophies. The rhythm is strongly marked, and rhyme is again employed to point up the message that collective attitudes constitute a form of indoctrination which has the most disastrous consequences; 'and kumrads won't (believe in life) ... because they are afraid to love' (CP, 413). These lines represent one of cummings's strongest critiques of the modern state, and the de-personalisation caused by acceptance of dogma and obedience to orthodoxy.

Another poem which contrasts institutional thinking with the plight of the individual is 'i sing of Olaf glad and big' (CP, 340). Again there is a strong rhythm and deftly placed rhyme, employed to make the message clear. Olaf is a principled individual, probably a second-generation Swedish American from the Mid-West farm belt, brought up in the Lutheran church. He is a heroic figure who dies for his beliefs after enduring barbaric treatment, including the ultimate obscenity with red-hot bayonets. American democracy and freedom suffer grievously at the hand of their supposed defendants, ironically described as '(a yearning nation's blueeyed pride)', while the pacifist traitor is lauded as 'more brave than me: more blond than you' (CP, 340). cummings is impartial in his attitude to regimes where correct attitudes are instilled and maintained by force. America and Russia are two faces of the same coin as far as he is concerned.

'a salesman is an it that stinks Excuse' (CP, 549) is an attack on commercialism in a modified sonnet, a hate poem on the negative side of America, expressed in a form traditionally reserved for love poems. The colloquial language of the salesman offers a further ironic contrast to the formal qualities normally expected of a sonnet. By its willingness to say anything and sell anything to make a quick profit, the whole of American life has been debased. Capitalism is rotten to the core, and so corrupt that democracy can be bought and sold like any other commodity. cummings says let the buyer beware, since only 'subhuman rights' are on offer here, not freedom or liberty. Rights belong to the free individual as typified by the lover, because in cummings's world only the free individual can be a lover, and only the lover is free.

Because he is such a good hater of what he perceives as the faults of the modern world, cummings is both a great lover and a great love poet. Poems about love or lovers make up some 25 per cent of his output, some 200 poems. His concept of love as a healing force in the world is more rigorous and less chauvinist than the often vacuous effusions on 'love' emanating from the poetry and music of the 60s counter-culture. Some 50 per cent of his poems on love are sonnets, modified and modernised in various ways, with a significant mixing of linguistic registers from traditional to formal to colloquial to standard Harvard to comic. This is cummings's largest subject area and it is appropriate that his versatility should be fully demonstrated in the subject which mattered most to him. 'my love' (CP, 33) is a surprisingly traditional tribute from the poet to his lady, addressed in the archaic 'thy' form, employing jewel and fertility imagery to make a poem rather like an Imagist Keats. 'it may not always be so and i say' (CP, 146) is a regular sonnet, a formal but tender address to his lady with a rather posed rhetorical quality. Some readers may not be completely convinced by the poet's demonstration of generosity towards his rival, but it is nevertheless a lovely and moving poem which shows cummings's mastery of form.

'i like my body when it is with your' (CP, 218) is a modern, more relaxed exercise in sonnet form with modern language to match. It is a celebration of the joys of physical love, a contemporary version of John Donne without the metaphysical overtones. It is both a young man's poem and an adult poem, enjoyment of the natural attributes without prurience, salaciousness, or a need to dominate the other person. It is entirely in the Whitmanian tradition, celebrating love, and opposed to the Platonist and Pauline attitudes to sexual pleasure. cummings upholds the modern post-Freudian view that to be spiritually happy, humans must be sexually fulfilled. (It should be noted, however, that generally cummings was not sympathetic to Freud.) 'she being Brand' (CP, 246) is one of the better-known poems, mainly because cummings's detractors hold it up as an example of his typographical eccentricities. In fact, critics who call attention to poems for this reason merely advertise their failure to come to terms with an important element of Modernist poetry from Pound onwards, the use of the capabilities of the typewriter to provide a score for the speaking voice. This is another sex poem with the emphasis on performance, the description of a new car being driven for the first time being a metaphor for a young woman's first full sexual experience. The poem also provides an illustration of the American obsession with automobiles, and the frequent equation of women and cars in American popular culture. (The American love affair with the car is documented in the lyrics of songwriters such as Chuck Berry and Bruce Springsteen.) Far from being eccentric or careless, the line lengths, word divisions and the stanzaic patterning are carefully designed and laid out on the page to give the reader a precise guide to the cadencing of the poem when read aloud. cummings's practice as a painter no doubt influenced his writing here. The visual devices are employed for non-visual purposes, and this poem is a reminder that nearly all of cummings's poems are speakable, with only a small handful offering real difficulties, although some rearrangement of the poem's element is sometimes necessary.

'if i have made, my lady, intricate' (CP, 307) is another sonnet, a lyric to his lady on a traditional theme, the poet's inability to write poems which do justice to her beauty. cummings's debt to the lyric tradition in English literature is plain here, yet the tone of the poem has a calm and tender beauty unique to cummings. It is entirely typical of his work as a poet of love and spring, whose April lies in a different world from that of Eliot's *The Waste Land*. 'may i feel said he' (CP, 399) is a high-spirited comic poem on a serious subject, the games people play which end up in adultery. As usual, cummings has a serious point to make in the last line, '(you are Mine said she)'. In his poetic world, people always have to face the consequences of their actions. Most of the love poems, however, involve relationships between free individuals, which accounts for the lack of guilt, violence or recrimination in the poems. '"sweet spring is your"' takes up the theme of the ending of 'if i have made, my lady, intricate', in rhymed four-line stanzas. For cummings, April is the gladdest month, full of new life and new energy after the long hibernation of winter, when the world belongs to lovers. Nature as process and rebirth is symbolised in that the last stanza is identical to the first, an affirmation that love does indeed make the world go round. The poem is not frivolous or irresponsible since this attitude, lived seriously, implies that people have no right to destroy the planet's ecosystem for profit, kill animals for their skins, or restrict other people's liberties. cummings's attitude to time, of living fully in the present and making the most of your time, is expressed in 'if everything happens that can't be done'. It is a celebration of growth and movement, and love. 'i carry your heart with me / i carry it in' is another lyric sonnet on a traditional theme, that of love as the motive force in the poet's life. Love and life as a cyclical process are again emphasised by making the last line identical to the first, an unusual device in a sonnet.

As well as personal and sexual love, cummings is a love poet in a more general sense. There are notable poems to his parents and poems about praiseworthy individuals, such as 'rain or hail' (CP, 568). There are also many sonnets on the nature of love. 'love's function is to fabricate unknowingness' (CP, 446) announces cummings's anti-rationalising philosophy in its first line. It is a poem where death is accepted as a natural process because love can transcend death and time. 'love is more thicker than forget' (CP, 530), in four short rhymed stanzas, gives a definition of love and the conditions under which love is encountered. Love is the permanent source of life and energy. 'nothing false and possible is love' (CP, 574) is another modernised sonnet, employed to define the truth of love and lovers. Love is the positive force in the world, with its own moral laws, 'love is a universe beyond obey / or command'. 'true lovers in each happening of their hearts' (CP, 576) is a sonnet where the normal form is only slightly modified by half rhymes. True lovers enjoy the secret of life, and heart wins over the mere mind's 'poor pretend'. The effect of 'loves own secret' is the subject of 'if (touched by love's own secret) we, like homing' (CP, 659). Mundane reality is negated by love and most people are 'contented fools' unable to 'envision the mystery of freedom'. The ordinary time-bound world is dismissed as a mechanical hoax. 'being as to timelessness as it's to time' (CP, 768) is a sonnet of affirmation, of faith in a world where love is a real presence. cummings's cyclical view is again on offer, but the second stanza answers a question some readers may wish to put to the poet,

> (do lovers suffer? all diversities
> proudly descending put on death pull flesh:
> are lovers glad? only their smallest joy's
> a universe emerging from a wish)
>
> (CP, 768)

The third stanza is a series of paradoxes designed to illustrate the all controlling, all conquering nature of love, and the poem ends with another swipe at intellectuals, whom cummings considers fools.

Many of the love poems are also a celebration of nature or the external world, and poems about nature make up some 20 per cent of his output. One of the best known, 'in Just' (CP, 27) celebrates the arrival of spring from a children's point of view and introduces the satyric lame balloonman, perhaps cummings's best-known creation. 'Spring is like a perhaps hand' (CP, 197) presents spring as the renewer of life made dull and familiar by winter, gently rearranging the world while people stare, as their faculties are awakened. 'may my heart always be open to little' (CP, 481) illustrates what cummings takes to be a proper attitude to nature, while 'anyone lived in a pretty howtown' (CP, 515) shows the townspeople living according to the natural procession of the seasons, with 'anyone' contracted to 'noone'. 'i thank You God for most this amazing' (CP, 663) is a sonnet of praise, one of the very few cummings poems in which God is addressed directly. It expresses delight and wonder 'for the leaping greenly spirits of trees', and alludes to the death and rebirth myth of Osiris, of which the Christ story is a version in anthropological terms. Nature is taken as proof of the existence of God, and the poem represents a precious moment of transcendent awareness.

Many more examples could be given, as very few of cummings's poems are located indoors, although some are spoken by drunks or set in bars. The most striking absence from his output is poems about work and routine. In this respect, more than any other poet of his generation, more so than either Pound or Hart Crane, cummings is one of Trotsky's 'bourgeois bohemians'. He probably regarded most work as useless toil, something which made individuals into most people or unpeople. For this reason cummings is not a social poet in the way Williams is. He is concerned to celebrate the lover and the individual, and attacks anyone or anything which threatens people's ability to achieve their full potential as individuals. The other striking absence is poems of meditation, since, apart from hate poems and love poems of various sorts, descriptive poems and poems of praise make up nearly half the total. Satire is also well represented, making up some 20 per cent of his output, with poems of reflection and persuasion representing smaller groupings. A typical cummings poem might well be a sonnet praising lovers and Spring.

cummings's language is probably the most varied of any modern American poet, yet he is often regarded as a comic or burlesque poet. He has, in fact, three main types of language, the mock or burlesque, a neutral register, and a formal or archaic tone. cummings is skilled at mixing linguistic registers within poems, and varying the effects within forms such as sonnets, and types such as satires. He is also famous for his use of typography, mixing capitals and lower case, and splitting phrases and words in unusual places. This is not an aberration, or an attempt to shock the reader. Although he has possibly the most highly developed visual sense of any modern poet, he breaks and remakes the visual mould of the poem for primarily auditory reasons. cummings has a scrupulous concern to aid the reader in realising the sound of the poem. A poem such as 'she being Brand', or 'ygUDuh' (CP, 547) is laid out for the purpose of giving the reader a precise guide to the sound of the text. 'ygUDuh' is spoken by an aggressive drunk, and is an exact portrait of the sort of bigot we all hope never to meet in a bar, and cummings presents this stream of bigotry without editorialising or comment. Poems like this show that cummings had a strong grasp of localism and objectivism, and could be as much the Modernist, in that sense, as the next poet when he chose.

cummings is also well known for the liberties he took with the English language, which fall into three main categories. The first is his characteristic variation of the normal subject – predicate – object word order in sentences. This is sometimes done for metrical reasons, although he very rarely resorted to old-fashioned poetic inversion: 'anyone lived in a pretty how town', is a good example. If the second line '(with up so floating many bells down)' (CP, 515) is reconstituted as 'with so many bells floating up [and] down', it not only destroys the rhythm but confuses the meaning. cummings's arrangement has rhythmic intensity, a visual image of the moving bells, and an idea of many different bells sounding simultaneously. We are also reminded that the normal linear word order in English locks our thinking about time and space into a mode which post-Einsteinian science has shown to be non-valid, however convenient for mundane use.

The second of cummings's characteristic strategies is his systematic conversion of verbs into nouns. These grammatical shifts convey both cummings's tone and his attitude to the world, as in 'he sang his didn't he danced his did' (CP, 515). In fact more parts of speech, such as adverbs, pronouns, adjectives and conjunctions, are converted into nouns. cummings also employs his conversion technique for rhythmical effects, and effects of rhetorical ambiguity, by inserting adverbs into subordinate adjectival clauses, so we get 'the slowly town' or 'your suddenly body'.

cummings's third strategy is more idiosyncratic, and perhaps derives from his classical education. His English behaves like an inflected language such as Greek or Latin, with their case endings. In these languages the same phrase can be modified and even reversed by the suffixes on each word (hence the old 'man bites dog' joke). By using prefixes such as 'un', cummings created a distinctive conceptual vocabulary, such as 'unmind', 'undeath', 'unpeople', and 'fools of unbeing'. The dislocations practised by cummings are carefully calculated and require a corresponding effort on the part of the reader, similar to the demands of Pound's ideogrammic method. Often, reading a cummings poem requires an analysis of the syntax and a synthesis of the poem into 'normal' word-order and arrangement. This more active reading process involves the reader in a creative partnership with the writer and was one of the prime aims of the Modernist project. In this sense, cummings's textual strategies are analogous to those of Bertolt Brecht's alienation effect, or the Russian Formalists whose notion of 'ostranenie' or making strange, a technique of defamiliarisation, was intended to renew both literature and the world for the reader. Like the French Surrealists, cummings was a profoundly serious artist, who employed wit and satire in his assault on the bourgeois value system most people were compromised into accepting. The view of cummings as the comic poet of Romantic humanism is finally a limiting one, although at times he appears to resemble W. C. Fields in his outrageous misanthropy.

cummings's love for the natural world and those free individuals who are able to love and be loved, makes him a true heir of

Emerson, and he represents the end of the New England Transcendentalist tradition. cummings was a radical in his metaphysics and his attitudes to society, like Emerson, but he is also radical in his use of poetic language in ways not available to Emerson. Although an anti-intellectual, a good proportion of his satires are concerned with ideas or concepts, albeit expressed in a playful fashion. cummings revitalised the lyric as a poetic form, and invented both a language and a way of using language which constitute a fresh look at the world. It is an invitation to readers to examine their own lives and the role of the individual in Western civilisation. While making full use of the English lyric tradition, cummings remains in many ways ahead of his time; he is at once the most modern of traditionalists and the most traditional of Modernists.

NOTE

1.　All quotations are taken from e. e. cummings, *The Complete Poems, 1910–1962*, ed. George James Firmage (London: Granada, 1981), page numbers are given after quotes, e.g. (CP, 515).

10

Objectivism

RICHARD BRADBURY

In the end, most of them decided Objectivism as a movement hadn't ever existed, even though it was how they themselves had been defined. What was more to the point was how they differed: what they thought they were when they were on their own with the paper or the typewriter; what they thought of Pound and how that had changed over the years and changed them with it. That's a thought we'd share with them, that difference was more important.

Not that they'd always thought that way. There had been a time, for one of them at least, when an identification outwards and to others had been the most important of all the materials out of which we weave.[1] But that had stopped him writing. For twenty-five years. Long enough to be forgotten, so that when he re-appeared it was like new. Of course, carrying on hadn't been a guarantee that they would be known or even just remembered (like some old corner of childhood when we are all younger, fresher and more naive and therefore can be forgiven for the grandiose illusion). Anthologisers went round them. They were behind the Sandburg hills, cul-de-sacs off Williams road, and then simply just not there, like the Native Americans in Asher B. Durand's painting 'Kindred Spirits'. 'The Groundhog' was in; *A*, 'Testimony', 'The Materials' out. And even when in, never near the heart and never with their best voice. But they come back, repeatedly and pressing their claim into ears never offered the chance. And when offered …

I sat all night at a kitchen table at my first encounter with Niedecker's *Condensary* and even now her opening lines stick with me.[2] My arms full of books, I meet a student in the trees and answer his question with

> And yet at night
Their weight is part of mine.
For we are all housed now, all in our apartments,

131

The world untended to, unwatched.
And there is nothing left out there
As night falls, but the rocks[3]

It happens repeatedly, that someone opens this door a crack and others follow, knowing this is what they want from the first taste. This precise sagacity. I can still hear a tape of Oppen reading 'Of Being Numerous', the distant New York car sounds counterpointing against the Wroclaw trams' nearer squeals and neither distracting the listening minds as the cities grated against each other.

It began with a constellation's forming, a gathering in of many parts. As Matthiessen said in another context, 'a good deal depended upon accidents'.[4] The irony of Harriet Monroe hiring Louis Zukofsky to arbitrate publication for *Poetry* magazine. The two-sided triangle (three-sided square?) which seemed to dominate American literary history when I first learned it – Pound, Williams, (Olson), ((Zukofsky)). Of course this doesn't work as a model, we learn more by learning more, but at the very least someone could have mentioned his name along the way, as in 'of course there was another poet of the time with whom Pound had bitter arguments about his economics, his anti-semitism'. Zukofsky's editorial policy touching a heart and mind in Wisconsin, sparking the confidence with which Lorine Niedecker toiled thereafter until final dumbness interrupted. The same policy giving the 'movement' its name – even though the word should always be apostrophised – *An 'Objectivists' Anthology*.

The objective was the object. Since Pound's sidling to H.D. and Richard Aldington's table to tell them that Imagism was born and they were it, the drive among the vanguard of the poets had been the pursuit of the object through the mechanism of straight talk with no slithering into unnecessary adjectives, metaphors or similes. 'Direct treatment of the thing whether subjective or objective'.[5] Pound's attention wandered, sectarianism proliferated and Imagism(e) ran into the desert sands. A trace left behind that we can see on the map but hardly a highway we'd follow.

Then four men sat down together in New York, in Brooklyn, and talked *Objectivism*.

the poem, like every other form of art, is an object, an object that in itself formally presents its case and its meaning by the very form it assumes. Therefore, being an object, it should be so treated and controlled. ... The poem being an object (like a symphony or a cubist painting) it must be the purpose of the poet to make of his words a new form: to invent, that is, an object consonant with his day. ... Oppen supplied the money, as much as any of us. We had some small success, but few followers. I for one believe that it was Gertrude Stein, for her formal insistence on words in their literal, structural quality of being words, who had strongly influenced us. ... Nothing much happened in the end.[6]

Much must mean many. Achievement can come in smaller packages, a line which sticks and holds in the memory when others fade into the endless page-turning.

Reznikoff had been writing some years by this point, and Zukofsky could find in a meditation out of his work another point for the manifesto (which never got written).

Writing occurs which is the detail, not mirage, of seeing, of thinking with the things as they exist, and of directing them along a line of melody.[7]

With the emphasis at different points, this sentence constitutes not just a statement, but almost a history of my object. The drive towards seeing straight, the gap that opens when the gaze shifts from the physical world to the social, the 340-page masque with which *A* concludes.

Seeing the object straight, seeing the poem as object, seeing words as literally there, all this means scraping away the detritus of expectation and habit until what is actually there liberates the intelligence. But what is actually there? Can we see gravity, or just its effects? Can we see society, or just its effects? We can see a skyscraper, but what does it mean? Is the object itself separable from what it means?

I spend my time telling students not to ask rhetorical questions. These are here because, bad rhetorical questions as I hope they are, their answers are always at least double.

Almost as soon as that small community of men assembled, it dispersed. (Where were the women? Flossie Williams wouldn't have gone, but Celia Zukofsky and Mary Oppen were co-authors, 'whose words are entangled inextricably'.)[8] The Oppens went East to France and the business of keeping the presses going, the Zukofskys went West to Wisconsin, Williams went back to Rutherford, New Jersey, even Reznikoff eventually went to Hollywood. Almost as soon as the first root was pushed into the fertile soil of Brooklyn, it was dug up and constantly transplanted. As far as I can tell, they never all sat down together again. And this is not just biographical information because movements need communities, people drinking wine and coffee, walking together, going on and on and on.[9] Letters are a poor replacement, the telephone a bare substitute, for that going on. They'll do, and when the parts were scattered as these were later they became lifelines thrown into the world's currents, but they are fossils of diversity without that verbal agreement that punctuates conversation. We readers acquire richness of difference now, but they had isolation for breakfast every day for years.

After the statements had been made, though, the work still remained to be done. The manifesto was written but, like any election promise, its words could be pushed aside.

For a work that was to go so far off the track that it wouldn't (couldn't) be seen by more than the fewest, *A* begins with a characteristic gesture, almost a cliché of modern poetry. The moment from the past held against the present to offer some handle on the present, something safe to clutch in the confusing days of the twentieth century. Here, it is Bach, playing in the very first line of this epic. Playing on the brink of the disaster. From here on for the first 20/25 pages, Zukofsky is getting his resources organised. Beginning to gain the momentum for a life's work, and part of that mobilisation is the conventional attitudes. Reading again at this poem, I was surprised by how conventional I found its opening. How conventional, and yet this time I could see the later major themes being practised in a minor key. The edge between the public world and the private space: if Ricky is Whittaker Chambers's brother, who is Kay?; can Bach's gestures at the grand order come over into this world two hundred and one years later?

In this it doesn't have the GRAB of the Cantos, no imperious voice demanding our attention early. But it is a little voice nagging at the fringe of the intelligence, suggesting that there is purpose here and that purpose is not setting Bach against Beiderbecke, Baroque against jazz, as a way of running down the second halves of the equation. No, history and change are the large presences. How we got here, how we go somewhere else. That idea, though, is always coming up against Art, against a will to order that goes outside history. That's the principle behind Kay, which gets argued out early (and then re-appears later, but we'll get to that).

So, while Pound arranges his authorities, Zukofsky arranges his early counterparts. And for a fair few of those sources gets the big stick from that happy band who read him before the 1978 complete edition at least made the efforts available. Duncan sees Stalin behind every reference to Marx and Lenin, even though Eric Homberger has made it clear that there was some deal of space between the CPUSA and poetry of this kind.[10] Burton Hatlen has to explain in words of one syllable to Reno Odlin that not every Marxist was/is a Stalinist.[11] And if that wasn't enough, the charge of obscurity, unreadability accelerates as the years and the poems pass. So, Zukofsky gets it from every way. When he's public and simple – he's attacked for what he's saying, and when he's private and difficult, he's attacked for the way in which he says whatever it is he's saying.[12]

What he's saying, it seems to me, is simple. One) that despite all the arguments to the contrary, art and its will to order can't be separated from the movement of history. Further) that that engagement with history looks the world in the eye and sees that change is only possible through labour, through activity. 'Men make their own history, but not in circumstances of their own choosing.' While Stalinism bears down hard on the latter half of this proposition, it seems to me blindingly obvious that anyone who devotes his life to writing an 826-page poem, at the very lowest level, sees the force of the first half, and further, that that commitment opens a philosophical space between Zukofsky and Stalinism. Last) (and this only comes slowly) that neither of these propositions is easy (simple, yes, but that's another matter) because there is a constant, a dialectical, interchange going on all the time between life's various demands. One of the courses *A* sketches is the routes taken by the political in the USA from 1930 to 1978; the rising and falling curve of activism and commitment to a world beyond domesticity.

Zukofsky's skill is in his depiction of the force with which each side of the equation strikes him. So, he's never apologetic for his thirties Marxism and he's never apologetic for his fifties love of Celia and Paul. Each side is real, not to be written out. It is with the reader to annotate this text by reference to the narratives beyond the poem.

One of those narratives is his engagement with Pound. As a co-worker, in letters, but above all in the poetics. When so many claim *A* as a Poundian poem, we need to see what that means. At the most obvious and to paraphrase Basil Bunting, Pound's work is the Alps. It is there, you can't go round it so you either have to sit down and wait for it to erode away, or you have to come to terms with it. In whatever way. Burton Hatlen divides Poundians into three groups: the neo-fascists; those who separate the poetry from the politics; and those who struggle to 'understand the sequence of events which led a by-no-means violent or authoritarian man to become an apologist, both in his poetry and elsewhere, for a political movement which glorifies violence and which was in practice both brutal and tyrannical'.[13] This is sharpened when we remember the paradoxical closeness of these two, the anti-communist anti-semite and the Marxist jew.[14]

So what did Zukofsky carry from Pound into *A*? The sense of the epic as a poem containing history, obviously, and a 'Poundian' mode which dominates *A1* to *A7*: juxtaposition and energy. But then there is the first of the caesuras I'm working towards. The gap from 1930 and *A7* to 1935 and *A8*. The Marxism, the activism becomes clearer. This poem, this *A8*, is James McLaughlin's 'epic of the class struggle' – that's history of a different order to Pound's sense – and it's also dialectical in the most slippery Hegelian sense. The theses aren't fixed, aren't transcendental in the way that they so often are in the *Cantos*. All is historicised, including the discipline of history. For the poetics, that means a move from a Poundian mode towards a Rukeyserian assembly of materials.[15] History goes up against and alongside other senses of history, autobiography. The gradation of importance and revelation is taken out, and everything begins to count.

It's an impossible aesthetic in the light of the Spanish defeat, the Stalin/Hitler pact, World War 2, Joe McCarthy, the bomb, the worst of the materials of the Forties. It's both too public and too private, at the same time. It's vulgar in the same way that Benjamin once described Brecht as being 'plumpes', daring those connections between phenomena into the light of scrutiny. Zukofsky begins to take long breaks from writing *A*, and when he comes back, each time it's a different poem he starts writing. Nothing from 1940 to 1948, a flurry from 1948 to 1951, and then again nothing until 1960, and then a stumbling sequence with shorter breaks until his death. Each time, he adjusts, goes further into himself until the home minutiae become a difficult allegory of that divorce between home and politics, of the burial of the Thirties and their legacy. And an allegory of the best kind, one in which the terms aren't interchangeable (this means that) but take on a force of their own. 'Love' 'does' 'replace' 'politics'.

That gradual substitution of personal terms for those more accessible is clearly at the root of Zukofsky's 'difficulty'. We just don't know enough, if anyone did know enough it would have been Celia and she was never sure of everything. The drift was towards a recognition that the private life, the internal world, was perhaps just not open for another, perhaps because its contours were not clear even/especially to the subject. What is clear, as we read on to the end of *A*, is that a substitution is taking place; one set of values is inexorably being complemented (rather than replaced) by another set. At its simplest, Karl (Marx) is joined by Paul (Zukofsky's son) in the sources of meaning. Other value systems begin to overlay that initial distinction between art and history, until the antagonism between static and dynamic becomes multiplicitous – a dynamic in itself. That dynamism is a constant, as is music. Together they make the broad outlines of this daybook 50 years in the writing, and then we can overlay history onto this study to see this autobiography (feeble word!) something like complete.

Part of that personalising was the severing of connections, the quarelling with the cohorts. A little of this comes from the internal dynamics of the small group, the way in which they take lukewarm tensions and boil them up in a small pot. Another part is the specifics of the case, the need to cut away the outside. Very, very few knew his name, his work by the late 50s and his paradoxical response was to pull away from most of them. The impulse inwards filled more than just the work.

Oppen's different voice consisted, at root, of the apparent absence of personality. His work looks and reads as objective and therefore as objectivist. Both the terms and the connection are false. They may look, they may read, as objective but in the hearing the tremble and rage obvious later are there from the first. Their (the Oppens were, in their own estimation, and are, in mine, a part) voice redefines objective. Not valueless but seeing clear. In every account and in every reading I make, George looks hard. Keeps still and looks until what is *there* appears from what seems. The technique is an eye for an 'I', and a prosody which heaves words apart before re-combining them in other ways. This is Hegel, Marx and his other philosophical sources at work. The chaos of reality is broken down into its abstract constituent parts and then re-assembled into coherence, into something which makes sense.

This method has little in common with the tub-thump and the moralising that passed for socialist writing in the Thirties. When Mike Gold was in charge of cultural production and Richard Wright's unfortunate 'I Have Seen Black Hands' was held as among the best examples for poetry, it is easy to see why George and Mary should have wanted to separate their writing from their politics. Seeing the imperative for political activity, they chose to be activists but equally well saw that they were incapable of filling Gold's prescriptions for what he saw as political writing and locked into self-denial for a quarter-century. One of the tinier prices we pay for the legacy of Stalinism is the poems lost in those years. Religious sentiment – with Stalin as the Father rather than just as Uncle Joe – supplanted philosophical understanding in so much of Stalinism and the faults were at their clearest in the debates about literature.

The first stage of that, not first stage in a chronological sense but in the sense of laying down a basis, was developing procedures for seeing clear and then speaking that clarity into poetry. It recurs right to the end of George and Mary's work, this need to go back and start over again with this basic, this clearing-out of the eyes.

It was also, of course, a clearing-out of the 'I's. The personal is there, of course it is, how could it not be, but it functions as representative. The political commitment, the going to war, the city. The range of the work reads almost as a history of the American twentieth century.

At the points when this work has been most completed and the poetry is achieved, the quality of pellucidity is such that it almost redefines what is poetic diction. It is quietly direct. Go over to the bookshelf, take down the *Collected Poems* and begin to read 'Of Being Numerous'. Is there anything here which is not immediately comprehensible? Pellucid, however, also implies a depth into which one would look repeatedly. Having looked in once, you will find yourself back at this pool's edge, pondering on that use of 'curious' as the sequence's last word.

This simplicity though is not simplistic, in the way that Mike Gold condescended to his audience. Stalinism assumed that only the lowest level of work was good enough for a proletarian audience; which makes for bad art and reveals a great deal about their thinking on the working class. Oppen assumed that a working-class reader would find no difficulty in his work because the hard labour had been done to make clear what was being said, and it didn't condescend.

If Reznikoff's work replaces Oppen's terse clarity with an exposition the narrative of which carries the work close to what we know more ordinarily as poetry, it does share roots in the urban and the drive to tell a history. *By the Waters of Manhattan*, a title to express the urge to collect together poems about the qualities of life within the city. *Testimony: the United States (1885–1915)* allows its characters, those people Reznikoff found in his endless reading of law texts, to speak for themselves and tell the history of a United States not so united, but rather, riven by contradictions.

In recording what he sees, Reznikoff's documentary has an accessibility of a different order from Oppen's. The former has a narrative which carries one forward with it, whilst the latter invites the reader to pause with an image. The difference may be that Reznikoff has little belief in the good society, seeing mostly how history's motion has carried utopias under, whilst Oppen holds close to the idea he found in Kierkegaard – 'He who will not work shall not eat ... but he who will work shall give birth to his own father.'[16] Carl Rakosi sums up Oppen in so many ways when he writes that he knew George for years even though they only met after nearly 40 years, and that when they did he had the impression of Oppen as a tree which stood still and endured. In the chosen silence was the refusal to participate in a world which danced on from one word, image, gesture to the next and the decision that there were, there are, words, images, gestures to which it is productive to return. Reznikoff's chronicle parallels the motions of capitalism's endless renewal whilst Oppen's sternly resists it.

By 1941, along with many another, the light of the first stage of objectivism had guttered out. Oppen's Communist Party activism led him into uniform, fighting in the good war, while the others were appalled by the news from Europe in other ways. Reznikoff found a mechanism in the documentary style of *Holocaust* which echoes Hannah Arendt's studies in the banality of evil in its use of detachment as the only way to look at this horror. For my other three subjects, though, silence or but the most oblique gesture were the only way of coming to terms with this denial of the taproot of their work, their humanism. This is speculation, of course, for silence is the human activity least open to interpretation.

These private silences were matched by a public silence which removed these writers and their influences from the anthologies, from readers. They sank beneath the surface of the postwar philistine mire. Their business did not cease, however. Oppen put as much into carpentry in his Mexico exile as he had into his activism, his poetry; Zukofsky kept on writing, even though the audience shrank until it was almost entirely perceptible; Reznikoff turned to publishing himself when no-one else would. The three kept going, beneath the surface. In that sense there were part of that drift which makes the Fifties so interesting. The surface shows so little, but there just beneath the surface – like the trout which patrolled us as I walked round a lake with my son – the work carried on.

Even when they did break surface it was only to cause small ripples. The first head up was none of these three but that voice from out there that Zukofsky had heard in the Thirties.

She was the unlikeliest poet, if one uses the banal measures. In a photograph, sitting in front of her house at Black Hawk Island, she is wearing a sensible house dress and wing-tipped glasses. A picture taken in 1967 and it's clear that she's not going to be wearing any flowers in her hair. A picture taken by Gail Roub, to whom a volume of the poetry had been given with the injunction to say nothing of its contents or author to anyone who might know her. A picture taken within a few miles of her birthplace and long-term home; she only travelled away to any physical distance once, to work in Milwaukee. And just to confirm the parallels to Emily Dickinson, there is the same tone of mixed hesitancy and confidence in her letter to Cid Corman offering poems as Dickinson had needed to Thomas Higginson. It's the same cultivated surface which draws no attention to itself, the air of conventionality behind which the poet's work goes on undistracted. Both pursued accuracy with a vengeance, by battering away day after day at language until it fitted the purpose, until the tool had been shaped to the hand.[17] The distances they construct between themselves and beyond are cunning because they conceal the connection between the two. So many critics assume that Emily Dickinson didn't go next door to meet Emerson because she didn't know, poor thing, who he was; perhaps she didn't need to go. The same pattern operates with Niedecker, who didn't need to travel because the world came to her. She is the prime example of the local poet who has entirely eschewed parochialism. Thoroughly rooted in place, but not tied down. Not hemmed in by the parish's narrow demand. The letters were her substitute for daily conversation, they are the medium which has the exact blend of intimacy and distance which makes her writing tick. She seems so distant from the machinery of the world, until she declares

> I am sick with the Time's buying sickness.
> The overdear oil drum now flanged to my house
> serves a stove not costing as much.
> I need a piano.[18]

And when she died, of course, she went unremarked within the institution, within the establishment, within the town where she had lived all her life. If that follows in Dickinson's footsteps, it also sketches a paradigm of the Objectivists. The ironic motions of literary history tied them together with Pound and they were convicted as guilty by association – about as just as a South African trial. What saves them is their fragmentation, their loss of a sense of collective purpose. What saves them is the death of Objectivism. That ended with the knowledge that that constellation had exploded, scattering its fragments so far that they were lost to each other.

Lost because the common purpose of writing poetry was never going to be enough to hold them together. They were so different, the urban Oppen, Lorine Niedecker from Fort Atkinson, the myopic and deeply learned Zukofsky, the toiling and equally learned Reznikoff. Objectivism gave them a respect for language and sight, but being Objectivists made them poets. Each one of them negotiated a relationship between the two terms which was, in the end, determined by their politics beyond the poem.

NOTES

1. George Oppen, 'Disasters', *Primitive* (London: Black Sparrow Press) p. 11.
2. Lorine Niedecker, 'Paen to Place', *From this Condensary*, pp. 215–16.
3. George Oppen, 'Myself I Sing', *Collected Poems*, p. 36.
4. F. O. Matthiessen, *From the Heart of Europe*, p. 72.
5. F. S. Flint, 'Imagisme', quoted in Richard Gray, *American Poetry in the Twentieth Century*, p. 54.
6. William Carlos Williams, *The Autobiography of William Carlos Williams*, pp. 264–5.
7. Louis Zukofsky, *Poetry*, February 1931, p. 273.
8. From the dedication to Mary Oppen of George Oppen's *Collected Poems*.
9. Russell Jacoby's *The Last Intellectuals* makes this point clear.
10. Eric Homberger, *American Writers and Radical Politics: 1900–1939* (London: Macmillan, 1986).
11. See especially, Burton Hatlen, 'Zukofsky and/or Stalin', *Paideuma*, vol. 8, 1, and 'Re Reno Odlin: a Riposte', *Paideuma*, vol. 9, no. 2.
12. Louis Zukofsky, *A*, p. 61.
13. Hatlen, 'Zukofsky and/or Stalin', p. 582.
14. I use the lower case version of the word to mean the absence of religious connection and the existence of a social positioning.
15. Read *A8* alongside *Theory of Flight* or *US 1* to see this!
16. Oppen, *Collected Poems*, p. 158.
17. The effect, I hope, of reading her work is that it infiltrates the writing of the reader; my copy of *From this Condensary* was bought cheap because it was not damaged but hurt.
18. Niedecker, *From this Condensary*, p. 96.

11

Frank O'Hara

ERIC MOTTRAM

How to create a demonstration of style under personal and social–political pressures, without absurd egoism or absurd poses of subsuming individuality in some totalitarian control of surface – by dogma of some kind that brandishes itself as impersonal, all artifice, resistant to inventive art and social change: that is Frank O'Hara's programme. How to say 'I', or to display 'I', without imposition, to resist that common dullness in poetry insistent on the poet's life and daily existence being interesting, without showing differences of experience to anyone else. How to include sexuality without the vulgar insistence, common today, that the author is the only one who really knows about it, one way or another. How to speak of enjoyment without gush or superiority. How to produce an object, the poem, which gives pleasure through constant poise, flexibility and humour, and resistant to the enslavements of closure. How to work out the desire for an urbane style in a society bent on accelerated desires for rapid consumption. Andrew Marvell, being inside both the state of Charles I and Oliver Cromwell, created a writing we still admire: 'the high speed, the succession of concentrated images', 'wit ... fused into the imagination', 'a balance and proportion of tones' (T. S. Eliot on Marvell in 1921).[1] How to create a body of work which is recognisably from one career, a career in style which resists oppressive self-engagement by creating an article that presents itself as spontaneity rather than a product of applied logic and pre-cooked subject material. Frank O'Hara, like the great jazz artists of the 1950s and 1960s, achieves his own skilled performance within the immediate sociality of a group, and within the poetics or history of his art – Bud Powell, Charlie Parker, Keith Jarrett, resister of consumerism, and of that condition defined by William Burroughs in 1961: 'The junk merchant does not sell his product to the consumer, he sells the consumer to his product'. The purpose of art is not propaganda and

143

addiction – forms of control by repetition: 'Assuming a self-right-eous position is nothing to the purpose unless your purpose is to keep the junk virus in operation. And junk is big industry ...'[2]

The characteristic mistake of critics against O'Hara is to condemn his work as 'little more than personality', 'a musing whimsy' of voice, the 'sanctification' of something called 'naturalness', and falsely contrived 'honesty' and 'directness'.[3] But in fact O'Hara is a social poet of constant alertness in the city, expressed through the analytical wit and humour of a man aware of the violence and decay of his environment. Replying to an aggressive attack on the poet in San Francisco, Bill Berkson, one of the best writers on his friend's poetry, said – and his irony is palpable:[4]

What strikes me reading any of his criticism or poems, is that his terminology for art is a terminology of social life. And his term-inology for social life he could also borrow from the stock pile of art criticism. That seems to make living in the total language more possible, make it total, rather than have specialized lan-guages for special experiences. ... We say De Kooning does this. We say Pollock ... A curiosity of art production is that it is done by people. You name the name and call up a body of work.

O'Hara's poems often use named composers of music, artists in the cinema, painters, poets, and friends who are not any of these. This is his social milieu: New York City, the Museum of Modern Art (MOMA) in New York, where he became a senior curator, and the poets and painters of the city in years when American painting and sculpture entered particular strengths into the history of twen-tieth-century Western art. It is a society that resisted, and resists, stasis, prefers mobility, loves first names and almost enforces so-ciality through them. Living in New York requires virtuosity if you intend to survive. O'Hara liked such virtuoso performance, an urban ideal. In his memoir of the poet, the composer Morton Feldman – he composed the music for the celebrated film of Pollock in action, and *For Frank O'Hara* in 1973[5] – wrote: 'He loved virtuos-ity, loved the pyrotechnics of it'. And: 'Frank O'Hara was the "poet Laureate" of the New York art world during the 1950s.'[6] The non-human Other – those growths and strata customarily termed 'nature', or even 'Nature' – had to be located in the urban, or dislo-cated, or practically parodied in poetic usages ('nature', in cities is parks and back yards). In his second book of poems, *Meditations in an Emergency* (1957), the title poem's humour is critical at just this point.[7]

> Even trees understand me! Good heavens, I lie under them, too, don't I? I'm just a pile of leaves.
> However, I have never clogged myself with the praises of pastoral life, nor with nostalgia for an innocent past of perverted acts in pastures. No. One need never leave the confines of New York to get all the greenery one wishes – I can't even enjoy a blade of grass unless I know there's a subway handy, or a record store or some other sign that people do not totally *regret* life. It is more important to affirm the least sincere; the clouds get enough attention as it is and even they continue to pass. Do they know what they're missing? Uh huh.

These are park trees. The erotics and nostalgias of romantic pastoral inheritance in art or cultural convention are relegated, along with the pseudo-innocence of 'living in nature', as the greedy phrase has it, leaves of grass yearnings, and identity with clouds or anything non-human, except in amused parody. The subway and record store reassure you that you can get across town quickly to see friends, reach work, buy music performances. When a comparison between human and non-human is included, it jars because it intervenes in social relations. More importantly, however, the issue is the quality of discriminating attention, and the production of a condensed discourse to articulate it:

> … it's my duty to be attentive, I am needed by things as the sky must be above the earth. And lately, so great has *their* anxiety become, I can spare myself little sleep.

Williams's 'no ideas except in things' has shifted to an environment of things in city contexts (as in fact most of his were); that is, human contexts within an emotional field of anxious attention. The sky is over the city which is on the earth. It just *is* there. In 1959, five years later, Alain Robbe-Grillet criticises the pathetic, insistent need 'to establish a constant relation between the universe and the being who inhabits it':[8]

> Nature … – mineral, animal, vegetable Nature – is first of all clogged with an anthropomorphic vocabulary. … This Nature –

mountain, sea, forest, desert, valley – is simultaneously our model and our heart. ... It encrusts us, judges us, and ensures our salvation.

In O'Hara's poems of sexuality, what is taken as sexual separation, so often called natural or unnatural by the sexually nervous or stupid, is mocked. The so-called 'tragic sense of life' is resisted because through that, in Robbe-Grillet's terms, 'everything is lacerated, fissured, divided, displaced'. For O'Hara, that is self-destruction, suicidal conclusion of love, and anti-social. The extensive poem 'Biotherm (For Bill Berkson)' (1961–2), combines montage, collage, cross-cutting and the variable chronologies of memory to make sure that the flexibilities and adjustments of a relationship are survived as well as enjoyed and left behind. Love itself can destroy: it 'hides you in the bosom of another and I am always springing forth from it like the lotus – the ecstasy of always bursting forth! (but one must not be distracted by it!)'. O'Hara's lotus and hyacinth in *Meditations* ... are flowers as symbols of beauty within 'the filth of life' – a Buddhist essential symbol and an ancient Greek flower from the blood of Hyacinthus, victim of erotic jealousy between Apollo and Zephyrus. They operate in a 'greenhouse' rather than 'nature' – artifice, man-controlled growth, as in art. He adds: 'Destroy yourself, if you don't know!' The poem's emergency is being caught in love as a finality:

I admire you, beloved, for the trap you've set. It's like a final chapter no one reads because the plot is over.

Then he quotes Mrs Thrale's journal, the passage on her love for Fanny Brown, who has just run off: 'I wish she had a good whipping and 10,000 pounds.' (Mrs Thrale was Samuel Johnson's erotic friend and helped him with his sexual needs, such as padlocks.) The poet also escapes disguised – 'I'll be back, I'll re-emerge, defeated. ... It's only afternoon, there's a lot ahead. There won't be any mail downstairs. Turning, I spit in the lock and the knot turns.' (Bruce Boone has nothing to say about this poem in his essay 'Gay Language as Political Praxis: The Poetry of Frank O'Hara'[9]). Resilience and a thoroughly urbane experience of how to handle such a situation retrieve what can be retrieved. The event is reconstituted and socially situated. This is a poem not a fragment of autobiography. This process is explicit in a long poem called *In*

Memory of my Feelings, addressed to the painter Grace Hartigan in 1956, as 'Biotherm' is addressed to the poet Bill Berkson. It is also the title poem of the book edited by Berkson for the Museum of Modern Art in 1967, combining each of thirty poems with works by American artists, most of whom appear directly in O'Hara's poetry: De Kooning, Helen Frankenthaler, Guston, Jasper Johns, Lichtenstein, Motherwell, Joan Mitchell, Nakian, Barnet Newman, Claes Oldenberg, Rauschenberg and Larry Rivers: a memorial tribute by friends of a thoroughly social poet and curator of their art.[10]

In the poem, 'loves' contains a range of experience from O'Hara's life, a definition of how active the word is in our lives. He began working at MOMA in 1951, and for *Art News* in 1953. By 1965 he became assistant curator. That is, he was professional of the visual arts without being a painter (the memorial volume is prefaced by his poem 'Why I am not a painter', 1956), a major organiser of exhibitions, and a central art critic whose language in that field is as creative as his language for poetry. His sense of organisation, in a large poem and in a characteristically large American painting of the 1945–65 decades, can be articulated through Harold Rosenberg, the finest American art critic of the period, especially in the procedures and products known as Action Painting: 'an arena in which to act', rather than a static object, an 'event' rather than a fixture, a record of process. And, it is consistently implied, a work to be 'read' as that, as a compositional procedure.[11] It is mistaken to speak of 'the mimickry of the painterly surface in the first generation of New York School poets (John Ashbery, Kenneth Koch, Frank O'Hara)' and 'experimentation where it may have reached a dead end in painterly surface or performance values'. Rosenberg's whole 1952 passage is salutary in opposition to such superficiality:

> … an area in which to act – rather than as a space in which to re-produce, re-design, analyse or 'express' an object, actual or imagined. What was to go on the canvas was not a picture but an event. The painter no longer approached his easel with an image in his mind; he went up to it with material in his hand to do something to that other piece of material in front of him. The image would be the result of this encounter.

Further, to enlarge an approach to O'Hara, in 'A Dialogue with Thomas B. Hess' in 1958, Rosenberg said: 'Action painting is not "personal", though its subject matter is the artist's individual poss-ibilities'.[12] O'Hara's curatorial responsibilities were also part of a major national sponsored event: the international promotion of American art. (Serge Guilbaut's critical account absurdly mentions him only once, in a list of 'friends, promoters, and admirers of the abstract expressionist artists'. Certainly, he knew what he gave his energies and skills to. A colleague at MOMA, Waldo Rasmussen, supplied necessary information in his contribution to *Homage to Frank O'Hara* (1978):[14]

> I think the painters and sculptors gave Frank confidence. ... Essentially he was the artist's spokesman ... he managed to work within [the organisation of the Museum] and yet keep a distinct separation from it. It was a special quality of grace he had, and no mean feat. He had a wonderful facility for collab-orating with others without losing his own identity or unduly imposing it.

It is the kind of power O'Hara speaks of in his essay on Franz Kline:[15] 'power to move and to be moved'. Rasmussen believes this 'fed into his poetry, both as a creative model and as part of his subject matter ... his sensibility operating in the specific New York art world arena which was part of his life'. The fact – which eludes his strident critics – is that he was a professional, or as another col-league at MOMA said: 'It always surprised me how the poet, the dreamer, the man about town would pay attention not just to the major problems but to every tiny detail as well'.[16]

O'Hara carried an aura about him; he was unmistakably charis-matic. This same colleague recalls that, at a poetry reading, when he entered 'a sudden hush, a "frisson", went through the room ... the expectation ... the aura of excitement'. René d'Harnoncourt's preface to the memorial volume offers one further comment on his social poise: O'Hara's reactions to works of art were secure enough for him to obviate aggression – 'he had absolute integrity without self-righteousness'. The conclusion of 'In Memory of My Feelings' shows these issues under poetic control, in 1956. The tensions many artists experience between daily life and the processes of art are far from the dichotomies Boone insists on.

In part 1 of the numbers sections of the poem, the self is a man of 'transparencies' (the world includes the photographic meaning), of 'naked selves' protected by 'weapons'. One scene is a race track, with shouting bettors, which leaves one self 'brushed by tails, masked in dirt's lust, definition'. The 'terror' is irresistible, and is also given as 'love of the serpent'. At the sight of a 'smooth' hunter, 'the serpent's eyes redden'. Then the image transforms into 'transparent selves' that 'flail about like vipers in a pail' while 'the aquiline serpent – the eagle-like serpent, with hooked or beak head – 'resembles a Medusa' – a figure with serpent hair, whose aspect turns men to stone. (Graves reports that the Gorgon-head could be a prophylactic mask.)[17] In parts 2, 3 and 4, the drama of self in society and in sexual relationships becomes transparencies of selves as multiplicities layered into a mobile process, in a field of scenes and figures voyaging, racing, competing in sports, foreign, sexually androgynous, morally free and frequently outrageous. This 1956 song of my self arises from an open road of possibilities, often humorous, partly from autobiography, partly from fictions of heroes. The multiple routines are layered into one another in exhilaration, and with a nervous sense of liberation from static identity, that 'identified' in part 1.

Then the fifth and last section begins in a present differing from the past, and the memory-feeling process of the previous passages: 'And now it is the serpent's turn.' This self is then addressed: 'I am not quite you, but almost, the opposite of visionary.' That is, a force which is continuous through the multiple scenes. It controls the energy centre of the transparent selves, the heart and its ghosts, the figures and scenes to the poem. 'Since to move is to love', the poem as 'scrutiny' has to be 'syllogistic' – that is, an assumed logical argument based on fixed premises towards an inevitable conclusion. An ironic joke, since 'syllogism' has overtones of a serious or tricky argument. The serpent surrounds the heart. Then the hunted small antelope ('dikdik'), the white flags of peace proposals in warfare, and the hunter, are summarised as 'our democracy'. The serpent's body ripples behind his head, 'the naked host to my many selves' 'shot by a guerrilla warrior' or dumped into ferns, 'themselves *journalières*' – that is, everyday occurrences. The body is exposed to other figures, a target, an object used by heroes – that is, exposed to society, work and art. Feelings drawn out of memory now have to settle for a complex syntax of inevitability and resistance to it. Any sense of liberation – 'my life and opportunity sense unenclosed' – now has to experience degrees of closure. Memory moves into forgetting, experience moves into art, 'against my will / against my love'. Love itself is liable to form as a diseased rigidity, a singularity, a statue; to change it into history is impossible.

The last lines of this long poem face the next stage beyond the poem, and move into a silence which is the next part of life, beyond youthful thirties. That is, the occasion of this poem as not so much a syllogism as a number of stratagems, and, form another meaning from hunting, a system of detours, the turning of the hunted crea-ture as it eludes the hunters. The poet becomes a hunter of his own brief past – an act of courage and necessity.

The serpent emerges as the force of all his energies, something original to him. O'Hara would know the mythic force of 'serpent' as the figure of wounding and healing combined, the homeopathic principle, sacred in its powers. In Book 15 of *Metamorphoses*, Ovid has the Greek archetype of medicine, Asklepios, appear in a dream:

> Be not afraid; I shall come, and leave my statues,
> But see this serpent, as it twines around
> The rod I carry ...

Perhaps O'Hara recalled Lawrence's passage in *Apocalypse* (1931): 'a rustle in the grass can startle the toughest 'modern' to depths he has no control over' (which is quoted by Kerényi[18]); and the 1959 'Poem', on page 334 of the *Collected Poems*, is a radical appreciation of Lawrence 'when he writes of lust springing from the bowels' and his sense of light and darkness in lust. O'Hara's serpent survives will, art, transience, the hunter and the condition of the hunted.

In Memory of my Feeling in fact needs an even more extensive con-sideration as an example of his poetry exercising the field between reporting feelings – which may falsify them, watching the self's selves and reporting them – and being alert to life as performances to be scrutinised in as detached a way as possible. He admired Boris Pasternak's *Doctor Zhivago* poems as forms in which the indi-vidual self is accomplished in articulation:[19]

> It is plain that this hero must be an artist; to Pasternak the artist is
> the last repository of individual conscience, and in his terms
> conscience is individual perception of life.

This is not self-glorification but

> the accomplishment of the individual in the face of almost insu-
> perable sufferings which are personal and emotionally real,

never melodramatic and official. And it is the poet's duty to accomplish this articulation.

Such is O'Hara's sense of the poet's responsibility, and his knowledge of its action bears a strong alliance with Merleau-Ponty's declarations of the phenomenology of perception and its necessary responsibilities.

> The human individual is the subject of historical events, not vice versa; he is the repository of life's forces ... he knows that events require his participation to occur.

Then O'Hara speaks of Pasternak's poems beyond Zhivago's:

> ... the role taking over the actor ... the word consuming the poet, the drama of the moaning, which the poet has found through the act of creating this meaning, transporting him to an area of realisation beyond his power ...

In his 1956 poem, 'Cambridge', reminded of Pasternak, 'the Master', during cold weather, O'Hara considers 'where health comes from! His breath in the Urals ...':[20]

>   ... sponsored
> by the greatest living Russian poet at incalculable cost.
> Across the street there is a house under construction,
> abandoned to the rain. Secretly, I shall go to work on it.

O'Hara remains always alert for the moment when self-performance becomes self-regard and self-pity, when the role takes over entirely, and the artist is killed. It is the subject of his James Dean poems; in fact, frequently movie stars and scenario clichés exemplify the absurd comedy of suffering, even death, reduced to display. In one of his most popular poems, the danger is only just subverted by a sense of the ridiculous: the 1962 'Poem: Lana Turner has Collapsed'.[21] Poetic skill here is in the control of tonal levels so that the text is strict as well as funny. To risk fussing over the obvious – not so obvious to some readers, apparently – a display of definitions and particulars – the weather, the poet caught in the traffic, and slowed down from meeting the 'you' of the poem – a capitalised bit of commonplace advertisement-news appears:

'LANA TURNER HAS COLLAPSED!' – shifts gear into analysis, the difference between Hollywood and here, the poet's own behaviour at parties. The star must be at a party; it's scenario; all she needs is the fans' encouragement – 'oh Lana Turner we love you get up'. It's a comedy of absurd resurrection, serious, humorous, poised. The headline intervenes and then generates a complete poem – which is a rarity for most poets – and one that shows O'Hara's admiration for Pierre Reverdy, another poet with close alliances with painters (Matisse, Picasso, Braque ...). It is clear, for example, in his translation of 'Pour le moment' – 'Just for Now'.[22]

Finding the generative is a concern in many of O'Hara's poems, and one of the finest examples is another long poem, 'Ode to Michael Goldberg ('s Birth and Other Births)' (1958), a work to compare with Charles Olson's 'Ode on Nativity'. Goldberg is a painter who appears in 'Why I am not a Painter',[23] and who contributed the cover and title page for O'Hara's *Odes* in 1960. Again the action is a field of events, an arena of discoveries constructed in varying densities and kinds, a variety of tonal levels and linguistic approached, from conversational to philosophically eloquent. The notation of measures is also highly varied. The whole virtuosic performance exhilarates from its confident imaginative invention – demonstrating no end to the generative. The syllogistic game of beginning–middle–end is replaced by a field opened, entered and cultivated with materials until its survival is assured. The 'Lana Turner ...' existential humour of survival is given an extended energy and information.[24] One structural method is to let a phrase evoke a range of developments so that it becomes a motif, as in certain music systems (O'Hara studied a wide range of music all his life). Image-resonance and image-variation rather than immediate symbol completion enables him to unify without over-definition. The poem is a dramatisation of mobility. The generative is not once but continuous. The plot is by train from coast to coast in World War 2; this Pacific voyage in the Navy – which leads to 'I'd sail with you anywhere'; love moving out of winds in voyage towards wind movement which sounds like Stravinsky's *Rite of Spring*, and from that to 'art / as wildness'; movement towards death, compulsively, to political movement and cells like germs, the growth of conspiracies, flying as writing poetry.

His own birth once – 27 June 1926 – is made highly mobile:

> when I came moaning into my mother's world
> and tried to make it mine immediately

by screaming, sucking, urinating
and carrying on generally
it was quite a day.

Once again, what the world persists in calling 'self' can only be the
kind of mobility an American Indian believes in:

> I am really an Indian at heart, knowing it is all
> all over but my own ceaseless going, never
> to be just a hill of dreams and flint for someone later
> but a hull laved by the brilliant Celebes response,
> empty of treasure to the explorers who sailed me not
> King Philip's trail

The points of motionlessness in the poem are invaded by motion
– the divided impulses of this self:

> I'd like to stay
>   in this field forever
>   and think of nothing
> but these sounds
>   these smells and the tickling grasses
>   'up your ass, Sport'

The vipers of 'In Memory of my Feelings' are now 'un repaire de
vipères', a den of vipers, an unhappy necessity of having to live in
his 'pays natal'. Life is a combination – 'too much endlessness /
stored up, and in store' – and the poem's structure dramatises precisely that. The notational lay-out or design is a stall of examples.
City life has become the very design of such a life, speeds of transition in continuity and discontinuity , as it is in 'Second Avenue',
O'Hara's long 1953 poem 'in memory of Vladimir Mayakovsky',
another admiration of his, written and to be read, at least initially,
with the speeds and variety of the street.

The node, the still relationship, is friendship within life accelera-
tions, different from sexual transience and anxiety, but sometimes
overlapping the erotic. 'Ode on Causality' (1958) is in one manuscript called 'Ode at the Grave of Jackson Pollock',[25] which fits with
O'Hara's book on the painter (1959). Cause in a work of art is every
thing, every gesture. Nothing is chance; there are no accidents. The
artist is an order-maker in his very being as artist. This is the stated

basis of composers as different as Charles Ives and Charles Mingus. Pollock's area of mobility is O'Hara's, and in this book the poet-curator quotes the painter's famous statement: 'When I am *in* my painting, I'm not aware of what I am doing ... I have no fears of making changes, destroying the image, etc., because the painting has a life of its own.' The art of gesture emerges from the body-mind continuum, a vital energy towards from, which is erotic and ecstatic. O'Hara's words invoke the painter he admired – mobile, substantial, intangible, and given to statement.[26]

In a 1959 statement for Donald Allen's *The New American Poetry*, O'Hara deftly places his compositional procedures as a field of discovery:[27]

> What is happening to me, allowing for lies and exaggerations, which I try to avoid, goes into my poem. I don't think my experiences are clarified or made beautiful for myself or anyone else, they are just there in whatever form I can find them. ... My formal 'stance' is found at the crossroads where what I know and can't get meets what is left of what I know and can hear without hatred. ...
>
> It may be that poetry makes life's nebulous events tangible to me and restores their details or conversely, that poetry brings forth the intangible quality of incidents which are all too concrete and circumstantial. Or each on specific oaccasions, or both all the time.

Probably he knew of Mayakovsky's statement – it is quoted by Walter Lowenfels in *Some Deaths* – 'One condition indispensable for the production of a poem is the existence in society of a problem whose solution is unimaginable except by a poem.'[28] A 1959 statement shows O'Hara's awareness of the wider social context of his collaborative work in poetry, theatre, painting and music:[29]

> The last ten years have seen American composers and printers and poets assuming leading roles in the world of international at to a degree hitherto unexpected. Led by the painters, our whole cultural milieu has changed and is still changing. ... The influence of aesthetic ideas has also been mutual: the very extremity of the differences between the arts has thrown their technical analogies into sharp relief. ... Although these analogues cease to be helpful if carried too far, it is in the framework of these mutual influences that Morton Feldman could cite, along with the playing of Fournier, Rachmaninoff and Tudor and the

friendship of John Cage, the painting of Philip Guston as important influences on his work. He adds, 'Guston made me aware of
the "Metaphysical place" which we all have but which so many
of us are not sensitive to by previous conviction.'

I interpret this 'metaphysical place', this land where Feldman's
pieces live as the area where spiritual growth in the work can
occur, where the form of a work may develop its inherent originality and the personal meaning of the composer may become
explicit. ... Like the artists involved in the new American painting, he was pursuing a personal search for expression which
could not be limited to any system.

In 1967 Feldman reciprocated with a tribute to O'Hara. After em-
phasising his virtuosity he adds:[30]

we recognised that his wisdom came from his own 'system' – the
dialectic of the heart. This was his secret. That was what made it
possible for him, without ever being merely eclectic, to write so
beautifully about both Pollock and Pasternak, to dedicate a poem
to Larry Rivers one day and to Philip Guston the next. ... Unlike
Auden or Eliot, who never stopped writing for the undergradu-
ate, Frank O'Hara dispenses with everything in his work but his
feelings. This kind of modesty always disappoints culture, which
time after time has mistaken coldness for Olympic objectivity. Let
us remember, however, that while culture has the initial say, it is
the artist who has the last word. ... In an extraordinary poem
Frank O'Hara describe his love for the poet Mayakovsky. After
an outburst of feeling, he writes, 'but I'm turning my verses /
and my heart is closing / like a fist.'

What he is telling us is something unbelievably painful.
Secreted in O'Hara's thought is the possibility that we create only
as dead men. Who but the dead know what it is to be alive? ...
these poems, so colloquial, nevertheless seem to be reaching us
from some other, infinitely distant place.

Robert Duncan reached into the nature of this site warily, and
with a characteristic thrust into the mythological, but with the
necessary sense of its sociality.[31] He speaks of O'Hara's attempt.

to keep the *demand* on the language as operative, so that something was at issue all the time, and, at the same time, to make it
almost like chatter on the telephone that nobody was going to

pay attention to before ... that the language gain was what was assumed before to be its *trivial* uses. I'm sort of fascinated that *trivial* means the same thing as *three* (Hecate). Trivial's the *crisis*, where it always blows. So that I think that one can build a picture, that in all the arts in America, they are *operative*. We think of art as *doing something*, taking hold of it as a *process*.

Duncan's presence prompts a comparison between his sociality, in 'Santa Cruz Propositions' (1968),[32] and O'Hara's in, for example, 'Biotherm (For Bill Berkson)' and 'Second Avenue'. In his Larry Rivers catalogue, Sam Hunter sensibly places the painting 'The Accident' with the poet's 'A Memoir', and, in his 'Introduction' describes it as 'a fresh vision of the agitated mosaic of urban life ... the colliding realities of art and life coexist ... the action of life and the medium of paint constantly interchange, and displace each other'.[33] Transposed to the medium of words, this helps to introduce the visual techniques and kaleidoscopic speeds of juxtaposition and interaction of event, image, syntax and memory in the poem. It was written while posing for Rivers in 1953, and works by him, Grace Hartigan and De Kooning enter the poem, whose order is a processive record:[34]

> everything in it either happened to me of I felt happening (saw, imagined) on Second Avenue. ... Perhaps the obscurity comes in here, in the relationship between the surface and the meaning, but I like it that way since the one is the other (you have use words) and I hope the poem to *be* subject, not just about it.

Turbulence and danger of surface to depth movements – between people and between the private and social functions of society – preoccupied O'Hara, as in fact they assume a constant preoccupation for most poets of any power today. In 'Franz Kline' (1960) O'Hara quotes the painter:[35]

> Hell, half the world wants to be like Thoreau at Walden worrying about the noise of traffic on the way to Boston; the half use up their lives being part of that noise. I like the second half. Right?
>
> To be right is the most terrific personal state that nobody is interested in ...

The nature of anguish is translated into different forms. What has happened is that we're not through the analytical period of learning what motivates things. If you can figure out the motivation, it's supposed to be all right. But when things are 'beside themselves' what matters is the care things are given by someone.

That care energises the extraordinary rapidity with which deeper emotions surface and return below in, for example, 'Adieu to Norman, Bon Jour to Joan and Jean-Paul' (1950), an arrival and departure poem, which thoroughly exemplifies Duncan's observations. The danger is in, for example, 'Song: Is it dirty' (1959).[36]

In *Meditations in an Emergency*, immediately following the passage quoted earlier on love: 'to keep the filth of life away', yes, there, 'even in the heart, where the filth is pumped in and slanders and pollutes and determines'. And at the end of 'Poem: Now the Violets are All Gone ...' (1959)[37]

> my head and the strange reality of our flesh in the rain
> so many parts of a strange existence independent but not
> searching in the night.
> nor in the morning when the rain has stopped

'For the Chinese New Year & For Bill Berkson' (1961),[38] one of his finest poems, dramatises the necessary urgency of participating in what is going on now, in the social and the political, and the grim possibilities of being subsumed by overwhelming contingency, manifest in threat not clearly perceived or not perceived until too late, that Henry James sense of the need to be 'free and uncommitted' but of not being 'too late in life altogether ... the wasting of life', that energy behind 'immediate and apparent life ... deeper and darker and unapparent, in which things *really* happen to us'.[39] O'Hara's epigraph from D. H. Lawrence is the devastating impulse: 'One or another / Is lost, since we fall apart / Endlessly, in one motion depart / From each other.' 'Should We Legalise Abortion?' (1964) concludes:

> What the . . .
> THERE'S NOBODY AT THE CONTROLS!
> Forget
> we ever met

But this poem is one of the eleven constituting *The End of the Far West*, which contain some of the funniest poems he wrote: O'Hara the poet as comedian satirist, with inflections from stand-up comedians like Mort Sahl, who functioned as social critics during the civil conflicts of the 1950–1970 decades. Ted Berrigan was right to publish them as a group in 1974; they have political indications in common, using a parodistic language of toadying journalists, western and other movie conventions, and arrogant authorities and those who believe them. And since they were to have been accompanied by drawings from Jan Cremer, they may serve here to introduce, and conclude with, the issues of collaboration.[40]

O'Hara may well have recalled Pasternak's repeated statement in *Safe Conduct* (1931) of his sense of life as a collaboration with Vladimir Mayakovsky. Certainly, John Ashbery, Kenneth Koch and O'Hara read *Safe Conduct* fervently and drew from it an ideal of 'personism' between poets as friends – reflected in the Summer 1961 collaboration issue of *Locus Solus*, as well as O'Hara's own 'Personism: A Manifesto' (1959).[41] The editor, Koch, included Peret, Breton, Eluard and Char, as well as work from Ashbery, James Schuyler, Williams Burroughs and Gregory Corso, Harry Mathews, and O'Hara. In his editorial essay he mentions the latter's collaboration with 'the French language' in 'Choses passagéres', and states the issue's continuity from Surrealism:[42]

> The act of collaborating on a literary work is inspiring, I think, because it gives objective form to a usually concealed subjective phenomenon and therefore it jars the mind into strange new positions. ... The strangeness of the collaborating situation, many have felt, might lead them to the unknown, or at least to some dazzling insights at which they could never have arrived consciously or alone. The surrealists were the first avowed practitioners of literary collaboration for this specific purpose.

O'Hara's collaborations with Larry Rivers and Jasper Johns certainly discover new forms out of resonances between individual practices, and enter the complex field of work as performance between author and addressees – not to mention Foucault's notorious 1969 criticism of 'the privileged moment of individualisation' and Roman Jakobson's 1960 sense that aesthetics includes collaboration with reader, viewer or receiver.[43] That is, the act of composition takes place within an existing and prospective site of collaboration, conscious and unconscious. It is not at all the necessarily anguished contest that Harold Bloom believes in *The Breaking of the Vessels* (1982).[44] Fine art is a creative synthesis in which conflicts of inheritance and the certainties and uncertainties of participating receivers are peculiarly ordered into a repeatable fertility. The academic criticism club persists in a triumph, jealous belief in 'the end of the individual author', but artists and poets practise authorship in collaboration creatively. In America, in the 1960s, Ron Padgett and Ted Berrigan with *C Magazine*, and then *Bean Spasms*, creatively disrupted 'the imperial self' into multiple creativities, and retrospectively condemn the irritated post-structuralist to sterility after the event. The collaborations of John Cage, Robert Rauschenberg and Merce Cunningham in dance should have alerted them; and, in writing, work of Borges, Stein, Pound and others.

O'Hara lives a collaborative life, as a poet within the *Locus Solus* field of writers, as curator of contemporary art at MOMA, and in his creative work with Rivers, Johns, Michael Goldberg and others in poetry, film, theatre and poetry-paintings: a city action, a New York excitement in a limited chosen community of virtuosity against democratic anonymity. His 'art chronicles' on Robert Motherwell, Pollock, Kline and others produced a further collaboration. Appropriately, therefore, Bill Berkson edited a memorial tribute to O'Hara in which a selection of his poems were each visually accompanied by a work from thirty artists. René d'Harnoncourt begins his preface with words to confound the nitpicking and dogmatic critics:

> Frank O'Hara the poet, was part of the community of artists who are giving form to the issues, tensions, and releases of our turbulent times and who, by doing so, are shaping the living fabric of the present.
>
> Frank O'Hara, the art critic and curator, was also part of that group who are called to use judgement and considerable action to make the artist's work accessible to all who may need it.
>
> Frank was one of the very few who are able to combine these two callings seemingly without conflict; on the contrary, his close associations with artists, as an artist himself, gave his work as critic and curator authority and warmth of personal experience.
>
> Frank was so sure of his own reactions towards works of art that he did not need to be aggressive ...

Bill Berkson, in his 'Afterword', quotes James Schuyler 'taking "Second Avenue" as an instance of connection between poetry and painting':[45]

> it's probably true to deduce that he'd read the Cantos and Whitman (he had); also Breton, and looked at De Koonings and Duchamp's great Dada installation at the Janis Gallery ... 'All enthusiasms aside, he opted for poetry as 'the highest art, everything else, however gratifying ... moving and grand, is less demanding, more indulgent, more casual, more gratuitous, more instantly apprehensible, which I assume isn't exactly what we are after'.

But the collaborative life remained essential. It enters the poetry, for instance, through social pressures – in Berkson's terms: 'the pressure of the syntax relates to the pressures of life. ... An O'Hara poem will always denote some change in the poet's world':

> the overriding particular virtues: sheer poetic finesse (so tactfully concealed), a speed almost synonymous with inspiration, the happy identification and excitement of real things – the utter range of noun and implied action; a jolting sophistication; the split-second enjambments ... sharp transitions, telescoped flourishes of imagery; the quick, specific truths.

The collaborative factors are particularised in 'How to Proceed in the Arts' (1961), that O'Hara wrote with Rivers (the 'text' includes two poem-paintings by O'Hara and Norman Bluhm, one each with John and Rivers):[46]

13. Youth wants to burn museum, we are in them – now what? ...
20. When asked about the old masters, be sure to include your theories of culture change, and how the existence of a work of art is only a small part of man's imaginations. ... We dream, and not impatient hoping for fame without labour, admiration without a contract, sex with an erection ...

The stances parallels Jasper Johns poking fun at individualist posturing in his 1960s *Painting with Two Balls, painted Bronze* – two heavy metal 'Ballantine cans' – and *Thermometer* – for measuring the heat of personal inspiration. Rivers recalled his O'Hara collaboration in 'Life Among the Stones' (1963):[47]

> Frank O'Hara wasn't going to write a poem that I would set a groovy little image to. Nor were we going to assume the world was waiting for his poetry and my drawing which is what the past 'collaborations' now seem to have been.

Their basis was improvisational, beginning with a little or a subject or a designated area. O'Hara's 'Memoir' in the Sam Hunter volume provides further detail, as does Rivers's poem collaborations, 'our great collaborative play *Kenneth Koch, a Tragedy*, and Rivers' encouraging his poet-models to compose while sitting for him'.[48]

O'Hara also knew of Jack Kerouac's inspiration from the collaborations in jazz, but did not share the interest. In a letter to Corso,[49] he says that what Kerouac

> feels as the content of jazz. ... I feel about painting with the corresponding difference in aspiration, that is where one takes Bird for inspiration I would take Bill de Kooning: partly because I feel that jazz is beautiful enough or too, but not fierce enough, and where jazz is fleeting (in time) and therefore poignant, de K is final and therefore tragic ... also, I don't have to see what I admire while I'm writing and would rather not hear it, which seems unavoidable in the jazz milieu.

Joe Brainard remembered collaborating with O'Hara: 'It was easy. Or so it seemed. Mostly they were cartoons. I would do the drawings and he would fill in the balloons instantly. On the spot. Sharp and funny and very frank.'[50] Peter Schjeldahl, also a poet and an art critic, realises the central function of these actions:[51]

> Collaboration, a direct extension of O'Hara's mode of living ... the manner of his relationships – an intimate competition in which each participant goads the other towards being at his best. ... Not everyone could cope for long with a mind that leapt at everything and missed nothing. ... If O'Hara had a motto, it was perhaps his own summary of his approach to poetic composition: 'You go on your nerve'. Or, meaning the same thing, a line of Pasternak's: 'It's past, you'll understand it later'.

The sheer nerve of 'Biotherm' is part of its unique concentrations and explosions as poetics. (That the method is deeply his own is clear from the unbeatably exhilarating letter from Belgrade to Joe Le Sueur in 1963, showing his ability to allow new places to penetrate his life. He was touring Europe with his Franz Kline exhibition.[52]) The five-month length of the writing is described in a letter to Donald Allen, which includes essential information as to the meaning of the title and the presence of 'plankton' in the text.[53] Initiated as a poem for Berkson's birthday – once again a nativity inspiration – it becomes a 464-line record of the collaborative life, in multiple meanings of 'collaborative'. The controlling issue is the relationships between health, fertility and protections. The title refers to 'a marvellous sunburn preparation' one of whose ingredients is plankton, 'practically the most health-giving substance ever rubbed into one's skin'. This locates poetic action: the beach, the sea, love; but it leaves the poet free to include a range of materials to generate the action, which raises the issue of how much of the information is probably opaque even to the most attentive reader. For instance: the Allen Letter includes, without citing the actual poem, 'This dedelie stroke, whereby shall seace / The harborid sighis within my herte'.[54] It is from one of many poems by Sir Thomas Wyatt concerning frustrated love, related to imprisonment, and, in this case especially, possible relief by suicide. Collisions between Berkson's birthday and its meanings for the poet, and Wyatt's violence projected the poem with enough energy to continue over the months. The existential time structuring of the opening shifts to 'What's the use', and then answers with several hundred lines! In an interview published after O'Hara's death. Ted Berrigan spoke of his many collaborations with Wyatt poems and cites 'The Harbormaster', which O'Hara told Allen was about Larry Rivers, which clearly uses Wyatt's 'My galy charged with forgetfulness'. This information initiates and certainly reinforces main themes in O'Hara characteristics of Wyatt: lonely anguish, threats of desperation and death, the force of involuntary and unrequited sexual enthralment, and related scenes from movies and from the contemporary colonial war in Algeria; Wallace Stevens themes (neatly parodied – 'an ordinary evening alone / with a lot of people'); the insistence that childhood is happy, shown to be fake – leading to 'what a strange life . . . what does it mean?' These are located in the O'Hara design: how to be fully alive to one's life and not be overwhelmed. Berrigan puts it very well, although this short passage

does not do justice to his appreciation (the syntax is that of improvised interview speech):[55]

> he believed ... that life, in the living of itself, fully aware and
> alert and fully as conscious as possible, with an eye almost to im-
> pulses to drift off into reflectiveness and fugue states of introver-
> sion and so on, that as being the enemy of reality, the enemy of
> being a real person ... if you stayed on top ... not on top of things
> in the sense of being in control ... that was the way you were in
> touch with the real light *and* the real darkness.

Shortage of space prevents a full analysis of this masterly poem.
Suffice it to say that the loneliness, the light and darkness, are detailed with buoyancy and confidence, articulated in remarkable and
beautiful flows of consciousness and inventive language. This, in
collaboration with other arts, is needed against self-degradation,
darkness, pollution, death always in the wings, and neurotic
egotism. Near the centre is an oedipal need to encounter being the
homosexual son (a further birthday location) and dealing with that
inevitability. Juxtaposed to: 'thank you for the dark and the shoulders'. The past thrusts in as inheritance of oedipal capitalism and
degrading human history, with 'an enormous sale of loneliness'.
But 'a health-giving substance', protective and generative, must be
found. The strategies of health are exuberant and recklessly fertile.
The sheer range of referentiality may be daunting sometimes but it
can be trusted. Montage, cross-cutting, collage and methods of imi-
tating memory are superbly organised into a poetics.

The place of momentary rest is preservative – 'pretty rose preserved in biotherm' – but, like Wyatt, O'Hara opts for continuing
life as itself preservative – 'merely continue' – but there is also a
duty to guard existence and art against 'mess and measure'. The
poem at last looks out from the beach towards a containing scene,
which is also a moral image. Beyond 'quicksand' and 'the ego-
ridden sea' are two lighthouse keepers.

NOTES

Most of the quotations of O'Hara's poems are from *The Collected Poems of Frank O'Hara*, ed. Donald Allen (New York: Knopf, 1972) hereinafter cited as *C.P.*

1. T. S. Eliot, 'Andrew Marvell', *Selected Essays* (London: Faber, 1934) pp. 292–304.
2. Eric Mottram, *William Burroughs: The Algebra of Need* (London: Marion Boyars, 1977) p. 62.
3. Charles Bernstein, 'Stray Straws and Straw Men', *Content's Dream: Essays 1975–1984* (Los Angeles: Sun & Moon Press, 1986, p. 41.
4. Bill Berkson, 'Talk', *Hills/Talks*, ed. Bob Perelman, *Hills*, 6/7 (spring 1982) pp. 12–15.
5. Morton Feldman, 'Lost Times and Future Hopes', in Bill Berkson and Joe Le Sueur (eds), *Homage to Frank O'Hara, Big Sky*, 11/12 (Colinas 1978).
6. Eric Mottram, 'Notes for Feldman Lecture, Tate Gallery', *Spanner*, vol. 3, no. 9, issue 29 (Hereford, 1990) p. 335.
7. *C.P.*, p. 197.
8. Alain Robbe-Grillet, 'Nature, Humanism, Tragedy', *For a New Novel* (New York: Grove Press, 1965).
9. Bruce Boone, 'Gay Language as Political Praxis: The Poetry of Frank O'Hara', *Social Text* vol. 1, no. 1 (Madison, 1979).
10. Bill Berkson (ed.), *In Memory of my Feelings* (New York: Museum of Modern Art, 1967).
11. Harold Rosenberg, 'The American Action Painters', *Art News*, December 1952; reprinted in *The Tradition of the New* (New York: Horizon Press, 1959).
12. Harold Rosenberg, 'A Dialogue with Thomas B. Hess', *The Tradition of the New*, p. 28.
13. Serge Guilbaut, *How New York Stole the Idea of Modern Art: Abstract Expressionism, Freedom and the Cold War* (University of Chicago, 1983).
14. Waldo Rasmussen, 'Frank O'Hara in the Museum', *Homage to Frank O'Hara*.
15. Frank O'Hara, 'Franz Kline', *Art Chronicles 1954–1966* (New York: George Braziller, 1975).
16. Renée S. Neu, 'With Frank at MOMA', *Homage to Frank O'Hara*.
17. Robert Graves, *The Greek Myths*, vol. 1 (Harmondsworth: Penguin, 1955) p. 244.
18. C. Kerényi, *Asklepios: Archetypal Image of the Physician's Existence* (New York: Pantheon, 1959) pp. 10, 13.
19. Frank O'Hara, 'About Zhivago and his Poems', *Evergreen Review*, vol. 11, no. 7 (Winter 1959); reprinted in *Standing Still and Walking in New York*, ed. Donald Allen (Bolinas: Grey Fox Press, 1975) p. 100.
20. *C.P.*, p. 239.
21. *C.P.*, p. 449.
22. Bill Berkson (ed.), *Best & Company* (published at 107E 10th St, New York, 1969) no page numbers.

23. *C.P.*, p. 261.
24. *C.P.*, p. 290.
25. Frank O'Hara, *Jackson Pollock* (New York: George Braziller, 1959) p. 32.
26. *C.P.*, p. 303. Neither Pollock's 'Bird' nor 'Bird Effort' much invoke flight. There appears to be a puzzle here; cf. S. Naifeh and G. W. Smith, *Jackson Pollock: An American Saga* (London: Barrie and Jenkins, 1989) pp. 354, 517–18, and plate between pp. 504 and 505.
27. Donald Allen (ed.), *The New American Poetry 1945–1960* (New York: Grove Press, 1960) p. 419.
28. Walter Lowenfels, *Some Deaths*, *Jargon*, 32 (The Nantahala Foundation, Highlands, NC, 1964) p. 27.
29. Eric Mottram, 'Notes for Feldman Lectures', pp. 335–6.
30. *Homage to Frank O'Hara*, pp. 13–14.
31. Ibid., p. 68.
32. Robert Duncan, 'Santa Cruz Propositions', *Ground Work: Before the War* (New York: New Directions, 1984) pp. 36–46.
33. Sam Hunter, 'Introduction', *Larry Rivers* (Massachusetts: Brandeis University, 1965) p. 28.
34. Frank O'Hara, 'A Memoir', *Larry Rivers*, pp. 8–17; *C.P.*, p. 497.
35. Frank O'Hara, *Art Chronicles*, p. 52.
36. *C.P.*, p. 327.
37. *C.P.*, p. 346.
38. *C.P.*, p. 386.
39. Eric Mottram, '"The Infected Air" and "The Guilt of Interference": Henry James's Short Stories', A. Robert Lee (ed.), *The Nineteenth-Century American Short Story* (London/New York: Vision and Barnes & Noble, 1986) pp. 164–6.
40. *C.P.*, p. 482; note on p. 556.
41. *C.P.*, pp. 498–9.
42. See also David Shapiro, 'Art as Collaboration: toward a Theory of Pluralist Aesthetics 1950–1980', *Artistic Collaboration in the Twentieth Century* (Washington: Smithsonian Institution Press, 1984) pp. 48–9.
43. Michel Foucault, 'What is an Author?', Donald F. Bouchard (ed.), *Michel Foucault: Language, Counter-Memory, Practice* (Oxford: Blackwell, 1977) pp. 113–38; Roman Jakobson, 'Linguistics and Poetics', Thomas A. Sebeok (ed.), *Style in Language* (Cambridge: MIT Press, 1960) pp. 350–78.
44. Harold Bloom, *The Breaking of the Vessels* (University of Chicago, 1982) p. 66, etc.
45. James Schuyler, 'Frank O'Hara: A Poet among Painters', *Art News*, May 1974, pp. 44–5.
46. Frank O'Hara, *Art Chronicles*, pp. 94–5.
47. Larry Rivers, 'Life Among the Stones', *Location*, Spring 1963, New York, pp. 90–8.
48. Frank O'Hara *Larry Rivers*, p. 17.
49. Marjorie Perloff, *Frank O'Hara: Poet among Painters* (New York: George Braziller, 1977) p. 110.
50. Joe Brainard, 'Frank O'Hara', *Homage to Frank O'Hara*, p. 168.

51. Peter Schjeldahl, 'Frank O'Hara: "He Made Things and People Sacred"', *Homage to Frank O'Hara*, p. 141.
52. Frank O'Hara, *Belgrade, November 19, 1963, Adventures in Poetry*, (New York, no date).
53. *C.P.*, pp. 553–4.
54. Kenneth Muir (ed.), *Sir Thomas Wyatt: The Collected Poems* (London: Routledge and Kegan Paul, 1949), no. 164.
55. Ted Berrigan, 'On Frank O'Hara's Birthday', *Homage to Frank O'Hara*, pp. 210, 212.

12

Charles Olson

GAVIN SELERIE

I said of Melville that his importance is that he comprehended man as mythological in an archaeological present

Charles Olson[1]

To approach Olson's work in the 1990s is – to borrow the archaeological imagery dear to the poet himself – a little like uncovering a familiar but buried pavement. Although more of Olson's writings are available than ever before, two recent forces in American poetry have diminished his reputation and influence. First, the championing of a new formalism and, paradoxically, the licence granted to confessional-type composition have involved a rejection, in some significant quarters, of the 'free' and experimental. (Helen Vendler's *Harvard/Faber Book of Contemporary American Poetry*[2] attempted to redefine the canon by excluding Olson and other late modernist or postmodern poets outright.) Secondly, the development of Language Poetry has shifted the experimental enterprise away from its previously oral base. Writers such as Charles Bernstein and Barrett Watten acknowledge Olson's key place in twentieth-century poetics but see the present possibilities for poetry as existing somewhere beyond the open field/breath-unit/mythohistorical practice associated with Olson.[3]

The breadth of Olson's concerns and the often awkward style of his critical statements present the uninitiated reader with a seemingly alien surface. Those who come to American poetry via Roethke, Bishop or Lowell are likely to experience some loss of bearings when confronted by the swirl of activity that typifies an Olson page. 'Projective Verse', as Olson called it, is 'COMPOSITION BY FIELD, as opposed to inherited line, stanza, over-all form'.[4] The intention is to maintain 'the act of instant' and so stay faithful to the track of perception. Commenting on his reading technique (i.e. to audiences) and by implication on the visual lay-out of his poetry, Olson said that he wanted to declare 'a behaviour for the word, as though *sometimes*, they better be shown as performing animals'.[5]

Apart from the poems, such as 'The Kingfishers', included in *The Distances* (1960),[6] Olson's major work is his epic sequence *The Maximus Poems*, begun at Black Mountain College in 1950 (at the start of a period of crucial correspondence with Robert Creeley) and continued, mainly in Gloucester, Massachusetts, until his death in 1970. Two volumes of *Maximus* were published during the poet's lifetime (in 1960 and 1968 respectively) and a third appeared, posthumously, in 1975. There is also a body of rejected *Maximus* material, some of great importance, which awaits publication in book form. Olson has been well served by his scrupulous and empathic editor, the late George Butterick, who wrote *A Guide to the Maximus Poems*[7] and edited the one-volume complete edition of *Maximus* which appeared in 1983.[8]

The bold experiments which culminated in such poems as 'rages/strain' (*Maximus*, III.38) had their origin in the form and, to a lesser extent, the content of Pound's *Cantos*. Compare, for example:

And I have told you of how things were under Duke Leopold in Siena
And of the true base of credit, that is the abundance of nature with the whole folk behind it.
'Goods that are needed' said Schacht (anno sedici)
commerciabili beni, deliverable things that are wanted.

(*Canto* LII)[9]

and

Off-shore, by islands, hidden in the blood
jewels & miracles, I, Maximus
a metal hot from boiling water, tell you
what is a lance, who obeys the figures of
the present dance

(Maximus, I.1)

Olson was attracted to the inclusiveness of the *Cantos* (Pound called his epic 'the tale of the tribe') and also to their apparently random juxtaposition of facts. Pound placed the burden of creating order on the reader, allowing things to stand in opposition and disharmony; if nature or history had a logic, it could not be seen by an avoidance of chaos. Nor could there be a simple separation between author and written product: the writer was attempting to trace the 'entire field of western culture and history',[10] yet remain close to his own experience – hence the use of the persona Odysseus, making his way back to order and light. The tentative nature of the overall structure was indicated by the early designation 'draft' (applied to the first thirty Cantos and later to Cantos CX–CXVII).

Aiming at precision but also fluidity of meaning, Pound had developed a way of opening up syntax so that the language could cohere in new patterns. Following the ideogrammic method as set out by Ernest Fenollosa, he departed from the logical arrangement of word units so that particulars could be charged with their own luminosity and allow for various instances of accretion or interfusion. As Fenollosa said, 'Complex ideas arise only gradually, as the power of holding them together arises.'[11] Olson absorbed the elliptical technique of the *Cantos* fairly early and by the time he was writing the first *Maximus* poems he knew how to incorporate fragments of biography, history and topography in a single structure. 'The Kingfishers' uses bird lore, cybernetics, pre-Socratic philosophy, central American history and contemporary politics to comment on the process of mutability in nature. Linguistically, Olson was working from equally Poundian principles. As he wrote in 1953: 'The quarrel is with discourse – and thus, up to a certain, but extreme point, with traditional syntax. Because it is not possible to say everything at once, is no reason, to my mind, to lose the advantage of this pressure (or compression) which speech is [,] which it wants to be: that it rushes into the mouth to crowd out to someone else what it is is pressing in the heart & mind to be said.'[12]

'The Kingfishers' glances back at the *Pisan Cantos* in several places, but it will be noticed that Olson's respect for Mao and his implied hatred of Fascism conflict with the master's vision. Despite his adherence to Pound's method, Olson could not take over rigidities of attitude which resulted in political conservatism. The two men became friends while Pound was imprisoned in Washington in 1946, and the confrontation with an irresponsible ego – as he termed the teacher's voice in the *Cantos* – was a source of anguish to the younger writer:

> I wondered then how long more I can hold out my hand to him as a poet and a man. I suppose I should tell him one day I am the son of immigrants, this influx of second class citizens whom Pegler and Pound think has made impure their Yankee America of pioneers and Biddles. That my father was killed fighting for the right of labor men to organise in unions. That decadent democracy gave me the chance to grope out of the American city into some understanding of what life is. … Meanwhile I shall do what I can, as long as I can, for this fool of hate because once he was also a fool of love.[13]

A further difference of approach, or at least of emphasis, is indicated by Olson's remark that Pound's reverence for 'past accomplishments' could result in a lack of emplacement in the present.[14] Olson was excited by the supra-chronological pattern of the *Cantos*, but he wanted to use the archaic more specifically for its relation to American experience now. Hence he seems to reject parts of the Classical and Renaissance inheritance which Pound reveres.[15]

The structural unit which Olson chose (or came upon) for his serial poem was the letter, a form which implies something less developmental and more instantaneous than the canto, which is equivalent to an instalment in an ongoing epic. In his *Paris Review* interview, Olson said that his interest was not in the canto but 'in another condition of song, which … has to do with absolute actuality. It's so completely temporal.'[16] Of course, there is a sense in which Pound's cantos have the spontaneous, digressive quality of Byron's in *Don Juan*; yet the inspiration is more strictly Dante's *Divine Comedy*, with its lofty 'spiritual' scheme. Olson's preferred vehicle, the letter, is less obviously 'high' art, and it carries opposite but not necessarily contradictory associations: the casual imparting of information and the delivery of a moral message. The voice of Maximus does both these things.

In creating his persona for *The Maximus Poems*, Olson was careful to avoid the well-known heroes who had appeared in other epics: the figure chosen could fit into any mythology as an archetypal *homo maximus* (the primordial self in alchemy)[17] but also had a historical dimension as the philosopher Maximus of Tyre. Moreover, the name had literal significance as a delineation of the poet's

titanic physique; wherever he went, Olson's size (height: six foot
seven) made him an object of wonder. Butterick has argued that
Maximus 'is as much a proposition, at the start of the poems, as
anything literal or referential'.[18] The speaker in 'Letter 3' (I.11) explicitly differentiates between his perspective and that of the
second century AD philosopher. Nevertheless, Olson did read this
eclectic Platonist (in the 1804 translation by Thomas Taylor) around
1950 and the content and tone of the *Dissertations* do have a bearing
on his epic. Like Plutarch and Apuleius, Maximus interpreted Plato
in an allegorical, mystic way. Thomas Lodge, defending the authenticity of the imagination against Stephen Gosson's assault on
the practice of poets and players, says in his *Defence of Poetry* (1579):

> You disprayse Maximus Tirius pollicey, and that thing that he
> wrott to manifest learned Poets mening you atribute to
> follye...why may not Iuno resemble the ayre? why not Alexander
> valour? why not Vllysses pollice? ... must men write that you
> maye know theyr meaning? as though your wytt were to wrest
> all things?[19]

The Elizabethans, then, regarded Maximus as an early instance of
the habit of layered thought.

As Frank Davey has shown, Olson may have derived inspiration
and corroboration for this ideas about non-exploitation of nature
and about communal vitality (particularly through a *polis*) from
Maximus's discourses.[20] Parallels exist also between the teachers'
respective bases of activity: Tyre, like Gloucester, was a port reliant
on the sea and central to the surrounding region; Maximus, like
Olson, travelled out to deliver his observations and reflections. The
philosopher's presence in *The Maximus Poems* is one means (at the
root) by which Olson reaches through time and space.

Beside or beyond his Tyrian context, Maximus is, in Butterick's
words, 'a magnification, a metaphor for human possibility'. He is
the sum of what the individual heroes – such as William Stevens
and Enyalion – amount to.[21] He is a man of action as well as a
careful thinker. Significantly, he exists in language, 'the Man in the
Word' (as the editorial note to the first volume has it),[22] a striding
force embodied in or cut into a glyph. He is a noun not limited by
pressures of grammatical conformance. At once the poet and not
the poet, he is an alternative to the 'EGO AS BEAK' which Olson
objected to in the *Cantos*.[23]

Olson departed from Pound's example in one other respect: he anchored myth in fact, avoiding as much as possible the accumulation of literary detail which blocked the immediacy of European verse. 'The Kingfishers' discards the known story – classical or Celtic – for a more concrete and investigative range of associations. This euhemeristic approach to myth enabled Olson to stick closer to the physical landscape, to the reality of one locale, something which his other mentor, William Carlos Williams, had proved indispensable to the development of an American epic. *Paterson* was clearly the model for Olson's concentration on the history of one town in New England, and Butterick has shown how the early intention to write an epic about the West modulated towards a more specific area of interest.[24], In later years, however, Olson remarked that he 'got nothing out of *Paterson*' and that he owed 'Bill Williams *nothing*'.[25] Whilst this is an overstatement, it does confirm distinctions which are frequently glossed over in writings about modern poetics. Just as Olson threw off the straitjacket of imagism, he refused to view the American experience in isolation. His sense of Gloucester as a place in time and history caused him to write about that complex which Edward Dorn (with a more pessimistic eye) calls 'The North Atlantic Turbine': the intercourse between those countries which share a North Atlantic seaboard. Gloucester could not be confined by the local because it was a centre of the fishing industry and because it seemed to exemplify key developments in the history of civilisation. The important thing is that Olson worked outward from his base concern; he did not start off with a set of theories and place them geographically; rather, he sought meaning in particulars and let larger ideas emerge from these discoveries.

Throughout *The Maximus Poems* there is a delicate balance between the literal and the symbolic, between material fact and imaginative truth. 'Letter 3' mixes childhood reminiscence with a sense of Gloucester as 'root city'; 'Letter 5' takes a local magazine editor to task for failing to bring out the nature of *polis* ('as a halibut knows its grounds'); Letters 11 and 14 deal with the early discovery of New England; 'First Letter on Georges' describes the experience of fishermen caught in a storm on the great bank east of Cape Cod; 'John Burke' shows a city councillor refusing to pass over issues of vital concern for the sake of politeness; and 'April Today Main Street' considers the second wave of white settlement in Gloucester in the 1640s.

Such a sample of themes in the first volume reveals little about Olson's pattern of writing. On looking more closely at individual poems, we see that he oscillates between passages of direct information and lines of comment; yet the strands of meaning cannot be separated in such an easy fashion. Olson was capable of conveying ideas without cross-currents of perception. Here is part of a *Maximus* poem that was left out of volume II:

> ... I will put back the people inside the city,
> away from the State, the modern filthy nation. They
> have to find out again that where they live, where their
> houses are, and their voices reach, where they can walk
> to, is their business. Or they live in a barnyard a suburb,
> their yards are dumps of Montgomery Ward, they look out windows
> on bulldozers, they are forever cutting down trees Their doors
> don't even keep out the wind. The eye of man – the soul of him –
> isn't even warm. They will build their houses again
> as though it were planting. Neither a government or a banker's
> loan, and no more shrines to make each house lot religion's
> sty. I will teach them to give themselves back sensation.
> They shall have shade, as gods could tell them, is necessary.
> How to place a house so it arrays itself in the morphology
> of its own landscape. The earth is the place we live on,
> it has its ice, and fire, and sedimentary sense. It does
> go up and down, and waters ways paths and roads flow and
> part. Even animals don't disobey their feet and noses.
> They go, as both lead them. ...
>   My Yankees,
> who have forgot what decent pastors and carpenters and ship captains
> knew, before investment ate away the leaves of money,
> and the scales of fish. Strontium lies as fat flakes of ash
> of fire on all foliage, to eat the cells of unborn children.
> I will give you genetics back but only if you will use it
> to find order.[26]

This is a fine poem in the Blakean tradition and its social comment is more acute than anything Ginsberg has written. Nevertheless, it does not give a representative picture of how the *Maximus* sequence operates.

The characteristic mode is better indicated in the poem 'On first Looking out through Juan de la Cosa's Eyes' (I.77–81), where the activities of various explorers and map-makers become an index of self-discovery. Olson speaks simultaneously about the opening up of fishing grounds and the possibility of saying something new in verse. By a careful use of syntax, history (the words and actions of fishermen) impinges directly on our present bearings. The title, of course, echoes Keats's enraptured discovery of Chapman's Homer in that sonnet in which the world of the imagination is compared to the New World. Olson wants his account of Gloucester to be (in Pound's words) a 'periplum, not as land looks on a map / but as sea bord seen by men sailing.'[27] Juan de la Cosa, the chart maker on Columbus's second voyage, drew the first map of North America which has been preserved – a rude but 'actual' representation.[28] Olson's poem enacts the experience of generations of sailors approaching the New World for the first time. The urge to recall and record (stretching back through John Cabot and the Portuguese) is traced in lines that catch the difficulty and wonder of voyaging:

> Heavy sea,
> snow, hail. At 8
> AM a tide rip. Sounded.
> had 20 fath. decreased from that to
> 15, 10. Wore ship.
>
> (They knew
> Cap Raz
>
> (As men, my town, my two towns
> talk, talked of Gades, talk
> of Cash's
>
> drew, on a table, in spelt,with a finger, in beer, a
> portulans

(I.77)

Heavy punctuation and short lines in a broken column accentuate the power of the elements communicated across time. The nouns here are chosen for their exact historical reference and for their physical sound properties: the Portuguese 'Cap Raz' (Cape Race, Newfoundland); the Latin 'Gades' (Cadiz, originally a Phoenician/Tyrian colony); the Anglo-Saxon 'spelt' (wheat: crumbs or brew); and the French 'portulans' (coastal charts).

The penultimate section of the poem deals with the tragedy of lives lost at sea and focuses specifically on the annual memorial ceremony in Gloucester. A very different mood is achieved here, as the longer, 'easier' lines indicate:

(4,670 fishermen's lives are noticed. In an outgoing tide of the
Annisquam River, each summer, at the August full, they throw
flowers, which, from the current there, at the Cut, reach the
harbor channel, and go …

out into

the Atlantic

(I.80)

The rhythm and diction testify both to the pain of death and to the
relief offered by the communal ritual. Daniel Hise has rightly noted
the tension between succession and simultaneity in this poem, and
looking at the shifts and concentrations in 'la Cosa' one is reminded
of Olson's early passion for the cinema.[29] But whatever artifice is
employed, the intention is to register the realities of seeing and
feeling for oneself.

As Sherman Paul has said, the flowers of the Annisquam ceremony anticipate the nasturtium ('nose-twist') in/out folds or
spirals of the next poem, a companion text, 'The Twist'.[30] Memories
and dreams of key phases in the poet's life – particularly his early
experience of Gloucester and emerging sexuality – combine to
produce a picture of a developing self:

As I had it in my first poem,
the Annisquam
fills itself, at its tides, as she did
the French dress, cut
on the bias

(I.82)

The value of the subjective is asserted in a way that side-steps the
interference of ego. Earlier in the book and elsewhere, Olson expresses fondness for the middle voice, intermediate between active
and passive, a means of expression aware of itself.[31] In 'The Twist'
we have a whole aware of its being in fragments. To analyse the
approach in these terms is not to ignore the beautifully lyrical
images ('English walnuts' and 'a paper village') or the phrases so
evocative of – especially – childhood ('the landscape / I go up-dilly,

elevated, tenement / down'). The poem is, in its way, as fresh as an Elizabethan lyric. Placed here in the sequence, it does none the less have a structural function: history twists back into layers of the person.

The idea of twisting structure has, in fact, already been raised in 'Letter 15' (I.68) where Olson quotes Paul Blackburn's criticism 'You go all around the subject' and his own reply: 'I didn't know it was a subject.' This difference of attitude goes to the heart of the modernist (or postmodernist) advance. Olson's aversion to subject as such is memorably restated by Robert Creeley – who shared the discovery of new procedures in the early 1950s – in *A Quick Graph*:

> The poem is not a signboard, pointing to a content ultimately to be regarded; but is, on the contrary, a form inhabited by intelligence and feeling. It is the way a poem speaks, not the matter, that proves its effect, and although this is an old insistence, it is one hard at times to remember when a great variety of desperations want a solution, a content capable of relief.[32]

Olson goes on to quote Blackburn's comment 'You twist' and his own response 'I do'. Instead of avoiding complexity and deviation, Olson allows his mind to wander through a variety of materials which then come to have a 'meaning'. Creeley again provides a useful gloss:

> I think that Olson was intrigued by Whitehead's tenet that the primary factor in experience was the process of the experience itself and that one could make useful predictions but one could not dictate the form that then came to be. And if one attempted to have too particular a purview or a preview then one was left arguing with what happened in some distracting way. ... The process for him was the primary instruction and content. At the same time, it wasn't wanting it to be speciously variable but he could in no way dictate its necessary overall pattern.[33]

Olson's continuing use of the flower metaphors testifies to the willed organicism of his method. Even the description metaphor here may be misleading, given Olson's insistence on inherent signification ('that which exists through itself is called meaning').[34]

Increasingly in this first volume, the poet's own experience releases the buried mass of the past:

I sit here on a Sunday
with grey water, the winter
staring me in the face

'the Snow lyes indeed
about a foot thicke
for ten weekes' John White

warns any prospective
planter

...

around what campfires
these fourteen Englishmen
managed

where I as a young man berthed
a skiff and scarfed
my legs to get up rocks

this coast is all it's
made of, not soil
not beaver

fish fish fish

(I.102–4)

Olson ranges through the classic works on New England, goes back
to the original documents (particularly the town records of
Gloucester), and makes this material come resoundingly alive. The
struggle between the original settlers and the Plymouth men, described in 'History is the Memory of Time' (I.112.–14), provides a
vivid insight into the foundations of 'the modern filthy nation'. The
Dorchester sailors want merely to live by the daily business of
fishing; they are opposed by a company that desires profit and
power. The combine forces the small-time fishermen to surrender
part of their livelihood, and Olson relates this to the process by
which wealth has been divorced from work in Western society.

The second volume of *The Maximus Poems* (sections IV, V, VI)
has a vastly increased range of inquiry, as the map on the cover
suggests. Instead of focusing solely on the history of Gloucester,
Olson traces 'the migratory act of man' which finishes on the shore
of that city.[35] This involves a study of Tyre (as an ancient counter-

part of Gloucester, a wellspring of civilisation in the Piscean age); a concern with nature as a whole, rather than human culture alone; a mapping of Dogtown – the wild common behind the city – as an image of earth fed by the sea; and a method of writing which suggests 'that no event / is not penetrated, in intersection or collision with, an eternal / event' (II.79). In this attempt Olson draws on an immense variety of myths, archaeological details, geological data, mystical theory and (as before) documentary material about Gloucester inhabitants. The style represents a radical advance on techniques used in the first volume; as Butterick points out, 'the poems seek a consciousness prior to the rational mind the Greeks may have invented'.[36] Maritime narratives exist side by side with Algonquin legend and alchemical philosophy. Moreover, the reader is confronted with a constant oscillation of structure: from pithy one-line poems to expansive chronicles. At first sight the arrangement is chaotic, but there is much evidence that the sequence was planned carefully. Olson laboured to preserve effects of randomness and gaps in sense, if such a lay-out made for further discovery on the reader's part. What he was aiming at was to let 'fact and story enter the poems in the sequence and strength with which they [came] to his attention'.[37] This is rather different from the stream of consciousness that we associate with, say, James Joyce. As indicated above, Olson does not start off with any informing structure; the form of the poems reveals itself as he goes along.

Olson was fascinated by the theory of synchronicity, as expounded by Jung, and the texture of sections IV, V, VI is perhaps most readily understood by looking at the psychologist's Foreword to *The I Ching*:

> The actual form ... seems to appeal more to the Chinese sage than the ideal one. The jumble of natural laws constituting empirical reality holds more significance for him than a causal explanation of events that, moreover, must usually be separated from one another in order to be properly dealt with. ...
>
> The moment under actual observation appears to the ancient Chinese view more of a chance hit than a clearly defined result of concurring causal chain processes. The matter of interest seems to be the configuration formed by chance events in the moment of observation, and not at all the hypothetical reasons that seemingly account for the coincidence. While the Western mind

carefully sifts, weighs, selects, classifies, isolates, the Chinese picture of the moment encompasses everything down to the minutest nonsensical detail, because all of the ingredients make up the observed moment. ...

Synchronicity takes the coincidence of events in space and time as meaning something more than mere chance, namely, a peculiar interdependence of objective events among themselves as well as with the subjective (psychic) states of the observer or observers.

The ancient Chinese mind contemplates the cosmos in a way comparable to that of the modern physicist, who cannot deny that his model of the world is a decidedly psychophysical structure.[38]

There are numerous points in the second *Maximus* volume where a 'pre-established parallelism of events' seems to operate alongside space, time, and causality, Although much artistry is put into the presentation of facts and ideas, the materials seem to complement each other by a process which lies beyond the author's control. An example is the humorous correspondence of myth and history in 'like', 'of old times' and 'they said' (II.20–2). Olson, like his carpenter hero who 'was the first Maximus', knew how to utilise the grain of the material at his disposal, letting natural features stand out when they happened to produce an interesting effect. The order of the poems depends largely on the chronology of their composition, and the length of lines is sometimes determined by the space available upon a sheet of paper or envelope.[39]

One point where a variety of themes and styles coalesce perfectly is the sequence of poems running from 'Maximus Letter # whatever' to 'A Maximus Song' (II.31–5). We have just heard the story of an early confrontation between white settlers and Indians; Olson's tone of voice brings out the two kinds of naivety involved: the pawns of imperialism caught suddenly in 'domestic / horror', and the red men reacting directly to a natural hazard. Now we are given (in slightly compressed form – 'chockablock') a season myth taken almost verbatim from Leland's *Algonquin Legends of New England*.[40] The designation 'whatever' instead of a particular number and date reminds us that myth universalises history; and, indeed, the tale of the man-with-the-house-on-his-head re-emerges as a paradigm of contact with the divine on II.141. The narrative goes as follows: a man, travelling through the woods, comes upon a

man and his wife who are dancing the ground away in order to
catch a raccoon which lies at the top of a tree; he shows them how
to cut the tree down in return for the skin of the captured animal;
later he meets a man who is bearing a house on his head; this
person desires the pelt of the raccoon so much that he offers to exchange the house for it; 'our man' is worried that he will not be able
to carry the house as the stranger does, but when he tries to lift the
dwelling it turns out to be 'as light as a basket'; the man carries his
cabin to an appropriate place for settlement and goes to sleep in
one of the rooms; in the morning he wakes up to find all manner of
provisions hanging from the beams; as he reaches out for them, his
bed (which now turns out to be snow) melts and his arms spread
forth into wings; he flies up to the food that hangs from birch-
boughs, for he is a partridge and it is spring.

Like most myths, this story relates both to the annual progress of
the seasons and to the journey of people through various stages of
life. There are the familiar motifs of initiation: travel into strange
territory; meetings and exchange of information; the carrying of a
prized possession; the revelation of its true significance and a metamorphosis which brings good news for all creatures. The 'man who
belonged somewhere else' may be a kind of shaman, since he
shows the hero an ability that he has not been aware of. The 'hard-
wood ridge near a good spring of water' is, in Algonquin terms, an
ideal place to live. The greater ease of movement that 'our man' has
after his transformation beautifully expresses the unlocking of
primal energies which occurs throughout nature at the start of
spring. However, there is some non-sequential element in the myth
that makes it different from similar accounts which exist in other
cultures. It was this sense of the human as part of nature, rather
than one who controls it, that appealed to Olson. Leland says
simply at the end of this tale:

> And he was a Partridge, who after the manner of his kind had
> been wintering under a snowdrift, and now came forth to greet
> the pleasant spring.[41]

We do not get much sense here of cause and effect, although
Leland explains in a note that 'birch buds are the food of the partridge'. Olson accentuates this touch of rightness that is enigmatic:
things happen according to a pattern that is glimpsed momentarily.
When we remember the poet's concern with territory we can see

why the Algonquin myth was incorporated into *The Maximus Poems*: it is a complex story told in the most fundamental way – in relation to its surroundings.[42] The physical details are uppermost, yet the meaning is ultimately 'spiritual'.

If we look at the etymology of 'chock-a-block', we find that the idea of things jammed close together comes from the nautical description of 'a tackle with the two blocks run close together so that they can touch each other – the limit of hoisting' (*O.E.D.*). Olson's use of the term here is a reference to the act of composition and also to the theme discussed: individuation. To hoist oneself up to the treetop of spring is to attain a more enlightened state; one is as close as possible to self-possession, but the act of metamorphosis shows that this involves a surrender of self (as against world). The paradox becomes clearer when we consider Olson's admiration for Stevens, who 'was the first to make things, / not just live off nature' (I.31). Again, 'A maker is one who equals. It is that difficult. To equal / yourself.[43] Olson honours the people who utilise nature's gifts as participators rather than exploiters; one example of a creative use of the environment is cutting down trees to make boats, specifically those which sail beautifully:

> Was Stevens not the
> head of something – the winning thing –
> got hidden all the years?

> (II.48)

One could pursue the subsidiary connotations of 'chockablock' further: the structure of a pulley is circular (as in season myth); on at least one occasion, Olson's pronunciation indicates that he has thought of the poem as a removal of obstacles ('*chuck* a block'). This theme is explored in the two related sections of 'Maximus, March 1961' (II.32–3). For the moment, however, it is enough to notice that the myth is told in concentrated form; Olson, even more than Leland and his Indian authority, wastes no words on minor, irrelevant detail. The tight method of presenting the story allows for many levels of interpretation; yet the smooth flow of the narrative and the lack of causal emphasis ('*and* he was a partridge') discourage any attempt to reduce the tale to allegory. The poet sustains a feeling of mystery throughout, but the story starts off in a naturalistic mode and becomes progressively more fantastic as it unfolds. Nowhere do we miss the presence of a moral or explanation; we are content with 'the thing itself' which flows directly into the succeeding versions of reality.

When Olson read the unpublished contents of volume II in Vancouver in 1963, 'Maximus Letter # whatever' was followed by 'First Stevens Song', a lyrical piece about shipbuilding, and 'Upward Choking', which ends:

> The world wheel down
> does spin my son says
>
> what does it look like
> now it's snow? It's
> all white with bushes
>
> stickingthrough[44]

The transition to 'present circumstances' was neatly handled; however, in the final version of the book Olson took the reader straight into 'Maximus, March 1961' after 'Chockablock'. The concerns of the latter poem feed so naturally into the problems of a winter-bound consciousness that one can only approve this tightening of the 'weave / of interlocking / pieces' (II.24–5). Whereas in the Algonquin myth nature provides all that one could desire, her representative here – 'the serpent' – refuses to arrange events until Man stops trying to contain her power by forcing things into shape. Maximus will not experience security till he lets go. It is appropriate that Olson returns to a maritime theme and in the text read at Vancouver he makes the connection with previous issues particularly apparent: 'Backward I compel / Gloucester / to yield / the Sea-Serpent.' We meet this beast elsewhere in the series in various guises: in her positive aspect she is Venus (I.57; II.13, 166); in her negative aspect she is Tiamat (I.35), Typhon (I.150; II.95–5, 166–72), Hydra (II.84) and the Gloucester sea-serpent (II.121; III.59–60).

It will be noticed that some of these serpent figures have male attributes. This may be due to Olson's preference for the ancient scheme in which the sea is male and the earth female. (One of the main motifs or *facts* in the book is, as J. H. Prynne has noted, 'the sea flooding into the serrated flanges of Gloucester'.)[45] Alternatively, the gender-ambiguity may be linked with the suppression of goddess worship by patriarchal societies. In this case the serpent is the female creatrix as viewed by male religion.

To quote Merlin Stone:

> In many of these [Indo-Aryan] myths the female deity is symbol-
> ized as a serpent or dragon, most often associated with darkness
> and evil. At times the gender of the dragon seems to be neuter, or
> even a male (closely associated with his mother or wife who is
> the Goddess). But the plot and the underlying symbolic theme of
> the story is so similar in each myth that, judging from the stories
> that do use the name of the female deity, we may surmise that
> the allegorical identity of the dragon or serpent is that of the
> Goddess religion. The Goddess, the original supreme deity of the
> people conquered and ruled by the invading Indo-Europeans,
> was not ignored, but was symbolically included in such a
> manner that these supposedly religious myths allow us to trace
> Her eventual disposition.[46]

Olson would have found a description of snake-girls 'of the great
salt water' in Leland (269–70); like mermaids, they are human
above the waist and serpent-shaped below. Moreover, the poet
makes extensive use of the HEPIT · NAGA · ATOSIS story (Leland,
273–5) in 'Of old times' (II.21), the poem which opens up the psychology of fear embedded in 'like' (II.20), an account of adultery
from the court records of Puritan New England. Clearly Olson is interested in the male fear of female sexuality which expresses itself
so often in these myths. He tries to uncover the positive attributes
of the serpent: the instinctual, the mysterious, and the generative
impulse in nature.

'Maximus, March 1961 – 1' (II.32) is partly an admission of wrong
behaviour and partly a triumphant realisation that nature is innocent ('The sea *does* / contain the beauty . . . The wonder is / limit-
less'). But the form of this poem, which is so much about
Gloucester and the sea, has its origin in Olson's experience under
the sacred mushroom. The Vancouver version actually refers to the
process of shaping the serpent 'out of / the watery mass with
mushroom eyes'.[47] It should be a 'ramp: / to eat God's food / raw'
(III.78). However, the act of grappling with the unconscious can be
unnerving, as Castaneda has shown. Images, seemingly discon-
nected, flash past; a thought sticks and cannot be dislodged; there is
a confusion between subject and object; clarity emerges then melts
away. Olson's mind is overlaid with isolated scenes that converge
and disperse by turns: the female goddess below 'the calm grey

waters'; the 'dragger, cleaning its fish,' idling into the scene and slipping 'across the empty water'; the snow which has dissolved or become something more than itself; the autos that have grown 'smaller, / and far away'. These are not just pictures to look at; the observer is inside each scene and feels the extremes of involvement and separation. Illumination comes when emotion is exchanged for feeling.

This last idea occurs is Olson's discussion of changes in consciousness at Gratwick Highlands (transcribed in *Muthologos*). Other comments from the same talk show how the responsible use of drugs may influence the language through which we communicate our perceptions to one another – a central concern of *The Maximus Poems*:

> I can capsulate it by [a quotation from] Herman Melville: 'By visible truth I mean the apprehension of the absolute condition of present things' ... And ... the advantage of the autonomic drugs ... is simply they restore the fact that we live in the autonomic system, which, as far as I understand, is to *preserve our organs from our will*.
> ... we inherited a complete system of discourse for two thousand years which has completely crapped motive. We have lost motive almost entirely out of our mental capacity and have had cause instead. So that the tendency of the objective world to go away from us has been extremely strong, because the objective world won't be treated that way. It just doesn't happen to be causal, it happens to be motible'[48]

Olson claims that there is a way of controlling perception which avoids the interference of the will–a total attentiveness provoked by the object – and perhaps it is in this sense that we should understand his attempt to turn snow back to snow and to define the *anima* of the depths in 'I forced the calm grey waters ...'. In other words, this poem (like the 'Juan de la Cosa' piece in volume I) describes Olson's effort to locate a clear-headed mode of discourse for his epic. The means, he concludes, are there in words and actions, if the writer is alert enough to see that 'An American / is a complex of occasions, / themselves a geometry / of spatial nature' (II.15). Confronting a submerged reality, wrestling with chaos, Olson comes back with coherence (both linguistic and psychophilosophical). The text vividly marks the track of this process, allowing expression to a flux of experience that might, in other hands, be rendered meaningless.

The second part of 'Maximus, March 1961' (II.33) also deals with an alteration of consciousness, but is different in mood and territorial focus. Instead of venturing out to sea, Maximus goes along the 'upper road' to Dogtown, a wild retreat which is associated, by implication, with Thoreau's faith in nature and Whitman's openness of expression. The movement is eastward, past Indian 'Lake' and otter ponds. A pioneer respectful of origins, Maximus orients himself on ground which can yield revelation.[49] The middle voice construction ('show me / myself') and the whole anti-linear arrangement of the poem's syntax help to create these changing terms.[50]

The poem which follows (II.34) seems to be parochial in the extreme; it is nothing but a summary of headings in an eighteenth–century merchant's account book. B. Ellery, however, is a key figure in Olson's research into the origins of Gloucester. One of the chief men of the city, he settled in Dogtown at a time when fishermen and merchants still lived some distance away from the harbour. His account book confirms that the business of fishing was largely conducted from this area ('A Southern Voyage / Each Year From What Sounded / Like His Back Door at the Green' – II.200). It is on such minutiae of history that the grander vision of *The Maximus Poems* must rest. As a later poem (II.47) suggests, Olson's encounter with B. Ellery is a way of transcending a gap in time; the road to Dogtown is a bridge through 'the lower region of earthy mist' from which one may know 'the Angel Matter'.[51]

The last poem in the sequence being discussed is 'A Maximus Song' (II.35), which returns us to the sea-shore. The occasion celebrated here is 'the annual ceremony of Phryne appearing before the people and going into the water in her full and original beauty'.[52] According to Athenaeus, this Greek courtesan was the model for Apelles' picture of Venus, and Olson imagines her as Aphrodite, whose representative indeed she must have been. The goddess of love and 'mother of all things', as Apuleius called her, is redeemed from the stigma of serpenthood by this song in her honour. We are reminded of the delicate generative power portrayed in an earlier lyric, 'The Ring Of' (1952), and also of the elemental theme which lies behind the *Maximus* series: that 'all things [are] engendered of water'.[53] It is interesting, in view of Olson's concern with the particular, that the poet linked his classical 'hymn' with an incident

involving Dr Leary's 'lovely daughter, who was the first woman to'
display her beauty openly in Gloucester:

> I wrote a poem on Phryne, the great mistress of Athens, walking
> into the sea yearly because men wished to see – men and women
> wished to see a perfect body. This was the model for Praxiteles'
> Cnidian Venus, that utterly beautiful thing. That woman, the
> Miss Suzanne Leary, appeared on the beach right out this house,
> the front beach of Gloucester, the Pavilion Beach, at fifteen years
> old, and the whole town blew up at seeing a body in a bikini'.[54]

Whether or not this event happened before the poem was written,
it makes a sharp comment on the feminine principle which figures
so prominently in this volume.

Despite the huge sweep of *Maximus Poems IV, V, VI*, there is a
constant pull towards crystallisation of viewpoint:

> and nature's gone away to furnaces men shoot
> bodies into, and our love is for ourselves alone
> I walk you paths of lives I'd share with
> you simply to make evident the world
> is an eternal event and this epoch solely
> the decline of fishes, such a decline Bayliss,
> my son calls her his first teacher, suggested
> to her husband Gorton's have an aquarium
> to show what fish look like – or it was already said
> it won't be long, with fish sticks, pictures
> will be necessary on the covers of the TV dinners
> to let children know that mackerel is a different
> looking thing than herrings

(II.38–9)

This is the Dogtown volume of the series because it is water under
rock that concerns the archaeologist of a Mediterranean culture
projected out into the Atlantic. Now that the decline of the Piscean
age is evident, it is vital to comprehend the process by which civil-
isations rise and fall. Hence the presence in these poems of Greek or
Egyptian deities, Sumerians, Hittites and Phoenicians; the culture
of the Eastern states of America is built largely on the dreams and
aspirations of adventurers or refugees from the ancient centre of

the world. Olson drives back to the source of travel, commerce and learning, but his mind is never far from the land and inhabitants of Gloucester. As J. H. Prynne has argued, the 'notion of age' here is not incremental (on the European model); rather, Olson's poem grows 'back into itself and its historic matrix'.[55]

When asked whether the end of the second volume marked the conclusion to the *Maximus* sequence, Olson explained that all his books 'end with an image of the vehicular'.[56] The last lines of this work ('I set out now / in a box upon the sea') refer both to the myth of Osiris and to the fate of Ishmael in *Moby-Dick*; like these figures, the poet has survived dismemberment and will tell further tales of the sea. After the structural complexity of the previous book, *Volume Three* impresses the reader with its clarity of vision. Although the material was collected in its present form after Olson's death, the scheme of advance had been manifest from three lines written as long ago as 1963 and designated as the opening of a third volume:

having descried the nation
to write a Republic
in gloom on Watch-House Point

(III.9)

The poet continues to experiment with the arrangement of words on the page (see, for example, III.104, 120–1); there is still packed meaning in such poems as 'AN ART CALLED GOTHONIC' (III.168–73); the anthropological concern continues under the influence of Heinrich Zimmer and G. R. Levy; political ideas have their counterpart on a mythic level; and particular events partake of a universal reality as before. Yet there is a more religious emphasis and a more spontaneous expression of daily observation. One feels closer to the man Olson, even though the public voice of Maximus extends the relevance of his thoughts. He is more integrated with the city, but at the same time a deep solitude is revealed behind the act of 'concentration' ('bitter / police cars turn my corner, no one in the world / close to me' – III.101, 80). The naked directness of a poem like 'Bottled up for days' (III.126) is something new in the series. Michael Bernstein has pointed out that, in its 'tone of controlled sorrow and lonely hope', Olson's more personal coda is 'akin to the closing parts of *Paterson* and Pound's *Drafts and Fragments*'.[57]

The last period of Olson's writing, then, constitutes a return to a more open mode of communication. If the 'tesserae' (pieces in a mosaic) are less tightly joined than formerly, this may not be due merely to the lack of Olson's editing impress. Within each unit a larger number of lines are double-spaced. Where there is pressure it is often of a tumbling colloquial character (as in the toy steam shovel episode, III.123). Syntactically, most of the poems come through with an, albeit desperate, ease (see, for example, III.108). Sometimes one feels that the matter is more interesting than its expression. However, themes from the previous volumes are picked up with freshness and lucidity, as in 'There was a salt-works at Stage Fort' (III.64–5) where the idea of cod as silver ore and of Gloucester as the mythical floating island of the Atlantic crops up again. Nor are we allowed to forget John Watts, an early hero of *The Maximus Poems* (III.45), the man with the house on his head (III.58), and the Sea-Serpent of local legend and world mythology (III.59–61). Enyalion reappears as the archetype of male glory in what is probably the most dextrous and muscular poem in the book (III.38–40). Hesiod's world of wilful, amoral forces – less humanised and refined than Homer's – remains an important source for the working out of father–mother–child relations.

The death of Olson's partner Betty in 1963 and the poet's problematic relationship with his father undoubtedly lie behind two poems about death, although it has to be said that the experiences are rendered in terms which invite interpretation beyond the bounds of a single person's life. 'O Quadriga' (451) refers in its title to Auriga, the Charioteer or Waggoner constellation. Maximus remembers how, in an earlier, happier year, he had to strain to see this form; now, in the summer night, he has clear apprehension of the underworld abductor (on one level a projection of his darker self):

> you are my instructor at last, there are no landings
> you also were Pluto, you did take my girl, you are
> triumph (trump before the Trump herself) I hail you, Driver,
> in your place upon the sky

Compact but fluent in structure, and quite unsentimental in tone, this poem enacts the shift to an acceptance of loss.

'COLES ISLAND', influenced perhaps by Chaucer's dream poems, describes a visit to 'a queer isolated and gated place' where game live unmolested by humans (III.69–70). The poet and his son are innocently observing the scenery when a stranger steps out from the woods; he is dressed more formally than Olson and he seems to be a sportsman. But beside this he is the figure of Death and 'a property-owner'. Maximus feels uncomfortable since he is trespassing; yet the country gentleman does not question his presence there. The two men 'regard each other' for a moment, then Death moves on without any drama occurring. Going about his normal business – the 'will / to know more of the topography' of the island, Maximus has crossed a barrier into Hades (coal's island) and come back alive. Is Death's materialisation and reaction a warning or a reassurance? With a fine balance, Olson's poem maintains the neutrality of dreams. On one level the story must be about the risks of venturing into unknown territory, and one is reminded of the second poem in the book, which quotes the response of a redoubtable neighbour, Mrs Tarantino:

> You have a long nose, meaning
> you stick it into every other person's
> business, do you not? And I couldn't
> say anything
> but that I
> do
>
> (III.10)

If it is the archaeologist's privilege to uproot hidden truths, there is a price to pay for such investigation.

Maximus the sage or moral authority is, in fact, more in evidence here than in the previous books. Looking back at the collapse of the settlers' ideals, he pays tribute to John Winthrop, 'who imagined / that men / cared / for what kind of world / they chose to / live in' (III.41). On a more immediate level, Maximus inveighs against the destruction of buildings such as the handsome Mansfield house in order to provide better commercial facilities. Too much of this prescriptive comment could prove tiresome (as poetry), but it finds its place here among other types of discourse. At times the zeal for preserving the *polis* gives rise to memorable and moving statement (as in III.202–3).

Alongside his awareness of decline, Maximus tries to locate an eternal aspect within the movement of the earth and its people. The image of the rose, associate with both mutability and the incorruptible, becomes increasingly important. The holograph version of 'Migration in fact' (III.104) is rose-shaped, reflecting migratory patterns. 'The winter the *Gen. Starks* was stuck' – dated December 21st, one day before the winter solstice – presents the Rose as a pattern in which renewal, even perfection, is figured (III.106). Olson is as much concerned with the future as the past; he labours to construct 'an actual earth of value' (III.190) so that people will know from *doing* how to live. This is the other nation whose foundations are laid bare in *The Maximus Poems*.

Critics otherwise sympathetic to Olson have pronounced *Volume Three* a failure or at least a disappointment after the tough ambition of the previous books. Hugh Kenner, Robert von Hallberg and Don Byrd express reservations about the conclusion of Olson's epic. The poems are said to flounder, to be too reliant on fancy, and to be at times 'talky'.[58] Nevertheless, in their perverse way these fragments have a lasting power. Lines and whole poems stick in the mind and resonate back through the preceding material. Completeness in a postmodern context may only be susceptible of expression as an *index* of the possible.

The effectiveness of *The Maximus Poems* depends first upon the authority of Olson's ideas and secondly upon the linguistic structure by which those ideas emerge. The two factors are, of course, intertwined. The issue of Olson's scholarship is tricky. Both Martin Duberman and Tom Clark emphasise the capriciousness of his procedures. Clark refers to Edward Dorn's view of Olson as a 'great intellectual punter constantly at the gaming tables of thought and literature'.[59] Dorn has spoken of Olson's 'passion for a scope of knowledge' but has distinguished that from the penetration of true scholarship: 'I don't think he was narrow enough to be a scholar. ... Olson was after a different kind of registration of his sensibility [from, say, Housman].'[60] Robert von Hallberg goes much further, suggesting that, in shifting from a historical to a mythological methodology, Olson is so wilful in his treatment of materials that he becomes as vulnerable as Pound to the charge that his text is ego-ruled.[61] Olson wanted to be taken seriously as a thinker; for him, poetry was not just a lyric or narrative entertainment but also a means of exploring and defining the world. His mode of operation in *Maximus* is anti-rational (or more precisely *ante*-rational) and this is likely to lead to difficulties when logical criteria of analysis are applied. It is significant that Olson paid homage to Pliny's *Natural History* as an example of 'pre-scientific' thought.[62] Pliny's investigation of things is particular up to a point, yet also inclusive and tolerant of imaginative realities. He has a willingness to define through story. Both *The Maximus Poems* and Olson's other utterances (for example, *Muthologos*) displays an energy of interest which is equivalent to Pliny's: references continually spark off others. This may not be scholarship in a singly directed sense, but it is a form of deep awareness.

Olson stresses that his business is the *enactment* of ideas and, while there is some masculine bluster in the position adopted, it is true that he tried, like Herodotus, to look 'for oneself for the evidence of / what is said' (*The Maximus Poems*, I.100–1). As a youngster Olson had worked on the Gloucester fisheries wharf and on local fishing vessels. Then, as a young adult, he sailed as a hand on a swordfishing schooner for three weeks.[63] The tread of Olson's feet on the Gloucester mainland is constantly evident in *Maximus*. Thus book knowledge was a supplement to direct experience, and the criticism which Bunting levelled at Zukofsky – that he wrote out of books rather than firsthand experience[64] – cannot so easily be applied to Olson. Pondering a shift in focus from the harbour to Dogtown in volume II, Olson writes: 'now I see what was up, / a year ago, chomping around these streets, / measuring off distances, looking into / records, disconsolately / making up things to do' (II.17). One can see how such methods lead to a poetics which is expressive and performative. When Olson speaks of the sentence as a 'capable animal … jumping all over the place, and growling',[65] the implication is that the vernacular, even in print, stays active from the *doing*.

One area in which Olson's ideas have aroused controversy is the depiction of women in *The Maximus Poems* – especially his treatment of the female principle, as embodied in figures such as the Lady of Good Voyage (I.2, 6; II.84), the Sea-Serpent, the Memphite Cow goddess (II.150) and the Mother city, Polis. The question is whether Olson's use of primitive story makes for a renegotiation of the power base between the sexes or leads merely to a re-application of patriarchal values. His stress on the recovery of elemental energies involves using language which has regressive associations in a more negative – i.e. gender – sense ('where ground itself is a fucking hole' II.151). The portrayal of 'that international doll' in the White House (I.35) seems not just a condemnation of surface fashion and corrupt manoeuvring but also an appeal to misogynist prejudices. Testimony concerning the poet's treatment of female students at Black Mountain is not irrelevant here.[66] Olson's attempt to re-establish 'the necessary goddess' (as he called her in 'In Cold Hell, in Thicket') means that he is dealing with archetypes which must, on one level, be a projection of male fears and desires. Drawing on Hesiod and anonymous ancient texts, interpreted in the light of commentaries by Jane Harrison, Jung, Erich Neumann and others, Olson presents powerful images of the Great Mother as nourishing and sustaining source, spiritual guardian, promiscuous venturer (II.143) and vengeful destroyer. Nevertheless, the poet's position towards these residual or inherent polarities is complex, as the example of the Sea-Serpent demonstrates. The figure is both threatening and consoling, and Olson attends carefully to the mental process of envisioning her. This self-reflexiveness continues in the third volume of *Maximus*, which gives the Father type greater prominence.

Maximus's critique of a certain kind of femininity (Jean Harlow as an instance of white 'Sunday supplement' falsity – a distortion of both male and female needs, I.55) is too important merely to be dismissed as patriarchal hypocrisy. As both Francine du Plessix Gray (an ex-student) and Susan Howe have argued, the oppressive aspects of Olson's masculine consciousness can provoke a valuable response. Howe writes that she is 'thrown into a confrontational relationship with the poet' at times, but that Olson's work is 'a necessary concentration of energy' which has provided her with 'a vocabulary for going forward into a past which is part of the living present'.[67]

The issue of gender and the more personal focus in *Maximus Poems Volume Three* invite speculation as to how we are to take Olson's approval of Keats's statement: 'A Man's life of any worth is a continual allegory – and very few eyes can see the Mystery of his life – a life like the scriptures, figurative'.[68] Olson appears to have it both ways in *The Special View of History*, a series of lectures given at Black Mountain in 1956. On the one hand, he admires Keats for unseating the unit 'I'; on the other hand, he applauds Keats's focus upon 'actual willful man'. It becomes clear that Olson approves what Keats extricates from 'the Man of Power – namely, the ability to be 'in uncertainties, Mysteries, doubts, without any irritable reaching after fact and reason'. This, Olson says, is a way of staying 'in process'.[69] Keats's concept of dynamic disinterestedness ('*Negative Capability*') is applicable to *The Maximus Poems* in that the poet aspires to 'hold off' and let materials have their own weight. This is, paradoxically, a kind of will or power.

In 'Maximus of Gloucester' (III.101), Olson says of this work on Gloucester: 'It is not I, / even if the life appeared / biographical.

The only thing / is if one can be / an image / of man, "The noble-ness and the arete".' The poet feels that the elements in his life's story are worth recording because they enable, on a manageable scale, some mapping of history; but those elements become trans-muted, or at least fused with other sources. Put simply, Maximus includes but stands for more than Olson. The biography of a poet will be flawed, as Tom Clark's account of Olson is, if it does not deal sufficiently with the physiology of the work.

The test for the success or greatness of poetry must ultimately be a matter of sound (the kind of words chosen, their rhythmic arrangement and so on). It might seem as if Olson deliberately sets himself against traditional notions of melody. *The Maximus Poems* do not yield the Provencal grace that persists even in the tough syn-tactical blocks of *The Cantos*: compare, for instance, 'I live under-neath / the light of day' (III.228) with the fragmentary Canto CXV. Nevertheless, Olson's long poem has distinctive aural patterns which range from the euphonious to the discordant. Silence also plays a part in this structure. Olson's approach to the voicing shapes of *Maximus* was influenced by the example of Pierre Boulez, whose views he quotes in a letter to Cid Corman: 'We are thus freed from all melody, all harmony and all counterpoint, since serial structure has caused all these (essentially modal and tonal) notions to disappear.'[70]

To hear recordings of Olson reading *The Maximus Poems* aloud is a revelation. The spatial deployment of words on the page comes to life with vivid point. The voice, a trifle breathless, hovers on the edge of incoherence but always delivers in an appropriately deep ('Maximal') tone. The Vancouver performance contains a particu-larly sensitive rendering of syllable and phrase, as in the slowed down energy of: '(socialism CulturISM LiberaISM jass is gysm) why I Don't Haven't Gotten / it all Further?' (II.23). The Folkways record, made at the instigation of the Beatles' company Apple in 1969, contains powerful readings of 'Maximus Letter # whatever' and 'Cashes', each delivered with the push of continuous narra-tive.[71] It is fortunate that these and other performances are pre-served on tape, since in many ways they provide the best entry into Olson's text.

Charles Olson has been accused of writing poems which run 'the risk of being notes on a subject of inquiry'.[72] Perhaps, in the case of *The Maximus Poems*, we need to broaden our definition of what poetry is. As the poet himself said:

I find it awkward to call myself a poet or a writer. If there are no walls there are no names. This is the morning, after the dispersion, and the work of the morning is methodology: how to use oneself, and on what. That is my profession. I am an archaeologist of morning.[73]

NOTES

1. 'Beginning of 3rd Institute', February 1953. Quoted by George Butterick in 'Charles Olson and the Postmodern Advance', *The Iowa Review*, 11, no. 4 (Fall 1980) 4–27. Hereafter cited as Butterick (1980).
2. Helen Vendler, *Harvard/Faber Book of Contemporary American Poetry* (Cambridge, Mass., 1985; London, 1986). The limitations and inconsistencies of this anthology are analysed by Marjorie Perloff in 'Of Canons and Contemporaries', *Sulfur*, 16 (May 1986) and by Dachine Rainer and Thomas Clark in *Agenda*, 24, no. 4/25, no. 1 (Winter 1987).
3. See, for instance, Charles Bernstein, *Content's Dream: Essays 1975–1984* (Los Angeles, 1986) pp. 321–39, and Barrett Watten, *Total Syntax* (Carbondale and Edwardsville, Ill., 1985) pp. 115–39. Michael Davidson provides a brief account of these attitudes in '"Skewed by Design": From Act to Speech Act in Language-Writing', *fragmente*, 2 (Autumn 1990), 44–9.
4. Charles Olson, *Human Universe and Other Essays* (New York, 1967) p. 52.
5. Charles Boer, *Charles Olson in Connecticut* (Chicago, 1975) p. 63
6. These poems are reprinted in *The Collected Poems of Charles Olson*, ed. G. Butterick (Berkeley and Los Angeles, 1987).
7. George Butterick, *A Guide to the Maximus Poems* (Berkeley and Los Angeles, 1978). Hereafter cited as Butterick 1978.
8. Charles Olson, *The Maximus Poems*, ed. G. Butterick (Berkeley and Los Angeles, 1983). References will be cited by the square bracketed numeration (coinciding with that in the original editions), except where new material has been added.
9. Ezra Pound, *The Cantos* (London: Faber, 1975) p. 257.
10. Pound, as relayed by Moni Moulick, 'The "Insane" Poet', *The Visva Bharati Quarterly*, 16 (1950).
11. Ezra Pound (ed.), *The Chinese Written Character as a Medium for Poetry* (San Francisco, n.d.) p. 30.
12. Letter to Ronald Mason, 13 July 1953; quoted in Butterick (1980), 21.
13. Quoted by Charles Boer, *Charles Olson in Connecticut*, p. 86. Olson's regular visits to St Elizabeth's Hospital evidently brought some animation and relief to the dispirited older poet. In a letter to his lawyer

dated January 1946 Pound wrote 'Olson save my life'. See Julian Cornell, *The Trial of Ezra Pound* (New York, 1966) p. 71.

14. Catherine Seelye (ed.), *Charles Olson and Ezra Pound: An Encounter at St Elizabeths* (New York, 1975) p. 89.

15. See, for example, *Pleistocene Man: Letters from Charles Olson to Jack Clarke* (Buffalo, 1968) p. 17.

16. Charles Olson, *Muthologos* (Bolinas, 1978–9) vol. 2, p. 122.

17. See C. G. Jung, *Alchemical Studies* (London, 1968) p. 131n. The phrase is derived from Pico della Mirandola, *Heptaplus* I, ch. vii and then from the writings of Paracelsus.

18. Butterick (1978), p. 6.

19. Gregory Smith (ed.), *Elizabethan Critical Essays* (London, 1937) vol. 1, p. 68. Part of Gosson's accusation is quoted on p. 365.

20. Frank Davey, 'Six Readings of Olson's *Maximus*', *Boundary 2*, 2, nos. 1 and 2 (Fall 1973/Winter 1974) 292–7.

21. Butterick (1980), 16.

22. Editor's Note [by Jonathan Williams], *The Maximus Poems* (New York, 1960) p. 162.

23. *Charles Olson and Robert Creeley: The Complete Correspondence*, ed. G. Butterick (Santa Barbara: Black Sparrow, 1980–9) vol. 5, p. 50 [8 March 1951]. It is interesting that this discussion of Pound's approach emerges alongside Olson's consideration of Mayan glyphs.

24. Butterick (1978), pp. xvi–xxxviii.

25. Boer, *Charles Olson in Connecticut*, p. 83.

26. Charles Olson, 'Maximus, to Gloucester, from Dogtown, after the Flood'; published in *OLSON: The Journal of the Charles Olson Archives*, 9 (1978), 8–9.

27. Pound, *The Cantos* (London: Faber, 1975) p. 324. The cover of the third volume of the *Maximus* Poems displays a *periplus* of the coast of Massachusetts from Gloucester to Marblehead, 'said to have been drawn by John Winthrop from the deck of the *Arbella* as he sailed south toward Boston in 1630'. No doubt Olson would have argued that this map, with its distortions, is more real than a modern equivalent produced by 'scientific' means.

28. This map is reproduced in C. Paullin, *Atlas of the Historical Geography of the United States*, ed. J. K. Wright (Washington and New York, 1932), a copy of which Olson used at Black Mountain. The map is also reproduced in Carl Sauer, *Sixteenth Century North America* (Berkeley and Los Angeles, 1971) p. 9.

29. Daniel G. Hise, 'Noticing Juan De La Cosa', *Boundary 2*, 2, nos. 1 and 2 (Fall 1973/Winter 1974), 330; Tom Clark, *Charles Olson: The Allegory of a Poet's Life* (New York, 1991) pp. 42, 127–9.

30. Sherman Paul, *Olson's Push* (Baton Rouge and London: University of Louisiana press, 1978) pp. 156–7.

31. See Olson, *The Maximus Poems*, I.36; Olson, *Muthologos*, vol. 1, 136; and Charles Olson, *Additional Prose* (Bolinas, 1974) p. 29.

32. Robert Creeley, *A Quick Graph* (San Francisco, 1970) p. 207. This essay was first published in 1961.

33. Unpublished interview with Gavin Selerie, Peter Middleton and Tom Pickard: The Riverside Interviews (May 1982).

34. Charles Olson, *Causal Mythology*, ed. Donald Allen (San Francisco, 1969) p. 2.

35. Olson, *Muthologos*, vol. 2, pp. 160–1.

36. Butterick (1978), p. x1.

37. Davey, 'Six Readings', 320.

38. C. G. Jung, *Psychology and Religion: West and East* (London, 1969) pp. 591–2. See also, the essays on synchronicity in C. G. Jung, *The Structure and Dynamics of the Psyche* (London, 1969) pp. 419–531. Olson was probably familiar with the comment: 'we have to go back to Heraclitus if we want to find something similar in our own civilisation, at least where philosophy is concerned. Only in astrology, alchemy, and the mantic procedures do we find no difference of principle between our attitude and the Chinese' (ibid., p. 485).

39. This is particularly true of the poems collected in *Volume Three of Maximus*; see Butterick (1978), p. 1i.

40. Olson's borrowings from other writers (in *The Maximus Poems* at least) are substantial; yet he is by no means merely a collector of other people's wares. Although he often follows his source closely, the choosing of extracts and presentation of material make 'found' work new. The minor shifts of emphasis in 'Of old times' (II.21) and the inspired compression in 'Cashes' (II.19) give these writings a fresh dramatic charge, even as the spirit of the original is retained. The subtlety of these alterations is revealed in Butterick's *Guide*; see, for instance, the documents which lie behind 'The Gulf of Maine' (quoted on pp. 397–400). Olson's use of nautical literature in the composition of 'Cashes' recalls that special relationship which existed between Shakespeare and Plutarch. Discussing Melville, Olson notes with approval Edward Dahlberg's definition of originality: 'Highborn Stealth' (*Call Me Ishmael*, London, 1967, p. 38). If the *Maximus* poems are dependent on a whole range of sources, Olson was a thorough investigator and absorbed knowledge in a creative manner. He knew what to appropriate for impact and relevance; and he knew how to bring things together in an interesting way. The grid, surfaces and core, is indeed a 'special view of history'.

41. Charles G. Leland, *The Algonquin Legends of New England* (Boston and New York, 1884) p. 292.

42. Sherman Paul notes that the 'hard-wood ridge near a good spring of water' is an approximation of Dogtown (*Olson's Push*, p. 202).

43. 'The Carpenter Poem I (Letter # 33)'; written for volume I but discarded from the series, this poem may be found in *OLSON*, 6 (1976), 52–4.

44. Published in *OLSON*, 9 (1978), 53–4.

45. J. H. Prynne, 'Charles Olson, Maximus Poems IV, V, VI', *The Park*, 4 and 5 (Summer 1969) 65.

46. Merlin Stone, *The Paradise Papers* (London, 1976) pp. 83–4. See also, Joseph Campbell, *The Masks of God: Occidental Mythology* (New York, 1964) pp. 72–92; and Robert Graves, *The White Goddess* (London,

1961) pp. 387–95. Olson was an admirer of Graves's researches into mythology; see Tom Clark, *Charles Olson: The Allegory of a Poet's Life*, pp. 164, 320, and *OLSON*, 2 (1974), 94–5.

47. The MS. draft is reproduced in *OLSON*, 3 (1975), 58. Olson participated in Timothy Leary's psilocybin research programme at Harvard in 1960–1.

48. Olson, *Muthologos*, vol. 1, pp. 49, 59.

49. Later in the book (II.90) Olson directs our attention to Obadiah Bruen's Island, where the Algonquins used to steep 'fly agaric in whortleberry juice, / to drink to see'.

50. See Don Byrd, *Charles Olson's 'Maximus'* (Chicago, 1980) pp. 127–30 for further elucidation of these points.

51. See Olson, *Muthologos*, vol. 1, pp. 15–16, 60–1, 74; Jane Harrison, *Themis* (Cambridge, 1927) pp. 391–2; Olson, *The Maximus Poems*, II.9, 148. It should be noted that Olson by no means assents to the view of life that is implied in Ellery's arrangement of 'categories'.

52. From an early version of 'Bk 11, chapter 37' (II.84) published in Olson, *Muthologos*, vol. 1, p. 19. Olson thought he had found literal confirmation of the Phyrne–Aphrodite analogy in Pausanias's description of 'a stone image of Aphrodite beside the sea' at Lerna. It would appear that this fascination with an embodiment of Venus represents a shift of emphasis, rather than a rejection of the stance outlined in *Maximus* I.57–8. The new approach to myth was no doubt encouraged by an intensive reading of Hesiod (see *Maximus* II.172 in particular).

53. Plutarch, *The Morals*, tr. Holland (1603) p. 805. Cf. Olson, *Call Me Ishmael*, pp. 106–11, and *The Maximus Poems*, II.72 ('the original unit / survives in the salt').

54. Olson, *Muthologos*, vol. 1, p. 192.

55. J. H. Prynne, 'Charles Olson, Maximus Poems IV, V, VI', 64.

56. Charles Boer, *Charles Olson in Connecticut*, p. 91.

57. Michael Bernstein, *The Tale of the Tribe: Ezra Pound and the Modern Verse Epic* (Princeton, 1980) p. 268.

58. Hugh Kenner, *A Homemade World* (New York, 1975) pp. 181–3; Robert von Hallberg, *Charles Olson: The Scholar's Art* (Cambridge, Mass., 1978) pp. 212–14; Don Byrd, *Charles Olson's Maximus*, pp. 191–3. Byrd's view is more positive than that of the others.

59. Tom Clark, *Charles Olsen: The Allegory of a Poet's Life*, x; Martin Duberman, *Black Mountain: An Exploration in Community* (London, 1974) pp. 369–71.

60. Edward Dorn, *Interviews* (Bolinas, 1980) p. 37; unpublished interview with Gavin Selerie: *The Riverside Interviews* (July 1981).

61. von Hallberg, op. cit., pp. 214–15.

62. Olson, *Muthologos*, vol. 1, p. 145.

63. See *OLSON*, 7 (1977), 3–42 and *Maximus* I.38, 91, 603.

64. C. F. Terrell (ed.), *Basil Bunting: Man and Poet* (Orono, 1981) pp. 266–7. See also Bunting's remarks on Pound, quoted in Peter Makin, *Basil Bunting: The Shaping of his Verse* (Oxford, 1992) pp. 38–9, 103.

65. Olson, *Human Universe and Other Essays*, p. 65.
66. Martin Duberman, *Black Mountain*, p. 380; Tom Clark, *Charles Olson: The Allegory of a Poet's Life*, pp. 209–10. See also Charles Boer, *Charles Olson in Connecticut*, pp. 53–6.
67. Susan Howe, 'Since A Dialogue We Are', *Acts*, 10 (1989), 169–71. Howe refers to the feelings of du Plessix Gray on p. 166.
68. *Letters of John Keats*, ed. R. Gittings (London, 1970) p. 218.
69. Charles Olson, *The Special View of History*, ed. Ann Charters (Berkeley, 1970) pp. 32–3, 15–16, 41–2. Keats, *Letters of John Keats*, p. 43.
70. Charles Olson, *Letters for Origin 1950–1955*, ed. A. Glover (London, 1969) p. 103; cf. Tom Clark, *Charles Olson: The Allegory of a Poet's Life*, p. 234.
71. Olson's reading of [the then unpublished] *Maximus Poems IV, V, VI* at the Vancouver Poetry Conference in August 1963 was taped by Fred Wah. Copies are held in the Olson Archive at University of Connecticut and at Essex University, England. The record entitled *Charles Olson reads from Maximus Poems IV, V, VI* (Folkways FL 9738) was recorded by Barry Miles in Gloucester. The title is slightly misleading since Olson also reads from *Mayan Letters* and from the projected third *Maximus* volume.
72. von Hallberg, op. cit., 185.
73. Charles Olson, *Additional Prose*, p. 40.

13

Allen Ginsberg

BRIAN DOCHERTY

Allen Ginsberg nowadays looks like a successful Jewish dentist since he cut his hair and beard and donned suit and tie at the instigation of his Guru Chögyam Trungpa Rinpoche. As the half-title page of his *Collected Poems* notes, he is a 'Member of the American Institute of Arts and Letters and co-founder of the Jack Kerouac School of Disembodied Poetics at the Naropa Institute'[1] and he describes himself gleefully in an interview with Jim Burns as 'a most respectable figure'.[2] A founder member of the Beat Generation, along with Jack Kerouac and William Burroughs, circa 1944, Ginsberg is still best known for *Howl*, *Kaddish* and the poems of his first ten years or so as a public figure. (The early poems written from 1945 to 1952 did not appear until 1972 as *Gates of Wrath*, since the 'ms was carried to London by lady friend early fifties, it disappeared and I had no complete copy till 1968 when old typescript was returned thru poet Bob Dylan – it passed into his hands years earlier'.)[3] Although Ginsberg clearly belongs to that neo-modernist grouping which derives its poetics from Ezra Pound and William Carlos Williams, he is a more social and political poet than either. He also derives parts of his poetics from William Blake, from the eighteenth–century poet Christopher Smart, the French Surrealists, Cézanne (whom he studied at Columbia with Meyer Shapiro), Herman Melville, Céline, and fellow Beats Kerouac and Burroughs. Another influence was his father Louis, a traditional lyric poet who appears in anthologies, such as *May Days* and *Unrest*, of radical poets of the 1920s and 1930s. He read his parents' magazines, such as *The New Masses* which published Mike Gold and Arturo Giovanitti, who used the long line and declamatory style of Walt Whitman and Carl Sandburg. Ginsberg also states that 'the poem from that period that had a big effect on me was Ben Maddow's *The City*. That influenced me a lot when I was writing "Howl"'.[4]

Along with the radical politics, and the complex matrix of literary influences, there is also the transcendentalist philosophy of Thoreau, Emerson and Whitman. According to John Tytell, 'the Romantic militancy of the Beats found its roots in American transcendentalism . . . the Beats' spiritual ancestors were Thoreau, Melville and Whitman optimistically proclaiming with egalitarian gusto the raw newness and velocity of self renewing change in America while joyously admiring the potential of the common man'.[5]

I would argue that the influence of Whitman has been most important to Ginsberg, and this essay will focus on Ginsberg's relation to Whitman, and the conjunction of sexuality and politics which informs their writing. There are, of course, several competing views of Whitman to be found and the view expressed in this essay does not aim to be full or complete. Whitman, of course, embraced contradiction and diversity and had no doubts about the value in social and political terms of an American poetry. Ginsberg, too, has from the start had a messianic faith in his ability to be a spokesman and chronicler, as set out in the opening line of *Howl*:

I saw the best minds of my generation destroyed by madness, starving hysterical naked.

(CP 126)

Nakedness; physical, emotional, psychological, was to become a recurrent theme of Ginsberg's poetry. This openness to life and experience is characteristic of the Beat project, and would in itself be enough to mark it as an oppositional tendency in the late 1940s and 1950s without the spirit of protest and revolt picked up on by most critics when *Howl and Other Poems* appeared in 1956. The shift in post-war values to Cold War hysteria and McCarthyite repression is well documented; the enemy without became the enemy within and the prosperity brought by the military–industrial complex had its accompanying tensions. Significantly, the major establishment poet of the fifties, Robert Lowell, talked of 'the tranquillised fifties', reflecting the Confessional poets' (Lowell, Berryman, Sexton *et al.*) obsession with interiority and public exorcism of private demons. Ginsberg's work has some superficial similarities with these poets, but it is always firmly grounded in the social and political as well as employing fundamentally different strategies (i.e. the ideogrammatic method of Pound rather than the procedures authorised by the New Criticism of Allan Tate and John Crowe Ransome).

Lifestyle and sexuality are celebrated, even paraded, in Beat writing, and their tender nakedness is quite different from, say, John Berryman's use of the poem as public psychoanalyst's couch. Since Ginsberg could be more open than Whitman, and was temperamentally inclined to be so, it quickly became apparent that this nakedness was offered as visions of the unspeakable individual, the homosexual. The love that dared not speak its name had not only come out of the closet, but followed Whitman's recommendation to 'unscrew the doors from the jamb' in a democratic gesture of inclusiveness, at least as far as men were concerned. There were, of course, other poets in the 1950s writing as gay men, notably Robert Duncan and Frank O'Hara, but Ginsberg is the pioneer closet dismantler. Whitman, however, is the American trailblazer.

It is in the 'Calamus' poems, even more than in the 'Children of Adam' poems, that Whitman's enduring quality as an American original resides. The first edition of *Leaves of Glass* makes clear Whitman's views on democracy and liberty, and many readers will consider that being the great poet of democracy is a sufficient claim to originality. We must look for more in a great poet, and I would argue that the open celebration of physicality and homosexuality, linked to democratic politics, constitutes Whitman's distinctive claim to be regarded as one of the major figures in world literature. This characteristic pluralism of expression, both personally and politically, represents the Whitmanian legacy to future writers, although the next generation, the poets of the 1890s such as Edwin Arlington Robinson, mainly conventional and conservative, turned away from Whitman's poetics. Even the arch-revolutionist of poetry, Ezra Pound, only came to terms with Whitman reluctantly, describing him as an exceeding great stench. Pound, in many ways a generous supporter of other poets, could also be a cantankerous bigot on occasion, and his remarks on homosexuality in *The Cantos* are in his crackerbarrel fascist mode. William Carlos Williams recognised Whitman as an innovator and major poetic force and resource, but he believed that Whitman had not succeeded in the search for a distinctive American vernacular which would form the basis of a specifically American poetry that owed nothing to Europe. Vachel Linsday, Robinson Jeffers and Carl Sandburg were virtually alone in pursuing a parallel course to Whitman in terms of

a long-breathed line, and, of the three, only Sandburg's early works
have much in common with Whitman. Lindsay's populism is that
of the music hall and tent show while Jeffers's iconoclasm and 'in-
humanism' are a severe corrective to Whitman's effusive optimism.

Whitman's qualities were undervalued or misunderstood by the
'New Critics', and were contrary to the prevailing spirit of the
1950s, characterised by Ginsberg as 'the syndrome of shutdown',
so it was perhaps natural, even inevitable, that Ginsberg should
have reached back past Williams and Communist versifiers such as
Mike Gold to Whitman as a source of inspiration. He must indeed
have screamed with joy reading Whitman for himself, since
Ginsberg has characterised the way Whitman was taught at
Columbia as stupidity and ignorance. Whitman also provided a
way out of the psychic impasse induced by his earlier Blake
fixation. Whilst a student at Columbia in June 1948, he had a mystical experience as a result of simultaneously reading Blake's 'Ah!
Sunflower' and masturbating. Ginsberg heard a voice he took to be
Blake's and, as Paul Portugés notes, 'suddenly he felt with Blake's
voice guiding him that he could penetrate the essence of the universe. He felt himself floating out of his body and thinking that
heaven was on earth.'[6] Soon afterwards he heard Blake's voice
chanting 'The Sick Rose', then a third experience of Blake chanting
'The Little Girl Lost'. Ginsberg gained a new sense of purpose from
this experience, feeling that everything which had happened in the
past few years, such as problems in his relationship with Neal
Cassady, and the illness of his mother, had been some sort of
preparation for the vision. Following this, Ginsberg, in an exalted
state of mind, attempted to communicate his experience to his
tutors, who doubted his sanity. During this period he had the opportunity of reading a collection of religious and mystical texts belonging to Russel Durgin, left in the flat where he was living. As
well as Blake, he was reading Marvell, St Teresa of Avila, Plotinus,
Martin Luther, St John of the Cross, Plato and St John Perse.

An intense reading of authors such as these is undoubtedly con-
ducive to mystical events, and Ginsberg had two further episodes,
one in the university bookshop, one in the field near the library.
After this he felt compelled to tell everyone he met, with the result
that people thought he was either lying or on the verge of a
nervous breakdown. Even Jack Kerouac failed to take him seriously. About a year later, Ginsberg was committed to Columbia
Psychiatric Institute, but this was the result of an incident where a

gangster living in his apartment managed to crash a stolen car full of stolen property. Ginsberg, who was in the car but not party to the robbery, was arrested but later escaped prison through the influence of his tutors at Columbia. *Howl* resulted from his stay in hospital, but, perhaps more importantly, his Blake experiences gave him a direction and role as a poet, that of visionary prophet. He spent the years from 1950 to 1953 mostly in his father's house in Paterson, and the poems of this period, collected in *Empty Mirror* and *Gates of Wrath* are largely a sustained attempt to record his experiences.

These early poems are mostly archaic and derivative, densely packed with mysticism and abstraction, although a few fine poems, such as 'The Bricklayers' Lunch Hour', show the influence of Williams. The influence and example of Williams was decisive, turning Ginsberg towards a poetry packed with closely observed detail from the everyday world, concerned with literal accuracy and less with expressing ideas or abstract concepts. Prose journals supplied the basic material for the new work, organised by the physical breath, not by literary rules. Ginsberg derived a theory of the poetic line from his understanding of William's practice. One breath equalled one line of spoken poem and the poems were transcribed to show this on the page. Williams, who was in his sixties by this time, had a somewhat sparer line than the rhapsodic young Ginsberg, who started to write a long Whitmanian line as well as the more 'controlled' short-line poems. Ginsberg's poetry has always been more varied than *Howl*, of course, and he has been a keen student of Pound's and Charles Olson's use of the facilities of the typewriter to provide a score for the reading voice.

Ginsberg's voice, manner and tone are quite distinct from Whitman's and their affinity lies in their affirmative responses to life, their proclamation of the physicality of life, and the insistence on the link between sexual freedom and political freedom. As Tytell remarks, 'Ginsberg is feared in America just as Whitman was feared: to believe in democracy is the first step toward making it possible, and such seriousness is dangerous.'[7] The extent of this fear became apparent in 1957 when Lawrence Ferlinghetti and Shigeyoshi Murao were prosecuted under Section 305 of the Tariff Act 1930, for allegedly selling or publishing obscene writings, namely *Howl and Other Poems* and issue 11/12 of *The Miscellaneous Man* (*The Miscellaneous Man* was actually published by William Margolis in Berkeley so this charge was dropped).[8] Ferlinghetti and

Murao (City Lights Bookshop Manager) were defended by three formidable lawyers as an ACLU test case, supported by testimony on the book's literary qualities from a variety of eminent critics and writers including Kenneth Rexroth, while the prosecution produced one tutor from a Catholic University and one private elocution teacher who proved totally inept. Hardly surprisingly the case was dismissed, but the judge established an important principle, namely that if a text could be demonstrated to have some literary value or worth, then the test of 'obscenity' could not be applied no matter what form of words was employed. It will not be forgotten that Whitman lost his job because of official disapproval of *Leaves of Grass*, and that in April 1882 his publisher James R. Osgood withdrew the 1881 edition after the Boston District Attorney ruled that certain poems were obscene. Whitman found another publisher in Philadelphia, and the publicity arising from this official censorship stimulated sales to the extent that he earned $1439.80 royalties that year, much more than in previous or subsequent years. Thus, in both cases, the state achieved exactly the opposite effect from what had been intended. Ginsberg's book sales run into millions world wide, he is probably the best selling poet ever.

It is clear that this last failed attempt at McCarthyite repression is a reflex of the corporate state's inability to deal with social criticism, and a recognition that Ginsberg stands in a long line of poets who have dissented publicly from the dominant values of their society or culture; and that, as Tytell reminds us, 'Ginsberg's most significant relation to Blake has been ideological – a sympathy with social concerns, a desire to transform consciousness to use poetry as an instrument of power or as sacramental invocation.'[9] This of course applies equally to his relationship with Whitman. The rejection of American values, or at least the bourgeois values of the post-World War II era, is clearly expressed in the 1949 poem 'Paterson' (CP 40).

The rejection of bourgeois values, whether the 'protestant work ethic', the immigrant (e.g. Jewish and Italian) drive for business success and suburban respectability, or the 'cleanliness is next to Godliness' ethos, contributed to the public perception of the Beats which saw them labelled as 'beatniks' or 'the great unwashed', and users of 'dangerous drugs'. The poem's second section features Ginsberg's vision of himself as a crucified and persecuted Christ figure, an expression of a desire for death or annihilation which is a recurrent characteristic of his poetry between 1948 and 1963, the year when Ginsberg finally rejected the influence of his Blake experiences, although Blake remained important in other ways. Nevertheless, in spite of the negativity of this poem it is clear that Ginsberg's poetry, as much as Kerouac's novels, epitomises the Beat desire *to be*, and that it is affirmative, if at times a rather grim celebration of existence as a positive value in an era of apathy and dull conformity. The poem's insistent anaphoric 'rather' does express a positive choice, a claiming of the freedom to live life to the full, to experience everything and reject nothing. Thus the Beats were able to claim saint-like status, and ascribe 'beatitude' to their way of life.

Living life to the full meant accepting all aspects of sexuality and refusing to be limited by heterosexuality and monogamous pair-bonding. In practice, as far as Ginsberg was concerned, this meant homosexuality or bi-sexuality. As in all the best American movies, the Beat story was very much a 'buddy' story, with women featured only as 'minor characters'.[10] Neal Cassady was the central figure in the drama, hero of *On the Road* and *Visions of Cody* and man of action who lacked Kerouac's Catholic inhibitions. Although basically heterosexual, he was capable of intimate relationships with men, including Ginsberg, who fell in love with him at first sight. The many poems to or about Cassady make it clear that Ginsberg virtually worshipped him. Marriage, first to Luanne, and then to Carolyn Cassady, did not restrain Neal Cassady, as the 1954 poem 'Love Poem on a Theme by Whitman' makes clear. This poem is in Ginsberg's most Whitmanian manner, yet there are clear differences in tone and style. The announced 'theme' is based on Whitman's own poem 'The Sleepers', particularly lines 11–20

The married couple sleep calmly in their beds, he with his palm on the hip of the wife, and she with her palm on the hip of the husband,
The sisters sleep lovingly side by side in their bed,
The men sleep side by side in theirs,
Another mother sleeps with her little child carefully wrapt[11]

…

I go from bedside to bedside, I sleep close with the other sleepers each in turn

Leaves of Grass, p. 441

...

I roll myself upon you as upon a bed, I resign myself to the dusk

Leaves of Grass, p. 442

The poem can be read as a celebration of homosexual love and companionship and a rejection of monogamy, and the 1855 edition contained a passage excised from subsequent editions, perhaps to avoid prosecution:

The cloth laps a first sweet eating and drinking,
Laps life-swelling yolks ... laps ear of rose-corn, milky
   and just ripened:
The white teeth stay, and the boss-tooth advances in darkness,
And liquor is spilled on lips and bosoms by touching the glass,
   and the best liquor afterward[12]

It seems clear that Whitman is describing the act of fellatio, probably by another man; Martin takes the view that nineteenth-century women were unlikely to indulge in fellatio, and that Whitman wrote 'The Sleepers' as an example of 'the role of sexuality in the establishment of a mystic sense of unity'.[13] This is close to Ginsberg's approach to sex, in so far as he views buggery as a means of achieving religious ecstasy and union with the godhead. Whitman's poem is structured as a vision, while Ginsberg enters unambiguously into the bedroom to interpose himself between the married couple (CP 115).

Ginsberg is more explicit and less mysterious than Whitman, but the poem gains from its directness, whilst having a strong rhythm and a solidity of expression which make it one of the best of the pre-'Howl' poems. Ginsberg's literary relationship, in the sense of writing poems to or about Whitman, is made plain in 'A Supermarket in California', which addresses Whitman directly as both a father figure and a lover. The poem is both funny and poignant, yet critics often describe Ginsberg's work as neurotic and joyless, usually failing completely to appreciate its moments of humour. Ginsberg speaks to Whitman man to man, but he also speaks poet to poet, inviting Whitman to share his view of modern America, where monopoly capitalism has turned the entire nation into a supermarket, where art and sex are commodities to be sold alongside the other 'frozen delicacies'.

One of Ginsberg's recurrent themes is that of bodily ageing and death, and it is significant that he imagines Whitman not as the brawny vigorous thirty-seven-year-old portrayed in section nine of 'I Sing the Body Electric', but as a 'lonely old grubber poking / among the meats in the refrigerator and eyeing the grocery boys' (CP 136). His sad old man is, however, funny rather than pathetic as he cruises the aisles with manic determination, accosting the grocery boys. Ginsberg does not mock Whitman, but rather uses the humour to offer an ironic critique of a mercenary society where a lonely old man whose desires are undiminished is no longer able to obtain sexual satisfaction. Ginsberg's own appetite for juvenile flesh is well documented in his writing, and it may be that he is expressing his own fear that as he grows older he will no longer be able to compete successfully in the sexual marketplace. His imaginative compensation of 'possessing every frozen delicacy, and never passing the cashier' (CP 136) is disturbed, but not prevented, by the figure of repressive authority, the store detective.

However, Whitman's expansive confidence and his faith in America's ability to achieve an egalitarian democracy where adhesive love would be the norm, is not available to Ginsberg. His America, even the golden state of California, is a place where 'we'll both be lonely' (CP 136). 'The lost America of love' has been replaced by 'blue automobiles in driveways' (CP 138), the suburban conformity which the Beats set out to subvert. For Ginsberg, Whitman is surrogate parent and teacher, the figure of liberation his own father Louis could not be. The affection for Whitman, and the recognition of his indebtedness, is clear in Ginsberg's poem, but it is also clear that the America of 1956 is not the America of 1856. The corporate state, dominating every aspect of people's lives, is a powerful and oppressive force in Ginsberg's poetry, just as it is absent in Whitman. The great industrial empires of such capitalist 'übermenschen' as Carnegie, Rockefeller, and Pierpont Morgan are not dealt with in Whitman's poetry, even though the various monopolies were well established by the time the later editions of *Leaves of Grass* were published. Instead he describes American working men as craftsmen and small masters, picturing them in heroic terms. Ginsberg, by contrast, grew up with the organised militant working class, taken to political meetings as a child by his mother. In 'America', one of his finest fusions of Jewish humour and social comments, he describe his cultural heritage. He grew up surrounded by the rich Jewish, Communist, and Anarchist political traditions and this background should not be forgotten even though poems like 'Kral Majales' show a demonstrable disenchantment with Communism in its Eastern European formulations.

'Kral Majales', written on 7 May 1965, is one of the texts where sexuality intersects with politics in Ginsberg's writing. He returns to the insistent anaphoric technique of 'Howl' to document his outrage at his treatment by the Czechoslovakian bureaucracy and its police henchmen. In Ginsberg's hands, the anaphora gives the impression that the poem has started in mid-sentence or mid-stanza. It gives the effect of a television news interview where what is transmitted is obviously an excerpt of the complete interview or statement. Geoffrey Thurley describes Ginsberg as 'the public drop-out, the guru, the subterranean jet-setter, the King of the May',[14] a sneer which imputes a lack of sincerity of Ginsberg's past. Thurley is, however, correct to point out the public stance of poems such as 'Kral Majales', as demonstrated by p. 355 of the *Collected Poems*, which is a reproduction of a broadsheet, with art by Robert La Vigne, showing the poem's text flanked by two silhouettes of a naked Ginsberg in tennis shoes, with six hands and finger cymbals. Each figure is enclosed in a large penis column. This broadsheet provides a conclusive answer to those critics who claim that Ginsberg's work is formless: form and content are perfectly fused in a gesture which not only illustrates his underlying principles, but also functions as a definitive reply to the Czechoslovakian authorities.

The poem condemns both State Communism and capitalism, and notes Ginsberg's dismay at discovering that the Communist State has a backward and repressive attitude towards homosexuality. Most of the poem, though, is a gesture of triumph, the personal being privileged over the narrowly political – 'And I am the King of May, which is the power of sexual youth' (CP 353) ... 'and I am the King of May, naturally, for I am of Slavic parentage and a / Buddhist Jew' (CP 354). 'Kral Majales' ends with the political reality, a Kafka-esque note of repression by the all-powerful and unaccountable bureaucratic state. The poem has a powerful symbolic force, because although Ginsberg has been beaten up and deported, he has turned the occasion into a ringing statement of his personal beliefs which invites comparison with Whitman's optimism. Whitman was never faced with this sort of state power, and indeed writes as if the state did not exist. The state cannot censor poems such as 'Kral Majales' and cannot prevent Ginsberg acting as witness to the change in consciousness he is helping to bring about. Twenty-five years after he was thrown out of Prague, Ginsberg returned to recover the notebooks confiscated by the secret police and reclaim his crown. Ginsberg was the last King of the May to be elected. In the new democratic Czechoslovakia, where the president is a former dissident playwriter (Vaclav Havel), his crown is 'ceremoniously handed back to him by the Major of Prague ("who just happens to be the Czech translator of Gary Snyder's poetry", Ginsberg adds to stress how the Beat poets were admired in Eastern Europe)'.[15] Poems such as this reached a huge audience and helped to radicalise attitudes, and give people the strength to start the process of changing their lives. Sexual liberation and political liberation are inseparably linked, and Ginsberg's poetry was an important part of delivering that message in the 1960s. The long Whitmanian line was essential to carry the stream of energy which flowed out as Ginsberg combined 'the rhetorical voice of American populist tradition with a passionate, personal intelligence and wit'.[16] However, as Ginsberg explains to Jim Burns, the reactionaries are fighting back.

'It's similar to McCarthyism', Ginsberg insists, and you can also draw parallels with Nazi book burning and Stalinist attacks on intellectuals broadcasting 'Howl', not to mention work by Kerouac, Genet, Henry Miller, and many others. Ginsberg sees it as part of a pattern which includes censorship of student publications, restrictions on press reporting of certain events, FBI surveillance of libraries and a long list of similar activities. 'It's an attack on language' he claims, and an attempt at thought control. 'Much of my poetry is specifically aimed to rouse the sense of liberty of thought and political social expression of that thought in young adolescents. I believe I am conducting spiritual war for liberation of their souls from mass homogenisation of greedy materialistic commerce and emotional desensitisation. Pseudo-religious legal intolerance with my speech amounts to setting up a state religion much in the mode of intolerant Ayatollah or a Stalinoid bureaucratic party line'. The interesting thing is, Ginsberg points out, that the neo-conservative and religious fanatics who are behind much of the drive for censorship are the types who, a few years ago, would have been in the forefront of anti communist agitation. Now they use the same tactics as their one time opponents 'to enforce the authority of their own

solidified thought police and ethical systems'. And is it strange
that this should happen? 'No', answers Ginsberg, 'Blake put his
finger on it when he said "They became what they beheld".'[17]

Ginsberg also tells Jim Burns that although he has not written
much poetry since *White Shroud* he is working on a collection of
photographs and that his opera *Hydrogen Box*, written with Philip
Glass, has been performed at the Spoleto Festival in Italy.[18] It is to
be hoped that the enemies of free speech, so intent on denying
Ginsberg's constitutional right of free speech and thought, are suit-
ably dismayed (or enraged) to note that in 1990 Ginsberg has a new
recording of poetry and music (*The Lion for Real* on Antilles
Records) and still draws audiences of thousands for public readings in London and elsewhere. The message of Blake and Whitman
is still being carried to all corners of the world in person and on
compact disc.

One of the ways in which Ginsberg differs from Whitman is in
the personalised nature of his poems. Whitman of course was not
in a position to write openly to, or about, Peter Doyle, or to dedicate a volume to him, because of the enormous social pressure
which made absolute discretion imperative. The year after
Whitman died, another notable homosexual, the Russian composer
Tchaikovsky, was forced to commit suicide. Ginsberg, writing one
hundred years later, and more concerned with recording his full
experience openly and honestly, rejected all constraints. There are
many beautiful passages depicting male intimacy in Whitman, but
nothing resembling Ginsberg's 'Many Loves'. Appropriately, the
poem has an epigraph from Whitman, 'Resolved to sing no songs
henceforth, but those of manly attachment'. Taking this as a starting point, 'Many Loves' is the first of a number of poems about
Ginsberg's relationship with Neal Cassady. It is explicit without
being pornographic, and answers the old question, 'what do homosexuals do in bed? (CP 156).

The poem details the physical pleasures of lovemaking with a
man as well as giving a potted biography of Cassady's youth in
Denver, and describes him in heroic terms. The emphasis on
Cassady's juvenile career as a car thief, and on his physical beauty,
no doubt contributed to the myths surrounding Cassady, and to an
underestimation of his talents, and his influence on the writing of
Ginsberg and Jack Kerouac. In May 1968, Ginsberg wrote 'Please
Master', another love poem to Cassady, but in a different mode. In

'Many Loves', Ginsberg writes that his 'first mistake' was to make Cassady his 'Master', a statement which a reading of their correspondence will bear out. 'Please Master' places Ginsberg in the position of acolyte, anxious to please even by acts of self-abasement. The tone is pleadingly submissive, expressing 'a desire to be fucked, a desire which one supposes is the equivalent to the poet's desire to be fucked by the universe, to be overcome by its sensations'.[19]

As Martin points out, this is a long way from anything in Whitman, where the sexual act is mutual and reciprocal, but he notes that 'Please Master' is a 'necessary political–sexual statement of the need to admit openly one's desire for anal intercourse'.[20] He goes on to make the curious statement that 'Ginsberg's master is unnamed, undescribed, totally anonymous; he is the coming to life of a statue, a fantasy embodied',[21] which suggests that his reading of Ginsberg has been somewhat cursory. It would be clear to anyone who had followed the careers of Ginsberg and other Beat figures, and who had read the poems, journals and letters attentively, that it is Cassady who is being addressed. Martin was also presumably unaware that Neal Cassady had died in miserable circumstances only four months before the poem was written. It was printed in *The Fall of America* as part of Section III, 'Elegies for Neal Cassady'. The first of these elegies is dated 10 Feb 1968, making it clear that Ginsberg was mourning the death of a friend and former lover. This knowledge gives the elegies a real poignancy, and point to the difficulties involved in coming to terms with the death of someone you have known for over twenty years.

Another important difference between Whitman and Ginsberg lies in their respective attitudes to women. Whitman believed in social and political equality for women, and he urged women to be open, frank, and active in their relationships. He was opposed to nineteenth-century concepts of femininity, and believed that his own greater openness about sex might make a contribution to women's emancipation by encouraging similar openness in women. In Section 5 of 'Song of Myself', he declares that all 'the women are my sisters and lovers', and in Section 21 claims

I am the poet of the woman the same as the man,
And I say it is as great to be a woman as to be a man,
And I say there is nothing greater than the mother of men.

Leaves of Grass, p. 83

In 'A Woman Waits for Me', he states 'all were lacking if sex were lacking' and

> Now I will dismiss myself from impassive women
> I will go stay with her who waits for me, and with those
> women that are warm-blooded and sufficient for me
>   *Leaves of Grass*, p. 136

However, although Whitman wanted American women to be 'warm-blooded', like most nineteenth-century men (and twentieth-century men?) he had a blank spot regarding female sexuality. 'Adhesiveness' was a male preserve, and active female desire, especially for other women, does not feature in Whitman's view of women's capacities. He may not have appreciated that a positive, active, emancipated woman might well be a lesbian. Apart from this limitation, Whitman's attitudes to women are considerably more progressive than most male writers. Ginsberg's attitudes in many respects form a sorry contrast, especially for a poet committed to Gay Liberation. The attitude of fear and disgust encountered in his poetry may derive in part from his reaction to Naomi Ginsberg's behaviour after her breakdown, but negative attitudes to women are commonplace among Beat writers. Burroughs, in particular, exhibits a particularly unpleasant brand of misogyny, and it is perhaps fortunate that it was not Burroughs who became the 'public guru' of the 60s counter-culture. Gary Snyder, although weak in his understanding of sexism, is one of the few Beat figures who actually likes and respects women.

The first poem the reader encounters in the *Collected Poems*, 'In Society', is dated Spring 1947, and the second stanza is an ugly tirade against a woman who says she doesn't like the speaker of the poem. In 'The Blue Angel', Marlene Dietrich is portrayed as a 'life sized toy' who needs 'a man / to occupy my mind' (CP 54). Women, for Ginsberg, are machines with no life of their own until they can capture a man, from whom they will drain the mental and emotional energies. This concept perhaps owes something to the Jewish idea of the 'golem'. Woman is seen as an object, the 'other' to be avoided by men if they wish to remain alive and independent, a view strikingly at variance with Whitman's. In 'How Come He Got Canned at the Ribbon Factory', a male apprentice intrudes into the female sphere of operations, and is perceived as 'this character', inadequate and incompetent, and dismissed by the women as 'not a real man any way but a goop' (CP 60). Relations between men and women are clearly problematic for Ginsberg and it is significant that he needed Whitman's guidance and example to write 'Love Poem on Theme by Whitman'. Neal Cassady and Jack Kerouac were both bisexual to some extent, and even Burroughs fathered a child by the wife he shot in Mexico City, but Ginsberg celebrates the exclusivity of sex with younger (blond) men, as the opening two poems in Section III testify. Ginsberg's partner for many years from 1954 on was Peter Orlovsky, and 'Malest Cornifici Tuo Catullo' presumably records the start of this relationship. 'Dream Record: June 1955' records the stereotype of casual relationships and drunken sex, a paradigm of pre-AIDS innocence. Versions of this poem, such as 'Sweet Boy Gimme Your Ass' are scattered throughout the *Collected Poems* and *White Shroud*.

'Kaddish', Ginsberg's elegy for his mother, written after her death in 1956, is in some senses an antiphon to 'Howl' and necessary to an understanding of the pressures which inform 'Howl'. It is a true epic in that it includes history; the history of Naomi Ginsberg's life in America, the history of her relations with her family, the history of her breakdown and treatment, the history of political radicalism in twentieth-century America, and the history of her troubled relationship with Allen. It is a complex occasion, and one of the few instances where Ginsberg actually makes use of his Jewish heritage, rather than merely referring to it. The response by Jewish literary critics was divided, with one critic denying the poet's right to use the ritual term 'kaddish', claiming that the use of tradition was illegitimate. Other critics were able to be more positive, and respond to the personal and historical imperatives of the poem. A selection of these responses to 'Kaddish' can be found in Lewis Hyde's invaluable compendium of Ginsberg criticism.[22]

The physical decline which accompanied Naomi Ginsberg's mental breakdown is graphically described, with the poet's attitudes to his mother portrayed as a mixture of disgust, compassion, indifference and Oedipal fascination. Nothing is withheld (CP 215). Although, according to the poem, her first breakdown occurred in 1919, the poem is mainly concerned with events from the mid 1930s to the late 1940s, the years of Ginsberg's adolescence and early manhood. Whitman demonstrated that male homosexuality could be compatible with positive attitudes to women, and Ginsberg's attitudes cannot be ascribed to his gayness. However, given the traumas of his family life as related in 'Kaddish', his views are understandable although not excusable. The contradictions in his position are revealed in 'This Form of Life Needs Sex', a poem which mixes fear of women with wry humour, and a knowledge of mutability. It starts out 'I will have to accept women / if I want to continue the race' and goes on to talk about 'ignorant Fuckery' asking 'why have I feared' the 'one hole that repelled me 1937 on' (CP 284/5). He can still, however, be wryly funny about both the joys and limitations of homosexuality (CP 285–6).

His 'situation' is that the sexual revolution and the accompanying revolution of consciousness has no place for women, since Ginsberg has difficulty seeing women as people, human beings in their own right. Given these attitudes from someone perceived as a leader of the American radical movement it is now clear why there was a feminist backlash from about 1968 onwards. I do not wish to caricature the complex history of Women's Movement, but that history is outside the scope of this chapter. However, as Gloria Steinem has said, 'the sexual revolution was not our revolution'.[23] Yet according to John Tytell, the Whitmanian adhesiveness which inspired Ginsberg was 'his feeling of Kinship with all classes and kinds of people'.[24] The Women's Movement was obliged to work out its own version of adhesiveness, often in angry rejection of men and male sexuality, but it may be that attitudes towards women encountered in Beat writing, and in Beat-influenced songwriters such as Bob Dylan, provided a necessary catalyst for the development of modern feminism.

In 1968, Ginsberg provided an eloquent definition of adhesiveness, in testimony before Judge Hoffman at the 'Chicago Seven' trial.[25] In reply to a question by prosecutor Foran on the religious significance of 'Love Poem on Theme by Whitman', he replied:

Whitman said that unless there was an infusion of feeling, of tenderness, of fearlessness, of spirituality, of natural sexuality of natural delight in each others bodies, into the hardened materialistic, cynical, life denying, clearly competitive, afraid, scared, armored bodies, there would be no chance for spiritual democracy to take root in America – and he defined that tenderness between the citizens as in his words, an 'Adhesiveness', a natural tenderness, flowing between all citizens, not only men and women, but also a tenderness between men and men as part of our democratic heritage, part of the Adhesiveness which would make the democracy function: that men could work together not

as competitive beats but as tender lovers and fellows. So he projected from his own desire and from his own unconscious a
sexual urge which he felt was normal to the unconscious of most
people, though forbidden for the most part

The obvious question must be, where are the women in all this,
except as adjuncts to men? Ginsberg's 'demos' – the people –
appears to be men only. No wonder Joyce Johnson called her book
Minor Characters, an accurate reflection of the importance of women
in the lives of the Beat writers, and of the part women were allowed
to play in the counter-culture revolution. If that revolution was a
failure, it was because any revolution which incorporated the oppression of women into its structure (as well as alienating the
working classes) could not succeed. Nevertheless there were
significant gains, and Ginsberg and the Beat writers achieved a
great deal in terms of sexual liberation and personal liberation, and
helped to bring about a change of consciousness which cannot be
reversed. As Kenneth Rexroth, who supported some aspects of the
counter-culture noted, the contempt for women and the Beat practice of 'treating a girl exactly as one would treat a casual homosexual pick up in a public convenience' cannot be ignored or glossed
over.[26] Rexroth also points out that

it is pretty hard to dismiss anyone who can fill the largest audito-
rium in any city he chooses to appear in like Joan Baez, Bob
Dylan, or the Beatles – and who has produced thousands of followers, in all the civilized and many uncivilized languages.[28]

Rexroth, who as both a major poet and a trenchant critic was
perhaps uniquely qualified to comment on the development of
American poetry, places Ginsberg as 'one of the most traditionalist
poets now living. His work is an almost perfect fulfillment of the
long Whitman, Populist, social revolutionary tradition in American
poetry. ... Ginsberg meant something of the greatest importance
and so his effects have endured and permeated the whole society.'[28]
Rexroth was the master of ceremonies at the historic Six Gallery
reading which launched the Beat Generation as a public phenomenon, and in the 1950s acted as Godfather to the San Francisco
poets. Although his initial enthusiasm waned, his judgement
recorded here must have been gratifying recognition, especially
after some of the things written by critics and academics, who have

largely failed to recognise the value of the Beat project. But then, Ginsberg expressed his attitude to Norman Podhoretz and other critics in *Notes for Howl and Other Poems*:

> A word on Academics; poetry has been attacked
> by an ignorant & frightened bunch of bores
> who don't understand how its made, & the trouble
> with these creeps is that they wouldn't know Poetry
> if it came up and buggered them in broad daylight[29]

Appropriately, this statement is dated Independence Day, the occasion of the celebration of the American Revolution.

NOTES

1. Allen Ginsberg, *Collected Poems, 1947–1980* (London: Penguin, 1984). All quotations from this book will be given as CP then the relevant page number.
2. *Beat Scene*, no. 10 (July 1990) p. 29.
3. Ginsberg, *Collected Poems*, p. 813.
4. *Beat Scene*, p. 27.
5. John Tytell, *Naked Angels* (New York: McGraw-Hill, 1974) p. 4.
6. Paul Portugés, *The Visionary Poetics of Allen Ginsberg* (Santa Barbara: Ross-Erikson, 1978).
7. Tytell, *Naked Angels*, p. 213.
8. See Lawrence Ferlinghetti, 'Horn on Howl', in *On the Poetry of Allen Ginsberg*, ed. Lewis Hyde (Ann Arbor: University of Michigan Press, 1984) pp. 42–53 for an account of the *Howl* trial.
9. Tytell, *Naked Angels*, p. 222.
10. See Joyce Johnson, *Minor Characters* (London: Picador, 1973) for an account of her relationship with Jack Kerouac and a discussion of this issue.
11. Walt Whitman, *The Complete Poems*, ed. Francis Murphy (London: Penguin, 1975) p. 440. All subsequent quotations are from this edition.
12. Quoted in Robert K. Martin, *The Homosexual Tradition in American Poetry* (Austin: University of Texas Press, 1979) p. 11.
13. Ibid., p. 12.
14. Geoffrey Thurley, *The American Moment* (London: Edward Arnold, 1977) p. 172.
15. *Beat Scene*, p. 27.
16. Thurley, *The American Moment*, p. 173.
17. *Beat Scene*, p. 29.
18. Ibid., p. 29.

19. Martin, *The Homosexual Tradition*, pp. 169–70.
20. Ibid., p. 170.
21. Ibid., p. 170.
22. Hyde (ed.), *On the Poetry of Allen Ginsberg*, pp. 85–117.
23. Quoted in the *Observer*, 22 February 1987, p. 52.
24. Tytell, *Naked Angels*, p. 226.
25. Ibid., p. 243.
26. Kenneth Rexroth, *The Alternative Society* (New York: Herder and Herder, 1972) p. 106.
27. Kenneth Rexroth, *American Poetry in the Twentieth Century* (New York: Herder and Herder, 1971) p. 170.
28. Ibid., pp. 170–1.
29. Quoted in Donald Allan and Warren Tallman (eds), *Poetics of the New American Poetry* (New York: Grove Press, 1972) p. 321.

14

Edward Dorn

GEOFF WARD

I

By my count, the word 'actionable' occurs twice in the published work of Edward Dorn, but in neither case with a meaning corresponding exactly to that given in the OED; 'subject or liable to an action at law'. The first use is early: interviewed by David Ossman in February 1961, around the time of publication of his first book *The Newly Fallen*, Dorn was quick to turn the conversation away from the then-fashionable debates about 'the line' and its relationship to the breath and to verse measure. These were preoccupations associated with Black Mountain College, from which Dorn had graduated, and Charles Olson, the College's last rector and Dorn's poetic mentor. To Dorn at this point, measure in poetry had become 'a technical preoccupation' about which 'I frankly know very little', a 'false problem':

> But I think it will become less important as the content of our speech becomes more important – as what we're saying becomes more vital to all of us.
> One of the things being more recognized now and listened to, I hope, is that poets are saying things important for every human being, and not being just poets so much. I guess I sound dogmatic, but I think we have to face, finally, that there has to be some hope for something actionable to come out of all of this.[1]

In the context of that interview and those times, 'all of this' means the short-lived and, from a contemporary perspective, prelapsarian conjunction of what Dorn terms 'a political poetry' and the attitude of protest brought to boiling point by the Civil Rights movement. What is at stake, what is 'actionable' here, is not so much the settlement of a grievance by recourse to law, as an identification of the

218

law itself as part of the grievance. At this stage Dorn was clearly able to share the giddy but combative optimism of what Allen Ginsberg termed 'the new consciousness', when interviewed by Ossman for the same radio series.[2]

This neo-Shelleyan model of poetry as unacknowledged legislation, as the intrepid act of a consciousness that may silently take forward the society that in a day-to-day sense ignores it, was to be both confirmed and denied by the accelerating social changes of the 1960s. The libertarian values promulgated by Ginsberg and the Beats, very much against the sullen and suburban conformism of the 50s (as shown by the temporary banning of that actionable document *Howl*), were to become common currency only a decade later in the widespread use of hallucinogenic drugs, unabashed sexual promiscuity, antagonism to the demands of America's military–industrial complex, and other manifestations of the *Zeitgeist*. Edward Dorn's second use of the term 'actionable' occurs in the first Book of *Gunslinger*, published first in 1968, at the peak of High Psychedelia. By now the struggle to rebuild what Ginsberg had called 'the lost America of love' had either been won or proved unwinnable, as, in the wake of the Chicago Trials, the American Left began its retreat from the rigours of a social, to the pleasures of a personal, agenda.[3] Dorn's sense of being able to compose poetry in anything resembling proximity to legislation, acknowledged or otherwise, had withered by now in the shade of more seductive and exotic growths.

He has spoken a number of times in interview about the hallucinatory nature of the Vietnam débâcle, which had only the flickering pseudo-reality of TV image for those not directly involved, and which for those who were, was not infrequently filtered by drug use. Meanwhile non-combatants under the age of forty tended, by a curious parallelism, to articulate their experiences under LSD and other stimulants as if they were reconnaissance missions through alien jungle. 'People still like to recount their trips, which are now largely past, much like Tales of War.'[4] For all its Pop-art lightness and brightness, this parallelism whereby mystery can turn to paranoia, comedy to Tales of War, is exactly the territory into which *Gunslinger* presses, in its urge to comb 'the country of our consciousness' (G 7–8).[5]

Miss Lil, a foul-mouthed but genial madam, a kind of poeticised Mae West, acts as social anchor to a text whose 'refugee' speakers are otherwise prone to tripping back and forth, through the metaphysical riddles and tongue-twisters that are the poem's stock in trade, from the cosmic to the microscopically local in defiance of all 'actionable' norms. The poem's first person, named only as 'I', will die part way through Book II, only to enjoy a post mortem revival under the influence of a 'five-gallon batch' of pure LSD, the property of the ambitiously named Kool Everything (G 60). A lute-strumming Poet and the dope-smoking *'marvelous creature'*, a talking horse who may or may not be called Claude Lévi-Strauss, accompany the 'Cautious Gunslinger / of impeccable personal smoothness' (G 3), the elegantly philosophical and psychedelicised self-image of a word-slinger, Ed Dorn, whose poetry has always drawn sustenance from the image of the deracinated stranger, and from the history and myths of the Far West.

That actionable town, Boston, will prove to be the East Coast domain of Robart, the only other character of substance in *Gunslinger*, or rather the only character to lack substance so entirely as to be invisible, forever moving through a black hole that shrouds in secrecy the operations of a predatory commerce. The proximity of 'Robart' to Robard, middle name of reclusive millionaire Howard Hughes, is no coincidence. *The Cycle*, an unnumbered Book occurring like a warp in relativity between the poem's second and third Books, is his anti-history, Dorn's dark and fantastic apprehension of the limits set on all legislation and civic action by the unstoppable and omnipresent logic of what has since been dubbed late capitalism. This *Cycle* ran roughshod over the leisurely hoof-prints of the talking horse. The final two Books of *Gunslinger* are edgy, off-key: what began so brightly ended in Dorn's most powerful political satire, but lost all narrative momentum, indeed all ease of movement, in the process.

What follows will be an attempt to situate Dorn's poetry in relation to the changes in political, cultural and literary consciousness during his writing lifetime. Dorn emerged as part of the great wave of postwar avant-garde writing, anthologised by Donald Allen as *The New American Poetry*, a Grove Press book of 1960 that brought most readers their first acquaintance with such varied innovations as the Black Mountain productions of Charles Olson, Robert Duncan and Robert Creeley, the Beat-ific absorption of jazz rhythms and Zen by such poets as Gary Snyder, and the more Surrealist and seemingly 'European' lyrics of the New York School, pre-eminently Frank O'Hara and John Ashbery. Then almost equally unknown, those writers have enjoyed or endured radically divergent careers and reputations in the succeeding thirty years. While John Ashbery is currently the most critically esteemed American poet since Wallace Stevens, Frank O'Hara is only now emerging from the cocoon of his posthumous reputation as a 'poet's poet', and Snyder's constituency can hardly extend outside California.

Whatever their (substantial) differences in style and theme, the work of the New American Poets was characterised by an extreme individualism. The right to develop a personal language, a highly interiorised lexicon and manner, is taken as read by that generation and makes a poem by Creeley or Olson instantly recognisable, if only from its typographical layout. This individualism finds its broad analogues in the technical radicalism of Abstract Expressionism ('Action Painting', as it was once called) and the self-searching improvisation of jazz in its cultural heyday of the late 50s and early 60s. The primacy of expressive gesture is all. While certain poets, for example Frank O'Hara and John Wieners, appear to have thrived in conditions where their exercise of an expressivist art appealed only to a strictly limited audience, it has to be asked in Dorn's case whether the call for an actionable poetry and the development of a stylistic individualism have not been damagingly at odds, particularly given the impoverishment of American politics and culture in which the work has had to find its place.

II

Edward Dorn's first book, *The Newly Fallen* (1961), was published at the invitation of Le Roi Jones; several pieces were written specially in order to bring the quantity of poetry that Dorn had in readiness up to book size. These careful, tentatively lyrical poems of observation initiate the first phase of Dorn's writing, which would carry him through the increasingly 'adamant practice' of *Hands Up!* and *From Gloucester Out* in the early 1960s, to its culmination in the 'earth writing' of *Geography* (1965). In *The North Atlantic Turbine* (1967), published by Fulcrum Press in London while Dorn was in residence at the University of Essex, what had been adamant becomes strident: 'overreached', as the poet has said in interview. (*I* 15ff). Towards the end of that book comes the mysterious and much cooler 'An Idle Visitation', in fact a first version of the opening of *Gunslinger*, with which Dorn would be busied for the next eight years – the second phase of his writing.

The first, early 1960s sequence of texts has an autobiographical basis in the somewhat off-centre locations where Dorn chose to live or was able to find work: Pocatello in Idaho, or Santa Fe. The poems frequently take as their observed subjects the displaced, migrant workers, or those excluded on racial grounds; this attention to estrangement is matched by Dorn's own location of himself as enabled to observe with accuracy precisely through being a stranger. The recurrent theme of his work has been that of not naturally belonging. He has written very little about his upbringing in Illinois farming country: 'Villa Grove ... a small town on a secret confluence of the Wabash.'[6] It was not until he attended Black Mountain College in 1950 and 1954 – which he did in order to avoid being drafted to Korea – that he met an American from the East Coast. Coming from such a rural background, where 'the first thing you're preoccupied with is ... how to exit', all writerly language can only be acquired, never natural (*I* 70). Dorn's language is not merely self-conscious, as any American poetry from Ashbery to Zukofsky may be said to be: it is watchful, positively wary. A poem such as *From Gloucester Out* (1964) is made and marred by the toils of expression, able spasmodically to let loose some vivid images, as in the evocation of carnival revellers or 'their provocative women, slender / like whips of / sex in the sousa filled night.'[7] Generally it is as inhibited as it is enabled by the pressures and self-consciousness of poetic composition.

If the content of Dorn's work emerges from the privileges and inhibitions of the stranger, then from a methodological perspective his early poetry offers the working out of a relationship with two key influences, William Carlos Williams, and Charles Olson, in whose direction *From Gloucester Out* gestures. Olson's importance to Dorn was that of a teacher; the main lesson, however, lay in the encouragement to the younger poet to find his own terms of expression, which in fact drove Dorn back to Williams. Dorn's best-known essay, 'What I See in *The Maximus Poems*', eschews all piety towards Olson's supposed topics – place, historical narrative, ways of mapping – and places emphasis chiefly on gesture, in relation to the locus of attention. Such a judgement, debated at the time, was shrewdly prescient: those poems by Olson that most visibly follow Dorn's account, the final volume of *The Maximus Poems*, were yet to be written when Dorn published his 1960 essay. It is a judgement that comes from a deep understanding of what truly animates Carlos Williams's apparent objectivism, and the self-renewing possibilities of that practice for younger poets. This verdict on the lyric poems of Robert Creeley, delivered many years later, confirms Dorn's sense of a historical line of descent from Williams to the present: 'Creeley's advancement on Williams has been radical: he discharged the soft locus of that attention and proceeded directly to the bone of human transaction.'[8] In these early books we are drawn back to the dual focus of a poem such as the lyric by Williams called 'Pastoral', in which he writes of admiring the clutter and weathered textures of improvised living in 'the houses / of the very poor'. The poem ends

> No one
> will believe this
> of vast import to the nation.[9]

The locus of attention is dual, based in the ambiguity of 'this': this shack, pushed out to the city limits, where 'the nation' won't have to be troubled by it – or is 'this' the poem, of an at best decorative importance in linguistic society? A similarly mournful yet exacting ambiguity inhabits the conclusion of a poem by Dorn such as 'Time Blonde' from *Hands Up!* (*CP* 80). The estrangement of people from the city, of human from human, of the poem from society, are mutually confirming. As often with Dorn, there is a disappointed idealism smarting behind the self-protective drawl. It is hard to see, even at this early stage, what actionable or legislative function might be restored to an art form so driven towards the margins by choice as well as lack of audience.

If *The North Atlantic Turbine* collapses in places under the pressure of its own stridency, that is traceable to problematic elements in Dorn's modification of Williams's conjunction of lyrical gesture and the culturally antipathetic vignette. All the Black Mountain poets are sons of Williams. Robert Duncan adapts the moment of dramatic utterance which defines Williams's preferred rhetoric, the excitable 'I must tell you' of 'Young Sycamore', and makes of it a moment of intellectual synthesis, just as feeling is discharged. The mainspring of Duncan's poetry is the discovery that essentially syncretic and teacherly modes of thought, derived chiefly from eclectic reading, can become so cross-bred and mutually pressuring as to raise themselves abruptly to the transcendent level of lyrical utterance. A poem such as 'Often I am Permitted to Return to a Meadow', with its conscious echoes of Corinthians, Whitman,

Freud, the Light Metaphysicians, Celtic folklore and so on, would be a case in point: the song-like quality of Duncan's expression is enabled by, and not at all in contradiction with, what amounts to a term's reading list from Black Mountain jammed into one page-long poem.[10] It is the forced compression of disparate materials that generates the lyric spark. This is a daring modification of Williams, in part because it denies the *raison d'être* of his long quarrel with Pound and Eliot over the question of cross-cultural literary allusion, while building on his rhythmical innovations, and his sense that the lyric is imperative, is what over-rides.

It might be concluded that all the younger attenders at Black Mountain – Dorn, John Wieners, Robert Creeley – were personally influenced by Olson, while writing in relation to Williams. Wieners writes – until the 1970s, at any rate – of what the nation would never believe to be of 'vast import', but his immersion in the overlapping night worlds of jazz, drugs, petty crime and homosexuality means that he is able to draw on a whole neo-Baudelairean tradition of the *poète maudit* in that very marginalisation. Dorn specifies this link in a short piece on Wieners's first book, *The Hotel Wentley Poems* (1958), by referring to it enthusiastically as 'the most famous testament in American poetry of the outlands of the modern city, of the ikons in the crumbled mansions of a half-lit drug world' of which, (*V* 90) the conclusion to 'A Poem for Vipers' may be taken as indicative. Indeed, a 'viper' is itself an old term for a pot-smoker (as in Fats Waller's genial 'Viper Blues').

Here, dark people' are friends of 'Jimmy the Pusher', their darkness of multiple sorts. And indeed, a simultaneity of coded operations is exactly what John Wieners takes as, to revive Dorn's phrase, the locus of attention. Words are hidden under 'the coats' of the 'tongue':[11] like the 'sacred' tablet in Communion, the secular speed bought in bars (*V* 90). The tongue is coated by drug-use, but in another pun it signifies language, of men and angels, as well as flesh. Meanwhile coats of another sort have hidden pockets; and so on: no-one will believe this of vast import to the nation, whether this be a drugs transaction set in motion by the code of hip slang, or a poetic negotiation with *its* own codes and forms ('law'). Melancholy and alienated, Wieners's early poetry is still able to draw on perversely positive resources.

Dorn is no *poète maudit* like Wieners, and although he has been employed as a university professor, is not a teacherly writer in the Duncanian or Olsonian sense, either. For all its intermittent eloquence, his pre-*Gunslinger* poetry can be raw and awkward, through its inability to build resourcefully on its own marginalisation, as the other sons of Williams were able to do. The post-*Gunslinger* Dorn has written knowledgeably and with a kind of wistful pleasure about eighteenth-century English writing, and one might detect there a nostalgia for what this poet has perhaps not enjoyed so far, except at Black Mountain and in the late 1960s when the prevailing cultural winds blew briefly in a Slingerish direction: a noisy, literary milieu, in which pugilistic but informed position-taking was a *modus operandi*; a place where writing mattered.

That said, the strongest poems by Dorn before the late 1960s do muster an emotional and intellectual range of tones and materials that can exceed in power any of the texts cited so far, as in his 'Song' from *Geography* (*CP* 141). The poem shows how Dorn is able to articulate his sense of what *is* of vast import to the nation, in terms of kinds of toxicity, in terms of the effects of a general economic plight on the interior of private life, both at the macro-level of rhetoric, trailing 'pointless' sentences like unfinished business, down to the micro-level of the syllable. The interconnectedness of an exploitative system and balked personal desires is conveyed by almost subliminal echoes and twists of sound. The heat of 'burns' is desire kept barely alive in the 'ember' of 'November', a dying coal stamped out by the turn into 'encumbered', as the 'sulphur' of the workplace, its 'burdensome smoke', is met by the casual self-poisoning of daily cigarettes and matches, and the 'smiles' that are as throwaway, in boxes so unlike homes they might as well nuclear shelters. Dorn's skill at disinvesting 'assigned' meanings in melancholy satire, while restoring power to expression through puns and layered meaning, is equal to Wieners's – and he arguably has the harder task, having no tradition of Bohemian rhapsody on which to draw. Part of the skill lies in switching the expected components of an image-cluster to create an effective poetic dissonance, as in the deliberate entrapment of 'I read Yeats', a hopeless exercise, between cloud-descriptions that draw alternately on the toxicity of the chemical factory and the unearthly idealism of Yeats's late Romanticism: the latter might as well have written 'time is wisdom, joy an endless song' for all the practical difference it can make. Again, the plea is for a writing that matters, socially, and that isn't merely struggling in an 'artful' way, in order to survive. Is that a dead snake, 'hooded', by the tanks: or one of the tanks themselves? Catastrophe waits, for the citizen and the *polis*, behind a surface of tiredness and repetitive labour. Like other poems in *Geography*, 'For the New Union Dead in Alabama' or 'Mourning Letter, March 29, 1963', and most of all 'Dark Ceiling', a revision of the 23rd Psalm, the ironically titled 'Song' is dependent on quite traditional structures of theological imagery, and Biblical echo. It has a tripartite structure: Yeats's Paradise is dismissed as unreal, displaced by the sulphurous Inferno of the chemical works, and the last, Purgatorial images of love doomed to 'suffer in the cross streets of this town'. The experimentalism and ingenuity of the *Gunslinger* period should not divert attention from the ways in which Dorn was able to mine more traditional veins of imagery and verbal association in the best of his earlier work.

III

The primacy of gestural individuality has been put in question by contemporary American poetry. The increasingly influential L-A-N-G-U-A-G-E group, in particular the writings of Charles Bernstein and Bruce Andrews, place a combative and thoroughly politicised emphasis on collective signifying practices at the expense of personal imagination. Meanwhile poets such as Sharon Olds or Thom Gunn produce impressive work, but convey their intense interest in personal experience within the kind of verse-frame that was traditional even in the 1950s. In contrast to both, *Gunslinger* was written at the high-point of the 'reading circuit', when a poet such as Robert Duncan could address a football stadium (whose human contents would, admittedly, have come for the most part to hear a rock band). Dorn's highly performative long poem is the most effective poetic writing of those years, and, by its very periodicity, dated (*G* 28–9).

The ontological, semantic, phenomenological and other somersaults that give the text its ceaseless intellectual vitality and comedy are almost always dependent on some hallucination of *voice*. Dorn has often compared *Gunslinger* to radio drama in interview, and one of the spin-offs of this long-term project was a film script (*Abilene! Abilene!*) for which avant-garde film-maker Stan Brakhage would have acted as cameraman, had it seen the light of day. Even Miss Lil, notwithstanding Dorn's repeated and preposterous assertions in interview about all women being one Woman, is basically a highly particularised form of vocal intonation, rather than a 'character', as is born out by his particular relish for her lines in recorded readings. In *Gunslinger* Dorn offers in different voices the community for which his writing has always wished, and which by the late 1960s it had begun creating for itself (*G* 46). Ironically, the most self-indulgent of Dorn's poetry seems to find the largest audience, through its cultural coincidence with the years of collective raga, yoga and hallucination. Drugs are certainly prevalent in the 'Gunslinger' poems, so much so that in what is marketed as a scholarly edition of the text, with a new critical introduction by Marjorie Perloff, the latter can remark authoritatively that 'Each of *Slinger*'s four books is devoted to a specific drug: the first to marijuana, the second to LSD, the third and fourth to cocaine (Lil is known as Cocaine Lil)' (*G* 12). This might imply a rather straightforwardly old-fashioned if not naive model of what constitutes 'devotion'. More cautiously, Dorn has described the role of drugs in the text as 'like the facade, or the molding on the building. ... They were very much in time'(*I* 92).

I would suggest that drugs in this text might with more accuracy be thought of as linguistic twists, synonymous with irony. Dorn has written on a number of occasions of his enthusiasm for a little-known American novelist, Douglas Woolf, whose ironies have a precise linguistic shape, a sentence 'curved, with a hook at the end' (*V* 58). Given the visual layout of *Gunslinger*'s text in relation to its vocalisation, one notices the brevity of the line and its consequent emphasis on the 'hook', or swerve of the line around the corner and into its successor. Incessantly playing off the linear flow of conversation and the narrow column of poetic text becomes a device of defamiliarisation, by its very nature likely to lead to irony; that is, to some incongruity between what was expected and what is delivered. This disparity finds a broad parallel in the action of mild hallucinogens, whose effects are bound up with unpredictable surges and discrepancies at the level of attention. To deconstruct Dorn's poem, one might conclude that drug use was the most evident cultural manifestation, at the time, of what would in rhetorical terms be thought of as the slippage of signifier from signified, of saying from meaning, of expression from convention. It is simply (or at least fundamentally) the case that the alienation of earlier texts, and their situation *vis-à-vis* an audience (or lack of it), is treated in this text with a genial rather than a negative disposition. In one sense this is the idiom of the time; in another nothing has changed.

One of the most powerful but least known prose pieces by Edward Dorn is his Introductory Note to *The Book of Daniel Drew*, a piece he chose not to reprint in his collected essays and criticism, *Views*.[12] Drew was effectively the first Wall Street shark, who began by living on his wits, proceeded to amass a fortune through deception and virtual gangsterism, and ended by founding a theological seminary, only to deprive it of funding after the loss of his ill-gotten gains. This outrageous but likeable figure, recalling by turns something from Dickens and Defoe, operated at an essentially public and visible level, even in his darker machinations. Dorn argues in the preface that modern capitalism has become characterised by an exactly contrary approach, typified by Howard Hughes, whereby financial operations, even those entailing massive public consequences, are by definition removed, unaccountable, unseen. Hughes's neurotic reclusiveness is therefore not an interesting or weird twist in his personal history, but the absolutely logical model of personal behaviour for an operator of this kind. Dorn's portrait of Hughes is intended to be set against Daniel Drew's story: effectively, however, it is a prose commentary on Robard of *The Cycle*, and the dark underside of the *Gunslinger* world, and the 60s:

> It isn't done like this anymore. Now *the thing, the pass, the action* is made another way, shudders behind very hard shades. Perhaps reflects where in fact you stand in your 'world', the eagle flies across the convex mirror lens – dig – in the sky it's a bird, no! and while you were looking of course somebody nailed your big toe to the floor. ... So nobody moves into the top of the Desert Inn either, or the Flamingo, or anyplace, it was a dummy on the stretcher, The Man ambled in behind with his mouth open like the rest of the spectators ... (*DD* vii–viii)

In the words of *The Cycle*, The Man (Robard/Hughes) 'aint never been seen':

> Still, there is no-one inside
> For inside there is no-One
> There is indeed inside only
> The No No No
> (*G* 99)

However, if Robart and his crew are very obviously to be read as the anti-type of Slinger's happy company, it is interesting that Dorn's language, in both the prose and *The Cycle*, does not stand satirically outside the paranoid style of the opposition, as Douglas Woolf's might have done, but inhabits it with a driven ferocity. The implication that in the figure of Robard we may read the anti-type of Dorn the poet, appears unavoidable. What was Howard Hughes but an unacknowledged legislator? No-one could be more socially marginal than a poet, unless, ironically, he were a key player in the operations of late capitalism, sequestered and barely known. 'Isolation is important, protection it is hoped, from the snipers' (*DD* viii).

The bitterness in the tone that marks these late 1960s texts has become almost the habitual manner of Dorn's more recent work, without unfortunately the strange *élan vital* of *The Cycle*. *Hello, La Jolla* (1978) and its uglier twin sister *Yellow Lola* (1989) try to mine a vein of impatience, a jaundiced *non serviam* that could only work if it had teeth. The jokes needed to be better: what follows is an entire poem, 'The Russian Quote':

> *Oh poet, you should*
> get a Jobooski.[13]

Dorn's latest collection, *Abhorrences*, goes further down the La Jolla road, towards self-parody, as in 'On Losing One's Coolant':

> Along about the 6th inning
> of game 7, intense loathing
> for the Mets and things 'New York'
> spilled out of me like
> dark, apoplectic lava
> whereupon I stuck a few pins
> in my Ed Koch doll.[14]

The trouble is that *Geography* or *The Cycle* really *were* full of 'dark, apoplectic lava', but were too absorbed in pouring it over the opposition to have time to turn around and admire their own eruptions. An ability to put marginalisation to creative use has turned, in Dorn's case, into mere provincialism and a sour withdrawal. The Gunslinger has traded in his leather boots and spurs for a pair of carpet slippers, in which to sit flipping the TV zapper on cultural flotsam that no-one needs his poetry in order to be jolted into disliking. Perhaps the problem is finally that there exists no sizeable community of readers who want his poetry, or any poetry, for any reasons other than those entailed by the higher education market. Of his extraordinarily gifted generation, Dorn was the New American Poet least able to draw sustenance from his forced estrangement from the mainstream. The best work, prior to his masterpiece *Gunslinger*, got its energy from the 'actionable', from jolting the reader into an *activation* of sympathetic imagination whose logical consequences were political. To paraphrase Dr Timothy Leary, it would seem that, having Tuned In to the 1960s, then Turned others On to the livelier idioms of the time, both this poet and the prospects for a legislative poetry just Dropped Out, lost to serious consideration.

NOTES

1. David Ossman (ed.), *The Sullen Art* (New York: Corinth Books, 1963) pp. 85.
2. Ibid., pp. 87 ff.
3. Allen Ginsberg, *The Collected Poems, 1947–1980* (New York: Harper and Row, 1985) p. 136.
4. Edward Dorn, *Interviews* (Bolinas: Four Seasons Foundation, 1980) pp. 89. All further page references to this book are contained in the essay, and prefaced *I*.
5. Edward Dorn, *Gunslinger* (Durham and London: Duke University Press, 1989) pp. 50. All further page references to this book are contained in the essay, and prefaced *G*.
6. Edward Dorn, *The North Atlantic Turbine* (London: Fulcrum Press, 1967). From the autobiographical statement on the inner dustjacket.
7. Edward Dorn, *The Collected Poems, 1956–1974* (Bolinas: Four Seasons Foundation, 1975) pp. 87. All further page references are contained in the essay, and prefaced CP.
8. Edward Dorn, *Views* (San Francisco: Four Seasons Foundation, 1980) pp. 123. All further references are contained in the essay, and prefaced *V*.
9. A. Walton Litz and Christopher MacGowan (eds), *William Carlos Williams: The Collected Poems 1909–1939* (Manchester: Carcanet Press, 1987) pp. 84–5.
10. Robert Duncan, *The Opening of the Field* (London: Jonathan Cape, 1969) pp. 7.
11. John Wieners, *Selected Poems, 1958–1984* (Santa Barbara: Black Sparrow Press, 1986) pp. 28.

12. Edward Dorn, *The Book of Daniel Drew* (New York: Frontier Press, 1969). All further references are prefaced *DD*.
13. Edward Dorn, *Hello, La Jolla* (Berkeley: Wingbow Press, 1978) pp. 48.
14. Edward Dorn, *Abhorrences* (Santa Rosa: Black Sparrow Press, 1990) pp. 101.

15

Robert Creeley

ALISTAIR WISKER

Robert Creeley read poems from a new volume, *Windows*, in a small café in London early in 1991.[1] It was obvious that he was at ease, had done this many times. But he wanted, and the audience sensed that he needed, to say something about his feelings as an American abroad at that particular moment in history. The instance[2] was projected as his present field of interest. In this particular he sensed the universal, very much in the mode of his obvious predecessors – Walt Whitman and William Carlos Williams. The speaker in Creeley's poetry, as in this London reading, is often intent and overwrought, relentless, uncertain but always seeking, confident in his uncertainty rather than reliant on previous certainties, interested in approaches to complexity rather than momentary resolutions. The eye in Creeley's poetry sees things his way.

Notions of thematic coherence, the development of imagistic patterns, the celebration of meaning as outcome, don't apply. Creeley gets going on a poem, settles into saying something as it goes, improvises. You can hear it in his voice. His artistic relatives definitely include Miles Davis, Charlie Parker, and Jackson Pollock, who described the activity of his work as 'When I am in my painting', but just as definitely don't include T. S. Eliot, John Crowe Ransom, or the Cleanth Brooks and Robert Penn Warren version of 'understanding poetry' and, therefore, poetry for understanding.[3] The tradition to which Creeley relates has to do with what Robert Duncan calls 'a well deeper than time'. Being a poet is for him the reverse of an ego-centred occupation and writing is an expression, 'a realization, reification, of *what is*'.[4] Creeley is in his poems and very definitely also in his/the world which he views as complex and not given to simple resolutions – 'If one's at a time when world consciousness seems to be shifting in its dispositions towards experience, I think it's time indeed to acknowledge the resources of a far more extensive modality of statement.'[5] He is preoccupied by matters of perception and the speaker who perceives, by the relationship between perception and expression, and his explorations very often seem to take place in an inner or mental space, that 'wood where / nobody goes'.[6] Over a number of poems, his reader shares in Creeley's struggle to shape or perhaps reclaim an idiom from the seemingly chaotic, often surprising, often painful, sometimes disreputable facts of what would otherwise be lost or dispossessed experience.

Many of the poems which he selected to read in London were centred on friendships, dedicated to friends, concerned with memories, ageing, death, with 'sad, sagging flesh'.[7] As such a poem proceeds, the speaker searches for a sigh or a sign that 'I'm still inside'. This being inside and out, exploring the nature of both the perceiver and the perceived, and the concern with ageing and death are not new in Creeley's work. Take these lines from *Later*, published in 1975, for instance:[8]

> in these days
> of physical change,
> I see
> ...
>   life grow
> ridiculous.

The available ways of knowing do grow ridiculous and chance is often substituted for intention in the work of Robert Creeley. He is amongst those who:[9]

> dissatisfied with the similes, metaphors, and personifications that assume man to be the measure and scale of a phenomenal world totally in his control, everything else being mere descriptive objects, look around them for that 'order' larger than man, to wit, the literal world – space, things, and among them people – realized in each moment of perception: the 'instant' recognized as 'both shape and law'.

Every successful poem and within it every line is an instant of perception caught by the pen of a poet whose view of life is that it is 'interesting insofar as it lacks intentional "control"'.[10]

For love – I would
split open your head and put
a candle in
behind the eyes.

Love is dead in us
if we forget
the virtues of an amulet
and quick surprise.

Sloth and indifference invite danger but 'chance and surprise are rites that quickly exorcise the evils of apathy'.[12] The poem is a warning with depth. Creeley often finds his language in that of the everyday exchange but it is altogether revitalised and wrenched into new meanings; often, as in 'The Warning', revealing new chasms beneath old assumptions. Tired and predictable ideas are deconstructed and invested with the dangers inherent in tiredness and apathy. In fact Creeley is always on his guard against the evils of apathy, questioning expectations, defying comfort and predictability, as in 'Do You Think':[13] The poem becomes an existential journey incorporating a constant attack on the ego-centred assumptions which we all tend to relax into. Creeley adds in one line to each paragraph so that there is a sense of the poem gaining both momentum and weight, piling up against us and ending with a straight attack on the ego.

In such ways does the poem focus incrementally on the human ego and its dependence, taking a view of isolation, relationship, loneliness, and commitment. It questions each of these and then, punishingly, at the end it questions the questioning – breaking up the repeated 'Do you think that if' and spoiling even the predictability of the phrasing: 'Do you / think that if …' and 'Do you think that / if …'. Of course it is all magic. Magic, or a sense of it, 'inhabits all the necessary, or even compulsive, acts of love or writing, when with suddenness the known changes, the unknown and mysterious become true and alive'.[14] We travel together with the poet, away, and often well away from the usual and into a new time, a new mind, a discovery which was not possible to foresee or to forestall.

A questioning of perception then, a questioning of identity and relationship, suffuses Creeley's writing. In his novel *The Island*,[15] there is an island which 'sits in the sea some two hundred miles from the mainland', a testing ground, and here John thinks of those changes by which an association is preserved, and tries 'to commit himself, in all senses, though not to all things. To his wife, to begin with, the first free association, bred of loneliness, then of sex, then of mutual necessity, being now too known and too wise, they though, to be innocent again.' So there is a working out of identity and relationship here, a focus on the individual footprint. This particular passage continues:

> The roads of this world, crossed by intersections of, 'but I meant,' 'didn't you say that,' laws, agreements, painful rein-statements, insistences, of value stratified by centuries of enforcement, are often very painful. To walk them, to move from *a* to *b*, to *have* a move, no choice but that within that necessity, was for the moment John's own approach. He had somehow to prove the reality of his own footprint, there being no one else who could.

The thought of the novel is consistent with that of the poetry. And, too, it is worth noting that all this is consistent with Creeley's belief that if a person is a writer, 'very often one will find the same intensity of possibility in all that he does'.[16] He is, for instance, very much against the specious division that led to D. H. Lawrence's poetry being ignored for such a long period during which his novels were so much appreciated, because 'some of Lawrence's poems are magnificent, and the kinds of intensity they possess are those familiar to me in his prose also'.

It is worth remembering that Creeley wrote an early poem for D. H. Lawrence. The focus here is on the insistences, the repetition, the strident and near-hysterical questioning and assertion of identity which, after all that, remains 'alone and unwanted'.[17] The repetition of 'because' puts a pressure on the logic, on the linking of identity, self, and being. Elsewhere Creeley has identified how this kind of exploration of identity and consciousness shapes the background for his generation. The disturbance of the war years came at the end of the Depression, 'the chaos of values and assumption of values, the definition of values, was very insistent'.[18] Creeley discusses the common friends which he and Allen Ginsberg had at that time although they themselves had not then met. One such friend had a compulsive need to kill himself and Creeley sees that need as almost a societal condition of the time:

it was almost the actual situation of feeling in those years; a sort of terrifying need to demonstrate the valuelessness of one's own life. Think of the parallel of Existentialism, for example; the whole context of thinking in that time is incredibly self-destructive.

Not surprising, then, that Creeley has been so preoccupied, as an American and, particularly, as a New Englander, with explorations of identity and perception. As he has said himself, this has nothing at all to do with any kind of do-it-yourself psychoanalysis; there is 'a deeper fact of revelation'. It has to do with acknowledging, sharing, and perhaps in part shaping our modern circumstance and changing consciousness. Of course Allen Ginsberg knew all about this when he wrote of seeing 'the best minds of my generation destroyed by madness, starving hysterical naked'.[19] And Creeley comes to a plain statement of his position in a conversation with Ginsberg at a University of British Columbia Poetry Conference in 1963:[20]

> my point is that the very premise on which consciousness operates is undergoing modifications that none of us, I think, are at the moment capable of defining. We can only recognize them. Let's say, that if Pound says artists are the antennae of the race, I think that any of us here is in a position to be responsive to this feeling that's so immense, so definite, and so insistent. Not because we can do anything with it. It simply is, it's a big change, it's a deep change in consciousness, and I'm curious to see what's going to happen – which is a mild way of putting it. Indeed!

Creeley's recognition of *what is* is explored in poems which often are or enact thoughts, possibilities, surprises, intentions, hypotheses, transfigurations, rather than results, outcomes, or answers.

Irony can imply entrapment, a fixity. Creeley's poetry is a poetry of exploration, exploring the boundaries between being and environment. It requires a method of apperception, a method, that is, of recognising what we perceive. Denise Levertov has described such 'organic' poetry as:[21]

> based on an intuition of an order, a form beyond forms, in which forms partake, and of which man's creative works are analogies, resemblances, natural allegories. Such poetry is exploratory.

This implies a necessary openness, a denial of the ego which is so likely to intervene and defend itself as a priority, rather than to prioritise adaptation and the exploratory. Creeley expressed such a credo of openness and concomitant denial of ego in 'The Immoral Proposition',[22] which might well be understood as a manifesto poem. The perception finds its own form, measured rhythmically, for the voice, by the couplet form. The poem explores the notion that staying away from other people spares a person the tragedy of relationship; it explores the paradoxes of incompleteness and dependence – 'nothing is / all there is'. The 'unsure egoist' may not be 'good for himself', but he is, as well, no good for anyone else. Whatever the poet has to say, if it is worth the saying, should be capable of making its own form as it goes.

At the beginning of his *Projective Verse*, Charles Olson identifies some simplicities that a man learns if he works in COMPOSITION BY FIELD rather than the inherited line. One of these has to do with the *kinetics* of the process: 'A poem is energy transferred from where the poet got it (he will have some several causations), by way of the poem itself to, all the way over to, the reader.'[23] Creeley is clearly instructed and instructing on this transference from poet, through poem, to reader. In modern critical terms, Creeley, Olson, Dorn, and their colleagues were early in on the transfer of interest from author to text and, beyond the text, to the reader. Another of Olson's simplicities has to do with the process itself, which he boils down to a statement pounded into his head by Edward Dahlberg: ONE PERCEPTION MUST IMMEDIATELY AND DIRECTLY LEAD TO A FURTHER PERCEPTION. Creeley's work maintains this tenet of what Olson describes as the dogma. It is apparent in each of the poems we have quoted. The last of the simplicities which Olson identifies as apparent to those who work in composition by field is:

FORM IS NEVER MORE THAN AN EXTENSION OF CONTENT.

This is the principle, the law underpinning Olson's projective verse, and it is attributed to one 'R. Creeley'. Creeley has played a key part in the development of American and international poetry in the second half of the twentieth century through his work itself, of course, and through his consistent propounding of this principle. This new poetics is far from anarchic, it insists that there are forms

inherent in reality itself which can be discovered because, as
Ginsberg says, 'Mind is shapely', 'the message is: widen the area of
consciousness'. In a rare little book titled *Charles Olson Reading at
Berkeley*, published in 1966, a transcript of the poet reading at the
Berkeley Poetry Conference in 1965, Olson speaks of how Creeley
had criticised him and 'taught me everything one might. He
knocked any wig I ever had off my head ... he knew exactly what
he was saying.'[24] It is clear from this and from other records, including the testament of a number of interviews,[25] just how central
Creeley was to what was going on, irrevocably, in the development
of poetry and the other arts from the 1950s onwards.

Creeley is immersed in the activity of poetry, exploring its limits,
limited only by its nature. This immersion is reminiscent of, and
parallel to, that of his counterparts, the artists of abstract expressionism and the musicians of modern jazz – the main proponents
being perhaps Jackson Pollock and Charlie Parker. His preoccupation has been with the art, the act of writing, and the scrupulous articulation of his effort is clear throughout his work and particularly
in the volumes *Words*, published in 1967, and *Pieces*, published in
1969. The fascination with the nature and processes of writing is
apparent in individual poems such as 'The Rhythm', 'The
Language', several 'Songs' and 'Diction'. but this fascination with
the activity of writing, its history, its technical challenges and
achievements and its forms, is not limited to specific works. Rather,
articulating his engagement with the poetic process becomes both
Creeley's subject and object; and his focus, as he puts it in the
opening poem in *Pieces*,[26] is on:

saying
something
as it goes.

'Saying' is an important verb here. For Creeley, poetry is 'the basic
art of speech, of utterance?.[27] Line and stanza arrangement indicate
what the poet is after rhythmically because for him 'lines and stanzas indicate my rhythmic intention ... the typographical context of
poetry is still simply the issue of how to score – in the musical sense
– to indicate how I want the poem to be read'. In his own reading
Creeley tends to pause after each line, even if it is a short one. These
terminal endings give him 'a way of both syncopating and indicat-
ing a rhythmic measure. I think of those lines as something akin to

the bar in music – they state the rhythmic modality. They indicate what the base rhythm of the poem is, hopefully, to be.' For Creeley, then, the quatrain or couplet are both a semantic and a rhythmic measure. He refers to Pound writing in a letter that 'Verse consists of a constant and a variant.' The quatrain or couplet is the constant and the variant can then occur in the line:[28]

> the base rhythm also has a constant which the quatrain in its totality indicates. I wanted something stable, and the quatrain offered it to me; as earlier the couplet form had. This, then, allows all the variability of what could be both said and indicated as rhythmic measure.

Discussions of poetry as speech soon move on to an emphasis on the relationship between form and content, a relationship which Creeley has always believed is of necessity intimate, kinetic. Form should never be allowed to become an assumption, static, because 'content has its own form'.

A poem founded on this principle of form is often described as 'organic', and we noticed that in the comments of Denise Levertov quoted above. Creeley has distinguished between the organic and the 'traditional' thus:[29]

> The traditional poem is after all the historical memory of a way of writing that's regarded as significant. And I'm sure again that all those poems were once otherwise – as Stendhal feels, Racine *was* modern at the time Racine was writing those plays. But then for his work to be respected in the nineteenth century as being *the* way of writing – this, of course, was something else again. This is a respect merely for the thing that has happened, not because it is still happening but because it did happen.

All this becomes compressed into a pithy question – 'What's the point of doing what we already know?' There is dead tradition and live tradition. 'Dead' tradition, a respect for and imitation of something that isn't happening any more, becomes a drag on progress:

> the traditional is, after all, the cumulative process of response. It has its uses without question. But it can only be admitted as the contemporary can respond to it.

Creeley's version of the contemporary responds to the traditional with an ironising edge. Whether it be irony about the mnemonic adhesiveness of rhyme[30] or irony about recognised forms, the traditional is admitted because it has to be responded to like other facts of existence. Irony in relation to tradition is apparent in, for instance, 'The Flower'. Here the language of the nursery rhyme ('she loves me / she loves me not / she loves me / she loves me not') is reconstituted into 'Pain is a flower like that one, / like this one, / like that one, / like this one.' This ironic strategy is also apparent in 'Hello',[31] which is a brilliant reconstitution of the typical language of the thriller. The exchanging of the expected 'dress' for 'eye' and the splitting of the two sentences into rhythmic fractions is remarkably effective here. The assumptions and expectations of the sex-and-violence potboiler are disassembled and assembled as something entirely new which amounts to a questioning of the genre. Creeley, in effect, unpicks the predictable. This is one of his most original contributions to the craft of poetry. In this context it is worth looking back at 'The Warning': 'For love – I would / split open your head and put / a candle in / behind the eyes.' Another extraordinary outcome of Creeley's present-day look at tradition is found in a poem which, like 'The Flower', involves a sinister re-working of the language of the nursery. 'If You'[32] begins by asking 'If you were going to get a pet / what kind of animal would you get.' The poem quickly evolves into a questioning of assumptions about animals, feelings and beliefs about animals, and the giving of animals as gifts. The tone of the poem is relentless in its questioning and because of this there is no need for question-marks. It moves mercilessly towards its brilliant conclusion that 'a form of otherwise vicious habit / can have long ears and be called a rabbit'. The fascination is in the unsuspected direction which 'If You' takes and the denial of the comfort of rhyme, for instance, or expectation.

Creeley talks about the means of poetry a great deal but the matter of his work, its content, and his commentary on it, is equally pointed. The poem is always a discovery, rescued from what would otherwise be silence – 'I can't remember ever setting out to write a poem literally about something that I was conscious of before I began to write.'[33] In fact, Creeley doesn't believe that poetry has 'subjects'. It has themes, but subjects are imposed on it by persons 'well distinct from the actual activity'. Creeley falls back on the sense of this recorded in *The Maximus Poems* by Charles Olson: 'He sd, "You go all around the subject." And I sd, "I didn't know it was a subject".'[34] Creeley worries about the categorisation of poetry by subject, and the judgement of its value in relation to what may at least sometimes be a spurious sense of profundity. He refers in this context to William Carlos Williams, who, at least during the 1940s and much of the 1950s, was received with a charge of being unprofound, of being concerned with unpoetic subjects, the paraphernalia of everyday life. Creeley sees this charge as 'a very, very silly way to think of poems'. The poem is essentially an instrument rather than a bearer of thought, the poet, as Carlos Williams says, 'thinks with his poem' and that in itself is the profundity. In thinking these issues through, Creeley is struck by a definition of 'meaning' offered by Olson – 'That which exists through itself is what is called meaning.' This is explored in what is one of the most interesting of the interviews with Creeley:[35]

> That kind of meaning, that kind of significant, is what a poem is. It *does* so exist through itself, through agency of its own activity; therefore, is; therefore, has meaning. What a poem says as some kind of instruction that can be understood and then thrown away – I find this kind of meaning to be very secondary, to be finally *not* that which qualifies poetry in the active manner.

Creeley's interest is very much in 'poetry in the active manner' and this is apparent in his poetry and in the many interviews with him. It also comes into focus in the number of references he makes to the sentence, the word, the pen; in his proposing truth as a scrawl, or America as an ode for reality, or in his considering a giggly ode on motherfuckers. Sometimes his declared hesitation about subjects becomes a subject itself, or at least a way of starting.[36] The way of starting develops into something articulated as it goes, leads to unsuspected possibilities, to discovery associated with a rejection of metaphors and the appropriation of plain saying. There is a nervous pressure in the voice of it, an openness combined with an almost irritable reaching after fact; indirection leading to a new clarity. The poem becomes an act of discovery during which it becomes clear that writing and environment impinge on each other. Writing, and perhaps all artistic activity, is body-centred and permits or provokes a sense of being *in the* world. Robert Bly, in a prose poem, creates a metaphorical portrait of Creeley's 'being' and 'work' thus:[37]

The beak is a crow beak, and the sideways look he gives, the head shoved slightly to the side by the bad eye, finishes it. And I suppose his language in poems is crow language – no long open vowels, like the owl, no howls like the wolf, but instead short, faintly hollow, harsh sounds, that all together make something genuine, crow speech coming up from every feather, every source of that crow body and crow life.

This, of course, offers a grounding in the poetry of Bly himself. It does, however, also say a lot about Creeley: that authentic speech 'coming up from every source', that contiguity between all being and its environment – human articulation being simply a related if higher form of exploration.

So where do Creeley's preoccupations come from? He was born in 1926 in Arlington, Massachusetts, a fact which he celebrated more than forty years later in the volume *Pieces*.[38] Sadly his father died when he was just four years old. He grew up on a small farm in West Acton where his mother worked as a public health nurse. Two things at least have fascinated Creeley about those years. His mother kept things in the house which were evidence of his father's life and, as a child, he was fascinated by people who 'traveled light'. These two things come together in the example which he gives of his father's bag which was full of the instrumentation of his work as a doctor:[39]

> The doctor's bag was an absolutely explicit instance of something you carry with you and work out of. As a kid, growing up without a father, I was always interested in men who came to the house with specific instrumentation of that sort – carpenters, re-pairmen – and I was fascinated by the idea that you could travel in the world that way with all you needed in your hands. All of this comes back to me when I find myself talking to people about writing. The scene is always this: 'What a great thing! To be a writer! Words are something you can carry in your head. You can really "travel light".'

Creeley takes a plain view of many things and I am reminded here of his lines on 'The Puritan Ethos' – 'Happy the man who loves what / he has and worked for it also'. The death of his father and the still earlier loss of his left eye presented 'two conditions I have unequivocally as content' as Creeley has put it, and it is of course the loss of his eye that brings about Robert Bly's comment about 'the sideways look he gives, the head shoved slightly to the side by the bad eye'. Creeley graduated from Holderness School in New Hampshire and attended Harvard until the beginning of his experience driving an ambulance for the American Field Service in India. It was on his return from India in the winter of 1945 that the first poem which he remembers having published appeared, and it is titled 'Return':[40]

> Quiet as is proper for such places;
> The street, subdued, half-snow, half-rain,
> Endless, but ending in the darkened doors.
> Inside, they who will be there always,
> Quiet as is proper for such people –
> Enough for now to be here, and
> To know my door is one of these.

Although he had returned to Harvard after the war, he left in 1947 without a degree. At this time he was married to Ann MacKinnon, with whom he tried subsistence farming in New Hampshire before they moved to Southern France and Majorca, which was the scene of *The Island*. Following his divorce from his first wife, Creeley married Bobbie Hall in 1957 and a creative relationship developed between Robert and Bobbie Creeley over the subsequent two decades. They worked together on a number of books. Poems by Robert Creeley, monoprints or collages by Bobbie Creeley, became a familiar signature to a number of volumes. On my shelf, in nostalgic rather than meticulous mood, I can see *The Finger* (1968), *St. Martin's* (1971), *A Day Book* (dedicated to Bobbie, 1972), *Listen* (1972), and *Thirty Things* (1974). The relationship is given expression in the juxtaposition of the poems and prints, it also enters many individual poems and is in plain focus in 'The Act of Love'.[41] Bobbie and Robert Creeley divorced. In 1977 he married Penelope Highton, to whom the volume *Windows* (1991) is dedicated.

During the late nineteen-forties, the fifties and the sixties, Creeley was writing poetry, stories, and letters, and teaching. He entered into a number of correspondences, most notably with Ezra Pound, who tended to write in injunctions – 'You do this. You do that. Read this. Read that.' – and William Carlos Williams, who was always much more specific. Creeley wasn't dismayed but his ego was sometimes set back:[42]

I remember one time I wrote him a very stern letter – some description about something I was going to do, or *this* was the way
things were, *blah blah*. And he returned me the sheets of the letter
and he had marked on the margin of particular sections, 'Fine.
Your style is tightening.' But I had the sense to know such comments were of more use to me than whether or not he approved
or what I had to say. He would do things like that which were
very good.

Letter-writing is undoubtedly important to Creeley. There are fasci-
nating and sustained exchanges with, for instance, Cid Corman,
editor of *Origin*, and Charles Olson, with whom he worked at Black
Mountain College. Creeley has often acknowledged the importance
of his work for and at Black Mountain – an experiment in education
located in the foothills of North Carolina and lasting from 1933 to
1956.[43] In his junior year at Harvard he had spent a few days there
but it wasn't until 1953–4 that his association with the College developed. Since its first appearance in 1951, *Origin* had been publishing many of the writers who were to be associated with Black
Mountain and it was clear that there was space for a new publication. Creeley agreed to edit *the Black Mountain Review* in 1953 although he was at that time living in Majorca and hadn't yet met
Charles Olson, who had moved to Black Mountain to stay in the
summer of 1951. Creeley joined the College faculty in the March of
1954.

The identification of a Black Mountain School of poetry really
begins in Donald Allen's *The New American Poetry*, published in
1960. Allen was careful in his grouping and six of the poets in his
anthology had some real connection with the College – Creeley
himself, and Charles Olson of course, Robert Duncan, Ed Dorn, Joel
Oppenheimer and Jonathan Williams. But the matter of grouping
was not apparent at the time. It was the finances and politics of the
College situation which were problematic:[44]

At the time I was there, the college was in very straitened circumstances, and had a great deal of difficulty in maintaining its
operation, so that I think everyone present felt a curiously useful
desperation. It finally proved the end of the college, of course,
but I think we all felt a seriousness and an openness of form and
intention that was extremely useful to all concerned. The students, I suppose, had a more difficult time than the faculty,

although the faculty seems to have had troubles enough, but we were very much concerned with the problems of experimental education and what could be done now. We wanted a kind of teaching that usually depended upon actually being involved in the materials that were being used. So that, for example, in painting or writing, we had people who were painters or writers, as opposed to those who might be more theoretically involved.

Creeley's emphasis has always been, at Black Mountain as now, on the activity, the practice of writing. Joel Oppenheimer has commented that the interest in the line and in the sound texture of the poem, the attempt to make the poem on the page read as if Joel Oppenheimer, or Charles Olson, or Robert Creeley were reading it, are common concerns of the Black Mountain poets. Oppenheimer believes that whilst there is a common texture to the work of these poets, equally they are distinct in their own ways. And it is the distinctive differences which occur to Creeley. He recognises that the Black Mountain poets used Olson as a locus, and were variously involved with Pound and Williams and, behind them, Whitman.[45] But this does not necessarily mean that there was a 'school' of poetry. In fact Creeley has written about the strangeness of hearing, in retrospect, of a Black Mountain School of Poets: 'literary history to that extent defines us in a sense we neither had time nor interest to consider'. The same understanding comes to Ed Dorn, in an interview in which he notes 'I don't see any superstructure that existed there which would relate people and what they subsequently did.'[46]

Creeley has been scathing, over the years, about literary criticism as an activity. No doubt he is fortunate to be able to say that 'Criticism for me is occasional writing. I'd never undertake it as anything more. It's my own attempt to respond to something that's moved me, and to give witness to that response and to that which has provoked it'[47] But he is clear that, so far as he is concerned, 'speaking particularly of the situation of poetry, there is *no* correspondence of any interest to me between the activities of contemporary criticism and that poetry I am myself most engaged with'.[48] The point, from Creeley's perspective, is in meeting with what he describes as an exceptional critical intelligence – and his immediate examples are Kenneth Burke, D. H. Lawrence, Edward Dahlberg and Ezra Pound. This attitude to literary criticism is in fact part of Creeley's resistance to the institutionalisation of the arts, and of literature in particular:[49]

I question the universities' trying to make the arts a *subject*. And I always will question it. I would much rather feel that the university was reflecting a public concern with the arts rather than some institutional concern that wants to gain them as materials for its own activity. Till they realize that the arts are not to be confined by their assumptions, there will always be rancor and a feeling or misuse.

Following his work at Black Mountain College, Creeley taught in Albuquerque, became a tutor in Guatemala, and took a tutorship at the University of New Mexico. Since 1978 he has been Gray Professor of Poetry and Letters and the Samuel P. Capen Professor of Poetry and Humanities at the State University of New York at Buffalo. He has been (1989–91) New York State Poet Laureate. During the 1950s he appeared widely in magazines and the small presses. His reputation was then consolidated in the 1960s and 1970s particularly – and this is a personal preference – with the publication of *Hello: A Journal* in 1978.

Hello results from a tour by Robert Creeley of nine countries in a little more than two months, between 29 February and 3 May 1976. He went to Fiji, New Zealand, Australia, Singapore, the Philippines, Malaysia, Hong Kong, Japan, and Korea. He went 'to look, to see, even if briefly, how people in those parts of the world made a reality, to talk of being American, of the past war, of power, of usual life in this country, of my fellow and sister poets, of my neighbours on Fargo Street in Buffalo, New York. I wanted, at last, to be human, however simplistic that wish. I took thus my own chances and remarkably found a company.' In the introduction to *Hello* Creeley is preoccupied, as he always is, with being American, with the American circumstance. He believes that there is a sense in which Americans presume the world as something to look at and use rather than to live in. Other cultures, Samoan, Chinese, Malaysian, or Filipino, cannot easily think of one as singular – 'such familiar concepts as the "nuclear family" or "alienation" had literally to be translated'. Creeley's feeling is that American habits of social value constantly promote an isolation–'the house in the country, the children in good schools' – whereas the cultures he was visiting tended to find 'center and strength in the collective, unless it has been perverted by Western exploitation and greed'.

Reading *Hello* in these other cultures results in startling moments of recognition and identification.[50] There is the moment when you realise that you are different, as well, because you don't look like anyone else. This happened to Creeley in a 'Hotel Lobby'; it happened to my wife and me in a supermarket. It is a startling human reminder of cultural difference which makes you reflect on your own state – personal and political. At another moment Creeley returns to a hotel room on a visit to Kuala Lumpur in a decidedly questioning mood. He goes through the particular and inevitable period of exhaustion, recreated in clipped phrasing like 'room I accepted' or 'bed I lay down on' gratefully. Next he asks himself if he can or should.[51] Here we see Creeley's characteristic movement between inside and outside, a movement between the perceiver and the perceived. The speaker is moved to question his sense of responsibility, to fix on his family – too late? – and then look at himself as others might or might not feel about him. This poem from *Hello* becomes, like those from *Later*, *Windows*, and the other collections which we have considered in this chapter, a collage of perceptions. Perceptions about place readily give way to others which question self, its values, relationships, attitudes, and humanity. Of course, undergoing this degree of questioning, the desire to be seen, to have your existence acknowledged, may well overtake you. In the same seventeenth-floor room it might well strike you that: [52]

> No one's going to
> see me naked up here.
> My only chance is
> to jump.

What gives these lines their peculiar force is the tension between the humorous and the tragic, pressurised nervousness and deceptive calm, the single place and the world it's a part of, the single experience and the need to connect.

The shape of *Hello* had been predicted by *A Day Book*, written between 1968 and 1971, and *Pieces*, published in 1969. Creeley has often set out to build from brief notations in an incremental manner registering the difficulties of consciousness and perception at the *present* time – 'saying / something / as it goes'. This produces the explorative diction and strategically broken lines, and the pace of speech as it is recorded in, for instance, 'Hotel Merlin' and 'Seventeenth Floor: Echoes of Singapore'. What we hear is a plain, authentic rendering of a particular internal perception or discovery. This is often brief, although there are more sustained articulations.[53]

Creeley has often been asked about, and has often described, the influences on him and his sense of locale, of place. As he put it at one time, the latter had to do with:[54]

> that place where one is open, where a sense of defensiveness or insecurity and all the other complexes of response to place can be finally dropped. Where one feels an intimate association with the ground under foot.

He acknowledges that this is something of an idealisation, of course – and many other factors have influenced his work. We have registered some of those which he often refers to in interviews – the loss of his father, the loss of his eye, specific friends, geography, his New England childhood. When it comes to responding to questions about the more immediate influence of other contemporary artists on his own poetry, Creeley is wont to identify Williams as his greatest example. But, equally, he is always moving on and he often cites Robert Duncan, Allen Ginsberg, Denise Levertov, Paul Blackburn and Ed Dorn as influences – or equally, Charlie Parker. He says he finds it difficult to make 'a hierarchy of persons'. But he does dispose of a question about the presence of cummings in his own work with a perceptive remark about their different relationship with an audience: 'I don't have an audience, and this qualifies what I write. My poems are limited, unhappily perhaps, by having to speak in a very single fashion. I don't speak for a generality of people. Now cummings, despite all his insistence on the single identity of the "i," is speaking for almost a class.'[55] There is no doubt, however, of Creeley's understanding of the influence of Charles Olson not only as a critic or a teacher, or whatever, but as a reader. He had been trying to write in the mode of Wallace Stevens, which just didn't work for him. Olson he describes as the first reader he had, 'the first man both sympathetic and articulate enough to give me a very clear sense of what the effect of my writing was ... I found him the ideal reader, and have always found him so. At the same time, his early senses of how I might make the line intimate to my own habits of speaking – that is, the groupings and whatnot that I was obviously involved with – was of great release to me.'[56]

As for literary influences from further back, there is a sometimes deceptive ease about identifying the likely contenders. This goes from Creeley's early admiration for Paul Valéry and William Carlos

Williams to his readings in European love poetry and his assimilation of Walt Whitman. Writing of Whitman, Creeley has emphasised 'his instruction that one speak for oneself'.[57] There is a pithy
version of this when, in a conversation with Charles Tomlinson,
Creeley is reminded that he has not mentioned Eliot and is asked if
he is still available to the American poet as a useful influence. The
answer is 'No. Eliot is far less available than the people we have
spoken of. And there is one much earlier poet who is far, far more
available than Eliot. ... That is the figure the New Critics and the
universities to this day have conspired to ignore: that is Walt
Whitman.'[58] In the 1940s it was considered bad taste to be interested in Whitman, whose embarrassing affirmations might disturb
one's own somewhat cynical wisdoms. In a time of intensively
didactic criticism it was difficult to know what to do with him:

> He went on and on, he seemed to lack 'structure', he yielded to
> no 'critical apparatus' then to hand. So, as students we were
> herded past him as quickly as possible, and our teachers used
> him only as an example of 'the American of that period' which,
> we were told, was a vast swamp of idealistic expansion and cor-
> ruption. Whitman, the dupe, the dumb-bell, the pathetically re-
> grettable instance of this country's dream and despair, the
> self-taught man.

But D. H. Lawrence and Hart Crane valued Whitman. So did three
of Creeley's fellow poets – Allen Ginsberg, Robert Duncan, and
Louis Zukofsky. Creeley had grown up habituated, as he puts it, to
the use of poetry as a compact, epiphanal instance of emotion or
insight and he valued its 'intensive compression' and ability to get
through a maze of conflict and confusion to some centre of clear
point. But the question Creeley keeps asking is what if the emotions
or terms of thought 'could not be so focused upon or isolated in
such singularity?'[59]

> Assuming a context in which the statement was of necessity mul-
> tiphasic, a circumstance the components of which were multiple,
> or, literally, a day in which various things *did* occur, not simply
> one thing – what did one do with that?

A solution to this dilemma comes to Creeley late in the 1950s when
he went back to graduate school and took a course titled Twain and

Whitman, given by John Gerber, a visiting professor at the University of New Mexico. The group of which Creeley was a part was asked to produce individual thematic outlines of 'Song of Myself' and, on the day these were due, to write them up on the blackboards round the room. No two of the outlines were the same, and this was the instructive point. Whitman's poem does not have a systematised logic of 'subject' nor did the poet 'organise' his materials with a set schedule in the poem. Creeley's understanding of this is that 'the situation of a "field" of activity, rather than some didactic imposition of a "line" of order, was very clear'. It still is.

NOTES

1. A reading organised by The Blue Nose Poets at the Blue Nose Café in North London, 29 January 1991.
2. This was at the time of the so-called Gulf War.
3. The reference is to Cleanth Brooks and Robert Penn Warren, *Understanding Poetry* (New York: Holt, Rinehart and Winston, 1960).
4. Robert Creeley, *Contexts of Poetry: Interviews 1961–1971* (Bolinas: Four Seasons Foundation, 1973) p. 180.
5. Ibid., p. 199.
6. Robert Creeley, 'The Flower', *The Collected Poems of Robert Creeley: 1945–1975* (Berkeley: University of California Press, 1982) p. 194. The volume is referred to as CP in subsequent notes.
7. Robert Creeley, *Windows* (London: Marion Boyars, 1991) p. 90.
8. Robert Creeley, *Later* (London: Marion Boyars, 1980) p. 119.
9. Ann Mandel, *Measures: Robert Creeley's Poetry*, Beaver Kosmos Folios, no. 6 (Toronto: The Coach House Press, 1974).
10. Creeley, *Contexts of Poetry*, p. 131.
11. Robert Creeley, in Donald M. Allen, *The New American Poetry* (New York: Grove Press, 1960); reprinted in CP, p. 140.
12. Mandel, *Measures: Robert Creeley's Poetry*.
13. Robert Creeley, *St. Martin's* (Black Sparrow Press, 1971). Reprinted in CP, p. 474.
14. Mandel, *Measures: Robert Creeley's Poetry*. See also, Robert Creeley, CP, pp. 111 and 125.
15. Robert Creeley, *The Island* (London: John Calder, 1964), following quotations pp. 23 and 32.
16. Creeley, *Contexts of Poetry*, p. 113.
17. Robert Creeley, *The Charm* (London: Calder and Boyars, 1971); reprinted in CP, pp. 7–8.
18. Creeley, *Contexts of Poetry*, p. 46.
19. Allen Ginsberg, *Howl*, in Allen, *The New American Poetry*, p. 182.
20. Creeley, *Contexts of Poetry*, p. 37.

21. Stephen Berg and Robert Mezey (eds), *Naked Poetry*, quoted in Charles Molesworth, *The Fierce Embrace* (Columbia: University of Missouri Press, 1979) p. 104.
22. Robert Creeley, CP, p. 125.
23. Charles Olson, *Human Universe and Other Essays* (New York: Grove Press, 1967) p. 52.
24. *Charles Olson Reading at Berkeley*, transcribed by Zoe Brown (Coyote, 1966) p. 3.
25. I have quoted from Creeley, *Contexts of Poetry*, which includes interviews with David Ossman, Charles Tomlinson, Allen Ginsberg, Linda Wagner and others. It is also valuable to refer to the collected notes and essays of Robert Creeley, titled *A Quick Graph* (Four Seasons Foundation, 1970). I have also been helped for the purposes of this chapter by seeing the manuscript of an interview with Creeley by Brian Docherty, co-editor of this volume.
26. Robert Creeley, CP, p. 379.
27. Creeley, *Contexts of Poetry*, p. 72.
28. Ibid., p. 77.
29. Ibid., p. 78.
30. The term comes from Donald Wesling, *The Chances of Rhyme: Device and Modernity* (Berkeley: University of California Press, 1980). Donald Wesling, who nurtured my interest in American poetry at the University of Essex, in turn, acknowledges that the term originates from Northrop Frye in his book *T. S. Eliot*.
31. Robert Creeley, CP, p. 286.
32. Ibid., p. 176.
33. Creeley, *Contexts of Poetry*, p. 95.
34. Ibid., p. 96.
35. Ibid., p. 93–4.
36. Robert Creeley, CP, p. 441.
37. Quoted in Molesworth, *The Fierce Embrace*, p. 112.
38. Robert Creeley, CP, p. 401.
39. Robert Creeley, in a composite interview by Linda Wagner and Lewis MacAdams, 'The Art of Poetry', *The Paris Review*, Fall 1968 p. 157.
40. Robert Creeley, CP, p. 5.
41. Ibid., p. 480.
42. Creeley, 'The Art of Poetry', pp. 159–60.
43. The history and the embattled philosophy of the college are recorded in Martin Duberman, *Black Mountain* (London: Wildwood House, 1974). Reception of Duberman's book has not been uncritical – see Charles Tomlinson, 'Black Mountain Revisited', in *The New Review*, June 1974. There are many reflections by Creeley, see in particular, *Contexts of Poetry*, p. 24.
44. Creeley, *Contexts of Poetry*, p. 3.
45. Robert Creeley wrote an unsurprisingly personal and engaged introduction to his selection from Whitman (Harmondsworth, Middx: Penguin, 1973). This opens with a telling sentence – 'One of the most lovely insistences in Whitman's poems seems to me his instruction that one speak for oneself.'

46. Ed Dorn, from the interview in David Ossman, *The Sullen Art* (New York: Corinth Books, 1963) p. 83.
47. Creeley, *Contexts of Poetry*, p. 111.
48. Ibid., p. 189.
49. Ibid., p. 119.
50. Gina, my wife, and I were working together training College lecturers from Ipoh and Penang where we read *Hello*.
51. 'Hotel Merlin', in *Hello: A Journal* (London: Marion Boyars, 1978) p. 48.
52. 'Seventeenth Floor: Echoes of Singapore', ibid., p. 49.
53. 'Men', ibid., pp. 28–9.
54. Creeley, *Contexts of Poetry*, pp. 117–18.
55. Ibid., p. 20.
56. Ibid., p. 121.
57. Robert Creeley, *Whitman* (Harmondsworth: Penguin, 1973) p. 7.
58. Creeley, *Contexts of Poetry*, p. 28.
59. Creeley, *Whitman*, p. 10.

16

Denise Levertov

NANCY K. GISH

The *American Poetry Review* of November/December 1990 includes seven new poems by Denise Levertov. Readers of her work will recognise familiar themes and images – reverent, astonished pleasure in the gift of moonlight unexpectedly filling her kitchen; horror at human violation of Earth, and of other humans; the possibilities and complexities of dreams and human relations. Like all her work, these poems sustain a balance between moments of joy and wonder at the presence of spirit, and despairing recognitions of suffering and pain. Immediately above her new work is an announcement that she is one of three winners of the Jerome J. Shestack Poetry Prizes for 1989 for 'For Ikon: The Harrowing of Hell and other poems'. *APR*'s juxtaposition of recognition for her recent religious poems with new work sustaining other concerns helps define Levertov's work in the 1980s. She has moved steadily towards a poetry of Christian belief while sustaining the personal, social and political concerns of her previous collections. Her most recent four books – *Candles in Babylon, Oblique Prayers, Breathing the Water*, and *A Door in the Hive* move from individual experiences of immanence to a form of Catholic belief. This development, on the one hand, deepens and contextualises her private sense of spirituality in a historic and communal frame work. On the other hand, it seems initially at odds with her tendency to question orthodoxies and, especially, her consistent choice to speak of and for women. While her increasingly traditional Christianity is consistent with her acknowledged tendency to 'mystical' or 'spiritual' poetry, and can be read as an extension – through the focus on liberation theology – of her political activism, it is less easily reconcilable with the feminism of her earlier work. For despite her own scepticism about some feminist positions and her questioning of the term for her own writing, she has written not simply as the voice of a woman but as a voice and perspective for women. My concern here is to consider whether and how that feminist act can be sustained in specifically Christian poetry. How, in other words, can she speak out of her own experience as a woman within the context of the church?

Levertov has described herself as having 'always written rather directly about my life and my concerns at any particular time'.[1] This attention to her own immediate experience has generally been addressed as the source of her authenticity, her ability to, in Harry Marten's words, '[uncover and make known] the relationship of self to the world',[2] or, in Alicia Ostriker's, to keep her mysticism 'grounded in this world by her love of "the authentic" of daily experience'.[3] It also keeps her grounded in the experience of women – of birth, of mothering, of wearing red velvet dresses or hanging the washing out to dry. For Levertov, however, '"the authentic" of daily experience' may well *be* the experience of presence or spirit; she avoids privileging physical experience over 'mysticism' just as she eschews the opposite.

In like manner, her assumption of a woman's voice and perspective has never precluded her use of male mentors as sources of techniques as well as formulators of experience. She has acknowledged and praised them in prose and poems, notably William Carlos Williams in the poem, 'Williams: An Essay'. *A Door in the Hive* includes 'To R.D., March 4th 1988', a eulogy for Robert Duncan written a month after his death, which fuses the themes of friendship, mentoring, and shared religious experience. Levertov, as speaker in the poem, acknowledges that Duncan was her mentor but that she outgrew such a need. After years of separation his death lacked 'resonance' for her. But in a dream he reappears beside her in the Lady Chapel, holding her hand and sharing the community of those who respond to ancient harmony manifested in the 'daily experience' of being 'brother' and 'sister'. No longer needing him as a model or guide, she experiences him as sibling in their shared response to an ancient history and human community. At the same time that Levertov returns again and again to specifically personal and female experience, she also seeks to imagine male experiences and to inscribe her own sense of 'human' experience, that is the brother/sister sharing of what she takes to be non-gendered relationship. In *A Door in the Hive*, for example, 'Inheritance' chronicles the act and later memory of a woman's gentle washing of another, remembered as one woman remembers another. 'St Thomas Didymus' is told in the voice of St Thomas, a voice assumed both as an imaginative leap and as a voice for shared doubt. And in 'Envy', she speaks of bare trees from a position assumed as non-gendered. 'I, human, have not as yet devised / how to obtain / such privilege.' This deliberate dispersal of voices, including but moving outside her own and that of other women, is not new. Her feminist poems have always appeared among others that were not focused specifically on women's experience, definitions, or point of view. Their relationship to her other work, however, may have appeared less complex when they were set among political poems and poems celebrating the physical world than when they are in a traditional religious framework.

A poetry speaking with consistent clarity and courage for experience as a woman, yet moving into a traditional male centred religion for its primary spiritual source, presents a potential paradox, a conflict not restricted to poets but defined by many feminist theologians. How does a woman find a place for her own experience in a patriarchal church? In the case of a poet, how can poetry 'authentically' speaking out of woman's experience also speak from the experience of Christian belief? Any answer, of course, depends on one's definition of woman's experience and one's assumptions about the meaning of traditional Christianity. In Levertov's recent work these potentially conflicting positions are arguably not only reconcilable but inseparable. The specific form of Levertov's feminism makes possible her extension of women's perspective into Christian poetry.

Despite her denial of any particular feminist ideology, Levertov has long employed feminist theories, images, and attitudes. Nor has she altered or abandoned them in her religious poems. Like women who struggle with the church as feminist theologians, she both embraces and distances the church through her careful analysis. For example, 'El Salvador: Requiem and Invocation' chronicles the changed role of nuns and priests in El Salvador, from support of oppressors to resistance on the side of the peasants. Here and in other poems, Levertov brings her political vision and activism into the fold of belief through new definitions of the church's purpose in the world. In a similar way her feminism has altered as it becomes a way to live as a woman within the history and community of the church. In order to define the relations of feminism and religion in her recent poetry, then, it is necessary to examine in what sense her specific use of woman's voice and experience is feminist and how she incorporates that into a revisionist rewriting of Christian material.

While Levertov's directly personal poems have been acknowledged as important contributions to an emerging tradition of women's poetry, their feminism has been read in diverse ways. Writing in 1981, Roberta Burke included Levertov in a chapter on the Black Mountain poets, focusing primarily on her use and revision of Olson's 'projective verse' theory and on her political poems. Almost as an aside she notes: 'Feminist issues also entered Levertov's poetry in the late sixties, and gave it a new candor and strength.' She adds as one example the 'struggle to contain diverse roles within one woman in poems such as "In Mind,"' including it as an example of Levertov's overall tendency to harmonise opposites.[4] Alicia Ostriker also comments on the divided female self in many such early poems as 'In Mind' and 'Sunday Afternoon'. Yet, though she admires much of Levertov's work, she adds, condescendingly, that 'young women of unrevolutionary temperament often warm to Levertov's work because it expresses both clearly and gently a dilemma they find in themselves'.[5] Later, however, she also describes Levertov as engaging in revisionist mythmaking – specifically re-imagining divinity, in poems like 'The Goddess' and 'Song for Ishtar', as reuniting flesh and spirit.[6] Susan Gubar praises Levertov's attitude towards creativity, claiming she 'seeks to consecrate her own repeated efforts to contribute to the blank pages of our [women's] future creativity'.[7]

These brief and sometimes reserved gestures towards Levertov's extensive and intensive expression of women's experience suggest that she is less easily analysed in feminist theoretical terms than poets like Sylvia Plath or Adrienne Rich who either spoke their rage or claimed, in overt terms, a female world. The problem is sharply delineated by Suzanne Juhasz, who devotes a chapter to Levertov in her book arguing for the emergence of a new tradition of American women's poetry, and places Levertov at a transition between 'the dominant masculine and the emerging feminine traditions'.[8]

Because she is arguing for a new tradition as a specifically female form of writing, Juhasz discounts work grounded in forms traditionally used by male poets. Thus she finds Levertov's techniques inherently suspect:

the strong influence of the masculine tradition often causes her to step away from the experience that her poem has revealed to abstract and generalize upon its greater significance.[9]

This abstracting and generalising Juhasz claims to be 'alien', even 'oppressive', to current feminist poetry; she validates almost exclusively a poetry of direct self-representation. Her broader point is to distinguish between women who merely write from their own experience and those who use it to 'raise consciousness about women'. Levertov, she points out, sees herself as a poet, not as a woman poet, and for Juhasz this limits the feminist element in her work.

Yet for Levertov, 'consciousness about women' may well include their relations with or mentoring by men. 'We think back through our mothers if we are women,' according to Virginia Woolf. Levertov attests to thinking back through her mother and father: her mother taught her to 'taste and see', her father to meditate on what her experience means. She thus affirms the dichotomy Juhasz posits; intense direct attention to her own immediate world, the immediacy Juhasz seems to consider authentic female experience, Levertov claims to have learned from her mother:

> it was she who, as I have written,
> taught me ...
> to watch the sublime metamorphoses ...
> over the walled back gardens of our street.[10]

But Levertov, having looked and named, meditates, sees 'sublime metamorphoses' as revelations of spirit. Juhasz, then, aptly describes her 'poetic format': 'the poem traces an experience and comes to an understanding of its significance'. Yet she notes that 'experiences that are specifically feminine do not form the majority of Levertov's work',[11] and she concludes that because Levertov assumes a 'masculine intellectual tradition of analysis and of the consequence and necessary condition of analysis – distance', her experience in the world as a woman is at odds with her poetic form.[12] Juhasz seems perpetually disappointed at Levertov's insistence on speaking in spiritual generalities. But to privilege the representation of specifically female experience as the exclusive form of a feminist poetic tradition is to reinstate limits as constricting as older conceptions of women's writing.

The issue is not whether Levertov's work fits a specific definition of how to write as a woman but whether her writing as a woman opens poetry to the range and complexity of women's voices. Her use of male as well as female mentors and her resistance to focusing

exclusively on awareness of being female do not displace what
more seriously marks her work: the choice to bear witness –
whether personal, political, or spiritual – from the position of a
woman, speaking on whatever theme she wishes and out of her
own sense of an authentic voice. Her poems are feminist not by
virtue of excluding all except female experience but by that of including all experience as women's. This is not to say that women
and men experience the world in the same way; rather, the sources
of experience in self, world, and spirit are equally hers to approach
in her way. If her mother taught her to 'taste and see', her father
taught her to meditate. But it is she who meditates; she can use his
knowledge as well as her mother's. In her recent religious poems,
however, the dichotomy of male sources and female experience
takes on a new and more complex form. It is not simply an opposition of her own experience and that of individual men but a historic
exclusion from the church of the experience on which she consistently draws. Moreover, in its defined framework of ideas, the
church would seem to limit the possibility of re-imagining
women's spiritual experience. Although Levertov has spoken directly on the problems of a poetry deriving from or using as its
source Christian faith, the question for her is political. Her remarks,
however, help frame the issue:

> I have been engaging, then, during the last few years, in my own
> version of the Pascalian wager, and finding that an avowal of
> Christian faith is not incompatible with my aesthetic nor with my
> political stance, since as an artist I was already in the service of
> the transcendent, and since Christian ethics (however betrayed
> in past and present history) uphold the same values I seek in a
> politics of racial and economic justice and nonviolence. How
> does the wager interact with my creative work? There the ques-
> tion remains: does a position of even moderate orthodoxy
> threaten an artist's exploratory aesthetic freedom and 'Negative
> Capability'? So far, from inside the creative process, I have not
> found that it does.[13]

The service of the transcendent has historically, however, been a
male preserve. In *Beyond Anger: On Being a Feminist in the Church*,
Carolyn Osiek defines both the problem and a series of responses.
The central issue, she claims, is whether the tradition is redeemable:
'Are the tradition, the institution which conveys it, and the people

who embody that tradition and perpetuate that institution capable of conversion from the sin of sexism?'[14] She outlines six ways women attempt to cope with a patriarchal church – rejectionist, marginalist, loyalist, symbolist, revisionist, and liberationist. While Levertov does not ask the question of redeemability in this way, both her form of connection with the church and her poetic use of it employ elements of the last three. Like Osiek's 'symbolist', she emphasises 'the symbolic function of the feminine in the tradition and in the religious imagination', and she uses feminine imagery.[15] Like the 'revisionist', she retells and reinterprets historical sources, 'learning to "read between the lines"' and to bring out 'the nearly hidden minor themes of women's experience'.[16] And like the 'liberationist', she finds in Christianity a foundation for establishing a just society and resisting oppression. She acknowledges, in fact, that her interest in Christianity was largely influenced by her admiration for 'such people as Archbishop Romero, Dorothy Day, Thomas Merton ... whose commitment to peace and justice is absolutely outstanding'.[17]

In the development of a Christian poetry consistent with both her earlier vision and her witness to woman's experience, Levertov uses all three of these tactics, most notably and powerfully a revisionist re-inscription of women in the church. If her symbolism and liberationism set up a framework of faith accessible to and inclusive of women, her revisionism redefines the position of women in relation to both the historic church and divinity.

Feminine imagery as a way to evoke spirit is not new to her work. But in recent poems, earlier material is carried over and reframed in traditional terms.

Images of seeds, flowering, and fruit, identified with a female divinity in 'The Goddess', reappear in poems like 'The God of Flowers' attributed to 'the unknown God of the gods', and in meditations on the parable of the mustard seed. Eggs, webs, weaving appear over and over as ways of knowing divinity. But in a broader sense, what her poems continually move away from and back toward is earth, flesh, living itself, in trees, plants, flowers, fruits, a world whose beauty is recurrently invoked as illuminated within and often specifically as female. In the sequence 'Of God and of the Gods', in *Oblique Prayers*, rivers are identified with 'god or goddess'; a tall poplar weaves a 'close-wrapped cloak, sewn / with tear drops of green' and is in its time of advent; a young woman in a class 'has conjured' a brown tree that is 'haloed'; the 'god of flowers' is a 'hen on her eggs'; 'God' is not an 'old man / always upstairs' but a weaver at the loom and works outside in the wilderness; 'all / utters itself, blessedness / soaks the ground and its wintering seeds'; and 'the spirit that walked upon the face of the water' passes like a swathe of silk. My point is not that these images define divinity as female but that it is closely linked with sewing, weaving, birthing.

Similarly, Levertov's commitment to liberation theology is not exclusively feminist nor is it specifically directed towards using the church to extend liberation to women. Yet it provides a way of defining the church more compatible with a feminist call for women's value and equality. Liberation feminism, in Osiek's terms, is an extension of liberation theology:

> Developed from the broader base of liberation theology as it has been employed in favor of the socially and economically oppressed, the liberation perspective openly advocates a stand on behalf of the disenfranchised and disinherited, which its adherents believe to be that of Jesus. It teaches that the reign of God proclaimed in the Gospels has a concrete historical dimension as well as a transcendent heavenly one. That historical dimension can be brought about only by the establishment of a just society which includes, besides the abolition of racism and classism, the end of sexism as well.[18]

Levertov's own move into Christian belief was deeply influenced by liberation theology, and her political poems increasingly present change and resistance in Christian terms, most particularly in 'El Salvador: Requiem and Invocation'. On the position of women she still equivocates theoretically, less certain of women priests or gender-neutral language than of commitment to the poor. Yet her poems tend simply to assume women's full equality, value, and participation in the church. Her 'Requiem' is for the nuns as for Romero; her longing for change is always for women and men; her acknowledgement of Jesus as male is defined historically, not theologically. And the Jesus of her poems is one who shares suffering, knows humanness by experience, participates in the world of seeds, webs, birth. Between the abstract 'Word' and the historic living flesh, Levertov consistently images the latter; 'He' is born to woman, known by woman, revealed most fully in 'his' meaning, within history, to Julian of Norwich. That revelation, for Levertov,

continues to occur for women and men equally. She concludes 'El
Salvador' with a series of voices – the chorus, Romero and the Four
Sisters together, and 'All'. The chorus defines their relation

> Those who were martyred –
> Romero,
>> Maura,
>>> Ita,
>>>> Dorothy,
>>>>> Jean –
> and those whose names
> are lost along with their bodies —
> all the Marias and Juans, the Josés and Pedros,
> Elenas and Glorias – they tell us,
>> We in El Salvador ...[19]

In the choices she makes Levertov turns persistently to a form of
Christianity accessible to and compatible with values historically
held by women – compassion, equality, sharing, love of the physical human world; in her depiction even of a male god or priest she
incorporates these values and links them with women. Her imagination is drawn to the living human Jesus who knows pain like that
of 'women and men who've held out / days and weeks on the rack
–', who showed 'his' meaning to Julian, who shares with friends
'food – fish and a honeycomb'.

If, in her female symbolism and her liberationism, Levertov
creates a context of meaning within which Christianity can be understood as by and for women, in her revisionist poems she constructs a specifically feminist religious experience. Osiek defines
'revisionism' as retelling:

> The revisionist holds that the patriarchal cast of the Judeo-
> Christian tradition is due more to historical and cultural causes
> than theological ones. . . . What is needed then is a retelling, a
> reinterpretation of the historical data in such a way that our story
> can be freed from a certain kind of unhelpful cultural baggage
> which is non-essential to its real message.
> The task takes the form of going back into the historical
> sources – Bible, Talmud, early Christian literature, art and arche-
> ology – and learning to 'read between the lines,' to interpret one
> against the background of the other.[20]

While I do not assume knowledge of Levertov's broader theological positions, many of her comments are consistent with this stance. She claims to have moved into the Catholic Church with all her objections, acknowledges the pain gender-biased language has caused many women, and emphasises historical and cultural reasons for the Incarnation being male. But more important, her poems frequently rewrite Biblical and religious figures and stories from a feminist perspective: as witness to women's religious experience, voice, vision – not as subordinate but as central. This witness is evident in the stories and themes she emphasises – Jesus's birth, his humanness, his shared suffering and pleasure, his status as guest or brother, and the claim of women to a personal spiritual quest not possessed and dispersed by the stories of men. Moreover, she redefines traditional notions about religious women by 'retelling' and 'reinterpreting' their stories. Each of the latest four collections includes poems assuming the centrality of women's spirituality to Christianity and the church.

While fascination with the birth and humanness of Jesus is not, in itself, necessarily a feminist position, Levertov's persistent placement of those themes at the centre of her spiritual poems displaces the patriarchal figure of God and the abstract logos as defining images of religious experience. This human, sorrowing, sharing, Jesus seems more amenable to women's historic concerns. As such he is, in many ways, a feminine figure – nurturing, loving, resisting power structures. 'On the Mystery of the Incarnation' translates the logos into 'our kind', and inclusive term (DH 50). If the 'Word' and 'God' remain in one sense abstract and male in this poem, other nouns, and more significantly pronouns, contextualise this masculinity. Humanity is 'we', 'our kind', 'our selves', and, collectively 'this creature'. Gender, that is, is absent from the language for humans who are polarised not as male/female but as collectively tainted in contrast to an 'innocent form'. 'This creature', not 'man' assumes its likeness to God and is entrusted with 'the Word'. 'The Word', moreover, is 'guest', 'brother', an equal, a sibling, a human. Both the displacement of 'man/he' and the reiterated plurals ('we', 'our', 'our own') evoke a shared access to the divine, *historically* male sibling. If Levertov accepts and uses the masculine for the Christian 'God' or Jesus, she none the less depicts the reception of spirit as a shared human act. Gender-neutral language in this context shifts the human–divine relation from its traditional male line. Many poems repeat this pattern. 'A Calvary Path' constructs a pilgrimage of 'souls', 'our lives'. In 'Two Threnodies and a Psalm', 'spirit' is repeatedly addressed by 'us'. In 'The Past (II)' the speaker places her hand in the print of a mason who worked on a nave centuries before and says ' ... that human trace / will burn my palm'. In 'Envy' she again assumes a shared human fate in contrast to bare trees: 'I, human, have not as yet devised / how to obtain / such privilege.' Whatever Levertov's reasons for abandoning gender-biased language, the effect, in her religious poems, is emphatically to assert women's equal relation with divinity.

The assumption of an inclusive humanity, female and male, equally engaged in a spiritual quest, becomes more direct in poems retelling Christian stories. Her representation of Jesus, for example, becomes more traditional but retains her emphasis on sisterhood/brotherhood, the shared kinship of women and men with Jesus. Moreover, this inclusive humanity may be imaged as female; individual women may stand for 'we'. *Candles in Babylon*, for example, while it includes primarily poems on politics and women's personal experience, shows a tentative movement towards Christian faith in the final long poem, 'Mass for the Day of St Thomas Didymus'. The 'God' of this poem is known only in and through the world, and a fundamental act of creation – naming – is shifted to the world itself. Things utter themselves, and in doing so write 'the name of the spirit'. More radically, 'God' as lamb needs human strength, is not only innocent but ignorant and helpless (CB 114–15).

The 'human' is imaged as female, giver of milk to the new-born lamb, who wished 'to nuzzle at milky dugs'. Similarly, 'The Cry' in *Oblique Prayers* joins longing for milk with need for eternity, fusing human, animal, and vegetable – the world we are destroying – in another possible Incarnation, a 'wholly / holy / holy / unmerited call' as 'newborn cry' for 'eternity: / being: / milk'. Levertov's representation of the Incarnation includes female engagement with divinity not only as Mary's giving birth but as nurturing within the world by a feminine act of humanity. In her depictions of Mary and Julian of Norwich, as well as of Jesus, Levertov creates a more specific context for women in Christian tradition by placing them at the centre of key historic moments and by attributing new meaning to their roles.

Breathing the Water includes a sequence of six poems on Julian of Norwich and a separate poem on Julian's perception of Jesus. Linked by the notion of Julian's understanding, these poems celebrate her 'lucid spirit' that 'leapt / to the difference' and realised what others have not seen or cannot see. Julian understands the meaning of the coexistence of violence and love, which appears as a fundamental problem in all of Levertov's work. By attributing the meaning of this to an understanding of Incarnation and the human insight into that meaning to Julian, Levertov places women's intellectual and emotional experience at the centre of the Christian tradition. To Julian she grants the understanding of suffering, love, the universe ('All that Is'), good and evil, and the interrelationship of the ordinary and the divine: dandelions, cream, and butter, with Jesus, Mary, and the cross. In Julian's *Revelations of Divine Love* Levertov finds a definition of Jesus that can encompass her persistent dichotomy. Julian's becomes a primary and defining text, recontextualising images and themes from earlier poems into a specific tradition: images of milk, eggs, nesting, mothering, the web, and of women and men in shared suffering and laughter are rewoven into Julian's understanding of the Incarnation.

In 'On a Theme from Julian's Chapter XX', for example, Christ's suffering on the cross is questioned; why is it exceptional when so many suffer torture? For Julian – and thus as a way of knowing for Levertov – this suffering is distinguished from all other by Christ's imaginative realisation of all suffering at once, ' ... when He took to Himself / the sum total of anguish and drank / even the lees of that cup'. Again the focus is on Jesus's kinship with women and men, separated only by seeing and knowing all of the humanness of which he is a part. And yet the knowledge of that knowledge is Julian's. In like manner, Julian grasps the mystery of the universe as a *'little thing, the size of a hazelnut'* in God's hand; she chooses, in her desire for these wounds, not neurosis but the enactment of metaphor so that her body will make known 'God's agony'; she must be understood as an ordinary child in a dairy, surrounded by rich cream and carrying cakes of butter. Her hand is a 'five-fingered human nest' into which God places 'the macrocosmic egg' as 'her mother might have given / into her two cupped palms / a new laid egg, warm from the hen'; her laughter at evil is the sudden source of joy for both nuns and priest, but it is her mind that moves on to full insight; she embodies the union of insight and flesh.

In the final poem of the series, Levertov shifts to Julian's own choices and their power as a model. The meditative method that Juhasz rejects as masculine, Levertov attributes to Julian as human and formative (BW 81). If this parallels Levertov's own method, it is defined here not as a move away from immediacy but as a constant return to sources of vision, deepening the immediate experiences each time. The assumption that there is depth behind experience, that meaning is layered and unfolds itself to reiterated examination, is open to challenge; but that it is a gendered assumption is equally questionable. Many women need and are satisfied by the historical community of traditional religion. In her Julian poems Levertov represents that historical community as defined, experienced, and understood by a woman who then stands within the tradition as a source for others. Julian herself engaged in rewriting, retelling, and reinterpreting Incarnation. Levertov finds in her a source to reshape her own story of suffering and possible understanding (BW 81–2).

She lived in dark times.

… I turn to [her]

In establishing this link between Julian and herself, human pain then and now, she places female experience at the centre of both tradition and definition rather than separating it out as marginal, yet she grants it a unique status. Both Julian and Mary are represented as experiencing, from the human side, the union of physical experience and awareness of the divine and eternal most fully figured in Jesus. Julian, that is, recognises the meaning of Christ's human/divine nature and chooses, herself, to 'enact metaphor' in order to know it directly. If, for cultural and historic reasons, 'God' enters history as a male, in another 'moment in our history' [he] placed the 'macrocosmic egg' in a woman's hand, revealed [his] meaning to her as witness. Mary, likewise, experienced infinity in her own body, opened herself to an 'astounding ministry'.

Perhaps the most explicit revisionist poem of Levertov's recent religious work, 'Annunciation' redefines the meaning of Mary's choice as courage rather than obedience, making Mary's unparalleled experience distinct in its power rather than its yielding. The language used to depict her, moreover, echoes that used for both Julian and Jesus: all three are characterised by courage, consent, vision, and the almost incomprehensible fusion of finite body and divine spirit.

The Virgin Mary is problematic for feminists; on the one hand she provides the single Christian image of a woman in an elevated quasi-divine role. On the other hand, her significance has been seen solely in her role as mother and as traditionally obedient, nurturing, and sorrowing female figure. In *The Second Sex*, Simone de Beauvoir claims that Mary is exalted solely as 'Woman Mother'. 'But she will be glorified only in accepting the subordinate role assigned to her. "I am the servant of the Lord." For the first time in human history the mother kneels before her son; she freely accepts her inferiority.'[21] De Beauvoir contrasts Mary with Ishtar, Astarte, and Cybele, who 'were powerful'. She quotes Medieval litanies to demonstrate the status of Mary as the epitome of the 'feminine', the ultimate figure of subservience, even masochism, who 'hears the words of the angel on her knees and replies: "Behold the *handmaid* of the Lord."'[22]

In *Gyn/Ecology* Mary Daly gives a more radical view of Mary but also as the displaced (raped) Goddess. The Mary of Christianity she defines as utterly abject: 'Dutifully dull and derivative, drained of divinity, she merits the reward of perpetual paralysis in patriarchal paradise.'[23] Carolyn Osiek, too, sees Mary as an ambiguous and disturbing figure:

> Even as an honoured creature, however, the Mary of tradition contains mixed signals, as feminists are quite aware. On one hand she is the most exalted of God's creation, motivating the exaltation of womanhood along with her to the 'pedestal.' On the other hand, she is thus held up as an impossible ideal to which no woman could attain, in comparison with whom all women are invited to feel inadequate. Moreover, in spite of the excellent theological attempts to distinguish the 'historical Mary' from the 'Mary of faith' and to portray her as glorified because of her superior faith and discipleship, the impression remains that her chief qualification for exaltation is maternity. Even for Mary, biology is destiny.[24]

Feminist unease about Mary, then, derives from the celebration and privileging of woman as 'feminine' in the most extreme and servile definitions: subjection, obedience, powerlessness, and maternity. Yet, in *Sexism and God-Talk*, Rosemary Reuther both acknowledges that these are the traditional definitions of Mary and suggests a basis for a revisionist representation. In the Mariological tradition, Reuther claims, Mary is the 'theological personification of Psyche and Mother Church as Virginal Bride and Mother of Christians'.

She becomes, in Luke, 'the "first believer" whose assent to God's will makes her the means of God's messianic redemption'. In the second century, moreover, she becomes the 'New Eve', 'the obedient female who reverses the disobedience of the First Eve and thus makes possible the advent of the New Adam, Christ'.[25] This definition of Mary assumes the female as the sexual source of sin and death and constructs Mary as archetype of pure nature before the fall, redeemed only through 'obedience' as a reversal of sin.

Yet Reuther asks whether an 'alternative Mariology' has a biblical basis for reinterpretation. She locates it in Luke's emphasis on Mary's act of free choice: 'Lucan Mariology suggests a real co-creatorship between God and humanity, or, in this case, woman. ...Only through that free human responsiveness to God is God enabled to become the transformer of history.'[26] The notion that God needs human cooperation and that their shared act is a co-creatorship provides a theoretical reframing for Levertov's representation of Mary and of women in the church. In 'Annunciation' God waits on Mary's will. Her act is characterised by freedom, understanding, courage, and a deliberate openness to the ultimate extreme of human experience – qualities attributed also to Julian and to Jesus as they participate in the 'astounding' interweaving of divine and human.

The poem is divided into sections, each of which meditates on a facet of the meaning of Mary's act. The first and third sections focus on God's suspension of creation while awaiting her response; the second and fourth contrast her consent with the closure of those who fear or lack knowledge or merely submit. That this is what Adrienne Rich calls a re-vision, a return to see again and anew, is ironically explicit in the epigraph: 'Hail, space for the uncontained God.' Woman as space, as womb or vessel only for the male to inhabit, is a concept consistently rejected by feminist theorists. Yet what becomes central to the poem is not so much 'space' as 'uncontained'; that is, God's lack without human cooperation. Mary's acceptance is not a passive condition but a form of agency, a willed co-action with God, embodied in the choice of verbs: 'to accept or to refuse', 'undertake', 'enact', 'took to heart', 'perceiving instantly', 'to bear', 'to carry', 'to contain', 'to bring forth', 'push out into air'. None of the verbs suggests a new event. Rather, they cumulatively dwell on conceiving and nourishing and giving birth as an action, the chosen 'labour' of childbearing known by women. My point is that the poem is expressly 'woman centred' in its reconceptualisation of Mary's role; it displaces the assumptions of obedience, subservience, and biological destiny traditionally held as key to Mary's role.

Levertov's resistance to Mary as passive servant frames the entire poem. Opening with the images traditionally present in scenes of the Annunciation, she explicitly challenges its assumed meaning. 'We know the scene,' she writes, listing the lectern, book, tall lily, and angel with great wings always present. But she immediately shifts the accustomed power relation, making the angel the object of the sentence, the 'ambassador ... / whom she acknowledges, a guest'. It is the angel who supplicates and who, like Jesus, is placed in a position of human relation as guest. As brother, guest, kin, Jesus repeatedly appears as one who is honoured as well as honours. The angel is thus immediately represented as receptive. Mary's choice is then explicitly rewritten as action and strength (DH 86), and is itself a human act, one God needs in order to act in the world with her.

The second section meditates on the annunciations in many lives and on failure to consent through fear or weakness, or acceptance without knowledge or willingness. Mary is rare in her courage, not only because of the extremity of her experience but also because of the intensity and power of her human qualities. Unlike the frightened or frail, she remained 'open'. This contrasting openness leads to the third section's focus on her likeness and unlikeness to other humans.

Most importantly, she was a child 'like any other', a claim made also and emphatically of Julian. In both cases it is not an essential separation or divine offering that marks them out in itself. They 'know and act' because of choice and bravery. If her destiny was 'more momentous than any in all of time', that makes her consent only more rare and courageous, when others quail at far less. But what she is called to do is none the less unique in human experience, demanding a unique capacity to endure the extreme and unknown: 'to bear in her womb ... God' (DH 87). One is reminded of Sojourner Truth's response to the claim that women could not have 'as much rights as men' because Christ wasn't a woman: 'Whar did your Christ come from? From God and a woman! Man had nothin' to do wid Him.'[27] Levertov's Mary is thus unique in her act of co-creation as well as her capacity for a brave and extreme choice.

Like the first section, the third closes on the fact of choice as a human (hence woman's) prerogative; choice on which God waits not only for the human will to faith but for God's own access to history and humanity; the need is mutual; spirit waits on body. Mary's act of consent is framed by passages on her freedom and God's dependence. Set apart by willed choice, not obedient accept- ance, she becomes emblematic of a place for women in traditional Christianity both enacted *as woman* and possible *as human*; ma- ternity is female; choice is ungendered. If this particular choice was and could have been only a woman's, it is not the nature of the choice but the character of consent that defines Mary's humanity and spirituality.

The final section carries Levertov's re-vision one step further: it returns to the opening scene of room, lily, angel, but they are now filled with a light originating in Mary's act. Even the angel wings are filled with the illumination of her spirit (DH 88). In rewriting Mary's most fundamental act, Levertov emblematically shifts the ground of women's relation to divinity in a specifically feminist way. Though her particular claim about Mary's free act is grounded in both the Bible and tradition, her selection, emphasis, and diction reconstruct its meaning from the position of women and for a changed perception of their role.

Traditionally – and especially in the church – males speak for all – taking, as it were, all parts on the stage. For a woman to do the same is an act as radical as to claim to speak for herself. The Christianity of Levertov's work in the 1980s includes a developed form of feminism as witness. The early personal voice of and for woman develops, in the 1980s, into a voice of and for woman's ex- perience within Christianity, placing the co-creatorship of Mary, the 'lucid insight' of Julian and the spiritual quest and receptivity of all women at the active centre of the church.

NOTES

1. Denise Levertov, interview with E. G. Burrows, *Michigan Quarterly*, quoted in Linda Wagner (ed.), *Denise Levertov: In Her Own Province* (New York: New Directions, 1979) p. 102.
2. Harry Marten, *Understanding Denise Levertov* (Columbia, SC: University of South Carolina Press, 1988) p. 5.
3. Alicia Ostriker, *Stealing the Language* (Boston, Mass.: Beacon, 1986) p. 77.
4. Roberta Burke, *Bounds Out of Bounds* (New York: Oxford University Press, 1981) p. 39.

5. Ostriker, *Stealing the Language*, pp. 79–80.
6. Ibid., p. 220.
7. Susan Gubar, '"The Blank Page" and the Issues of Female Creativity', Elaine Showalter (ed.), *The New Feminist Criticism* (New York: Pantheon, 1985) p. 309.
8. Suzanne Juhasz, *Naked and Fiery Forms: Modern American Poetry by Women, A New Tradition* (New York: Octagon Books, 1978) p. 58.
9. Ibid., p. 62.
10. Denise Levertov, 'Beatrice Levertoff', *Light Up the Cave* (New York: New Directions, 1981) p. 243.
11. Juhasz, *Naked and Fiery Forms*, p. 68.
12. Ibid., p. 82.
13. Denise Levertov, 'A Poet's View', *Religion and Intellectual Life*, 1 (1984), 50.
14. Carolyn Osiek, *Beyond Anger: On Being a Feminist in the Church* (New York: Paulist Press, 1986) p. 27.
15. Ibid., p. 33, 34.
16. Ibid., p. 37, 38.
17. Denise Levertov, personal interview, September 1990.
18. Osiek, *Beyond Anger*, p. 40.
19. Denise Levertov, *A Door in the Hive* (New York: New Directions, 1989) pp. 37–8. All further references to Levertov's poems are from the following: *Candles in Babylon* (New York: New Directions, 1982), *Oblique Prayers* (New York: New Directions, 1984), *Breathing the Water* (New York: New Directions, 1987), and *A Door in the Hive*, and will be listed in the text as CB, OP, BW, and DH, respectively.
20. Osiek, *Beyond Anger*, p. 37.
21. Simone de Beauvoir, *The Second Sex*, trans. and ed. H. M. Parshley (New York: Bantam, 1953) p. 160.
22. Ibid., pp. 271.
23. Mary Daly, *Gyn/Ecology* (Boston, Mass.: Beacon, 1978) p. 88.
24. Osiek, *Beyond Anger*, pp. 19–20.
25. Rosemary Reuther, *Sexism and God-Talk* (Boston: Beacon, 1983) pp. 149–50.
26. Ibid., p. 154.
27. Frances D. Gage, 'The Akron Convention', *The Feminist Papers*, ed. Alice S. Rossi (New York: Bantam, 1974) p. 428.

Index